MARKETING IN THE
NEW PUBLIC SECTOR

Other titles in the
public sector management series

Accruals accounting in the public sector by V. Archibald

Managing change in the new public sector by R. Lovell

Purchasing in Government by P. Behan

Strategic management and planning in the public sector by R. Smith

Marketing in the
new public sector

by
Lionel Titman

Published by Pitman Publishing in association with
The Civil Service College.

MARKETING IN THE NEW PUBLIC SECTOR

PITMAN PUBLISHING, 128, Long Acre, London WC2E 9AN.
Telephone: +44(0) 171 379 7838; Facsimile: +44(0) 171 240 5771;
Telex: 261367 Pitman G.
A division of Pearson Professional Limited.

A catalogue record for this book is available from The British Library.

ISBN 0-273-61615-3

Printed and bound in Great Britain by Bookcraft (Bath) Ltd.

Contents

Chapter 5 was written in collaboration with Chris Cooper and Chapter 13 was written by Iain Cameron. Chris Cooper is a Senior Lecturer at the Civil Service College. Iain Cameron is Director of Senior Programmes and Director of Marketing at the Civil Service College.

Series foreword

This book is one of a series of texts on Management in the Public Sector which covers many of the most important topics on the current management agenda, in central Government and in the public sector as a whole. In the past many of these topics may have been the preserve of specialists. Finance was for Finance Division, human resource issues were for the Personnel Group, contracts were Contracts Branch. Increasingly all managers, at senior, middle and junior management levels, find themselves drawn into these, previously specialist, topics. With flatter management structures and increased delegation, all managers need a broad understanding of a range of management topics. This series of books has been produced with their needs in mind.

The texts are intended to be straightforward to understand, to provide a good summary of current understanding and best practice, and to illustrate the key points with examples from the public sector. There will still be room for the specialist, but these texts should enable every manager to talk intelligently with the specialist and understand him or her better.

At one time marketing was a concept entirely alien to the public sector, perhaps, in part at least, because the word was closely associated with ideas of selling, even of hard selling. Recent changes in the public sector have placed a great deal of emphasis on arms length relationships, on trading or quasi-trading relationships, and on allowing managers more freedom to decide on where they should obtain the services which require. As a result many more managers have had to start to think seriously about how best to inform potential purchasers about the services which they can provide and how to ensure that the services offered meet the needs of those purchasers. The Citizen's Charter has also increased the emphasis on service to the public, on establishing the public's needs and ensuring that they are met, issues close to the heart of marketing professionals. Whether you are providing services or information to others in the public sector, to private sector organisations or to individual citizens, this book is intended to give you an awareness of the appropriate key elements of marketing.

Robert J. Smith
Sunningdale
December 1994

Author's foreword

More and more managers outside the private sector find themselves involved in aspects of marketing. For some, this will be a new experience. As such, it can be pleasurable or daunting, depending on personality and experience. This book is intended for all those managers who need to know about marketing.

The aim of the book is to give enough of the flavour of marketing to give a solid basis of knowledge in both theory and practice. It attempts to combine the best features of an academic treatise, a practical road map and a bluffer's guide. Research suggests that only 12% of newspaper buyers actually read the leader column. The figure for an author's foreword in a book must be even lower. Therefore to those who want an academic emphasis, we can only say *lectori benevolo salutem*. To those who want practical advice we would say read no further, buy this book at once. It will enhance your life, improve your promotion prospects, and impress your colleagues.

I would like to thank Robert Smith and Ana Rostohar for their enlightening comments on the original script, Iain Cameron and Chris Cooper for their chapters, and Kerry Johnston, Alison Graham and Bob Pike for producing the text under great pressure. Any mistakes, maladroitness and malaproposness remain mine.

Lionel G. Titman
Sunningdale

Chapter 1

Marketing in management and strategy

Weakness comes from having to prepare against possible attacks ... strength from compelling our adversary to make these preparations against us.

Sun Tzu, The Art of War, c. 500 B.C.

You will always find some Eskimos ready to instruct the Congolese on how to cope with heat-waves.

Stanislaw Lec, Unkempt Thoughts, 1962.

In *Alice's Adventures in Wonderland*, Alice has a discussion with the Cheshire Cat about strategy along these lines:

'Would you tell me, please, which way I ought to go from here?'

'That depends a good deal on where you want to get to', said the Cat.

'I don't much care where', said Alice.

'Then it doesn't matter which way you go', said the Cat.

This sentiment was shortened by Peter Drucker to his famous epigram (Drucker, 1973):

If you don't know where you're going, any plan will do.

Defining strategy seems to cause some people difficulties. A football manager was asked what the team's strategy had been for a particular match, to which he replied:

We kicked them a bit, they kicked us a bit – that was the strategy.

The manager was wrong; he described tactics, not strategy. A more acceptable way of thinking about strategy was given by Tom Cannon (1990) when he stated that strategic decisions had certain characteristics. He said that strategic decisions are:

- important
- have a long time horizon
- involve top decision makers

- match activities to resources
- demand major resources
- deal with unstructured and unique problems
- shape the organisation's activities
- involve subjective judgement
- are complex
- make evaluation difficult.

Some items on this list may seem to emphasise the rather fuzzy nature of so much in management. In fact, we continually have to balance our 'experience-intuition' against 'facts-arithmetic' and use both dimensions simultaneously. This may be the reason so many public sector people in the past rejected marketing as alien; they preferred to use the third dimension of 'past policy-political realities'. The very idea of civil servants *marketing* something is a far cry from Sir Edward Bridges' (1950) concept of the 'storehouses of departmental experience'. It is perhaps even further from Sir William Armstrong's comment to Edward Heath's cabinet in 1973 that the business of the Civil Service was 'the orderly management of decline' (Hennessy, 1989).

However, it is not even enough to have a robust strategy plus willing management. Other details must be in place as well, such as an acceptable product. In October 1987, the town of Slough went ahead to launch itself as a tourist attraction. They marketed a 'dream weekend in Slough' with the advertising copy of:

> Why bother with Paris, Venice or Mustique when you can spend a once-in-a-lifetime weekend in Slough, the Cannes of the north and the Hollywood of Berkshire for only £75?

Leaflets were printed which offered a package weekend at the Holiday Inn and included a season ticket to the Maybox cinema. The all-inclusive price included a guided tour of the Slough Trading Estate and the Slough Community Centre ('once the home of the Ada Unsworth Formation Dance Team'). As if that were not excitement enough, the tour also included a visit to the car park next to a Mars bar factory ('used as the location for a dramatic scene in a seven-minute sci-fi film made in 1986 by a student at the National Film School'). It is now claimed that all this was tongue-in-cheek stuff. Whether this is true or not hardly matters. In the event, not a single enquiry was received, so we may safely judge the marketing and the product as a failure.

The Slough weekend raises an important distinction. In the public sector, much of the marketing is concerned with promoting a service rather than a physical product. Indeed, much of the marketing is even further along the spectrum, being concerned with selling an *idea* rather than goods. This is sometimes the selling of a change in conduct by the public (e.g. keep Britain tidy). At times, this change in conduct can have the backing of the law, such as the use of seat belts in cars. To try to change people's actual conduct can be more challenging, more exciting, than trying to get them to switch their brand of hair-spray.

The marketing strategies

It might be thought that there exists broad agreement on what constitutes and what drives marketing strategy. Regrettably, this is far from being true. There are many prescriptions. So many that there is even disagreement as to how all the different strategies should be categorised. There is no shortage of writings that examine the nature of marketing strategies (Cravens, 1986; Wright et al, 1991), that complain of people failing to think strategically (Yeskey, 1986), and that complain about academics who fail to address sufficiently the real world (Walker and Reukert, 1987). There are those who consider that it was not until the 1970s that marketers truly moved from thinking tactically and short-term to thinking strategically (Jain, 1986). Although there are many definitions of marketing strategy, most of them agree that it means a plan of using an organisation's resources to gain market-based aims. It states a direction or theme when deciding on the target markets and the 'marketing mix' (described later). There are three key questions that have to be addressed at the strategic level, and these are:

- where are we going to compete (the chosen markets or 'segments')
- on what are we going to compete (the service, goods or ideas on offer)
- when are we going to compete (market entry and development, new products)?

❏ Key elements of marketing strategies

A well-designed strategy needs to have certain characteristics:

- a medium and long-term focus (not just short-termism)
- good co-ordination across all the functions of the organisation
- integration of all the marketing decision-making areas
- a combination of customer needs and competitive advantage
- a combination of planning and flexibility
- a good marketing mix
- an awareness of external opportunities and threats, and internal strengths, weaknesses and resources.

If this list looks daunting, it should be pointed out that nobody said that marketing strategy is easy. Nor is it trivial. There are times when an entrepreneur has to 'bet the organisation'. If one analyses actual strategic plans, it is noticeable that comparatively few of them go right back to square one unless the organisation or product line is brand new. They are usually driven by a particular marketing component depending on circumstances. A useful, though slightly technical, list of product-market approaches is that outlined by Morris and Pitt (1993):

- product-market adaptability (based on intended rate of change)
- competitive posture (for market leaders, followers, challengers, or nichers)
- competitive advantage (cost leadership, differentiation or focus)
- product/market expansion (new/existing products, new/existing markets)
- product positioning (how one wants customers to view oneself)
- market concentration (the degree of going after particular market segments)
- product specialisation (the depth and breadth of what is being offered)
- types of demand (specifically, primary versus selective demand)
- price positioning (with respect to the competition and to customer perception)
- demand stimulation (where in the added-value chain one directs resources).

If any of this is unfamiliar territory, it should become clearer as we progress.

❑ Managing the marketing strategy

Over the years, the emphasis of all strategic thinking has evolved somewhat. In the 1950s the main concern was budgeting and control. In the 1960s it was long-range forecasting and precise planning. By the 1970s the emphasis was on for-mula-oriented planning. In the 1980s the concern was on managing the external influences. The early 1990s saw competitive advantage as a mainspring. Now the emphasis is on getting close to the customer needs, innovation and change, and the learning organisation. The cynics might say that they will wait for the next change and climb aboard the next bandwagon. However, the truth is that each new wave did not abandon the previous ideas, it added to them.

The starting point for any strategy formulation has to be in analysing the external forces that affect the organisation as well as the internal situation of the organisation. This is usually done by carrying out the well-known SWOT analysis, environment scanning and market identification. A SWOT analysis examines the external opportunities and threats as well as the internal strengths and weaknesses of the organisation. SWOT is certainly far from being new. It is however one of the basic tools of management, and should on no account be abandoned just because it is not novel.

Having looked at the outside and inside of the organisation, one can then see more clearly just what steps must be taken. These can be anything from improving margins and cash flow to pruning the product line and introducing new services. If no improvements at all are found to be needed, then one should think about changing one's employer since the present one is heading for trouble and does not know it!

Over the years, there has been some disagreement as to whether one starts with some effective tactics which lead to an overall strategy (Ries and Trout, 1986) or whether this approach is counter-productive (German et al, 1991). There is also some disagreement as to how many organisations really use marketing strategy or just think that they do. Research suggests that one's competitors tend to think that one does less strategic thinking than one does oneself. Our own thinking on strategy is:

- know where you are (by examining opportunities, threats, strengths, weaknesses)
- know where you want to get to (sales volume, budgets, markets, products)
- have a plan for getting there
- plan the introduction of new services or products
- feedback information on how well you and the competition are doing
- win; winning is much more fun than losing, especially in marketing.

Organisations vary considerably in the amount of detailed planning that goes into strategy, compared with what might be called an intuitive approach. From observation, it seems that the organisations that use extensive planning are those that exist in a stable environment.

Those organisations that live in a fast-changing or chaotic environment seem less enmeshed in detailed plans. The Royal Mint may be able to plan effectively since previous history gives a reasonably accurate picture of anticipated turnover and costs (a doubling or halving of either would come as quite a surprise). On the other hand, some NHS Trusts found budgetary planning difficult initially, especially if they lacked the data and control information on which to change decisions. The

Civil Service College inhabits a half-way position; it certainly carries out a lot of planning but the plans are not set in stone.

For many people in marketing, the strategy is represented by just one plan with one dominant theme. Research (Morris and Pitt, 1993) suggests that in practice there are five categories of dominant theme:

- a plan to achieve specified turnover/profits and/or growth objectives
- an approach to achieve clear competitive advantage
- a way of identifying and then pursuing specific target market segments
- a plan to identify and then to achieve how the organisation wants itself to be perceived or positioned within its environment
- a way of exploiting trends and opportunities.

Marketing and public sector change

The public sector has, since the early 1980s, undergone a number of major changes throughout the world. Perhaps the main one has been that of privatisation. Circumstances vary from country to country, but there are two over-riding aims. One is to reduce the size of the public sector and the other is to raise capital (Economist, 1993). One of the pioneers was New Zealand, while one of the biggest privatisations was in Japan (Nippon Telegraph and Telephone in 1986 at $12.4 bn). The process has been pursued irrespective of the shade of the political party in power. It has taken place in free market economies as well as the ex-socialist countries of eastern and central Europe.

It could be held that once an organisation has been privatised it is no longer our concern here. However, there are a number of factors that render this untrue. Firstly, many of the staff involved are the same. Secondly, some privatised concerns effectively or actually remain monopolies and so are still similar to the public sector. Thirdly, privatisation often means that parts of the public sector find themselves in competition with private firms and, most importantly, find themselves judged on how well they meet this competition. Fourthly, an environment of competition for public sector staff has been engendered by the atmosphere of privatisation. Fifthly, many organisations find that aspects of marketing have been introduced into their operations (the NHS, for example). All this means that the world-wide move to privatisation is forcing whole swathes of the public sector into marketing.

❑ Competition, buying and selling

Some public sector enterprises find themselves threatened not just by private firms but also by liberalisation and by technology. There has been a period in which the U.K. Royal Mail has been firmly in the public sector while the Dutch mail operator had been privatised. As a result, British firms found that it could be cheaper to ship their direct mail shots to Europe for onward delivery to Britain than to use the U.K. mail service direct. Throughout Europe, 10% of postal traffic is household-to-household, 60% is business-to-household, while the remaining 30% is business-to-business. The Royal Mail has seen itself as facing competition in each of its market segments (Financial Times, 1994):

Market by contents	Competition (examples)	Royal Mail share (%)
Social	Telephone calls, Interflora, hand delivery.	30%
Financial	Fax, EDI, credit cards, direct debit, courier.	36%
Commercial	Retail shops, home delivery, telephone.	13%
Advertising	TV, press, radio, posters, Ceefax.	31%

Privatisation may be the most obvious change to the public sector in the world but it is far from being alone, especially in the U.K. A large part of the British Civil Service has been turned into executive agencies. Many of these consider that they have become very different in nature – they have to sell their services and either break even or make a profit. Much of the NHS now has Trust status and is buying and selling services. Many educational establishments realise that they now have to sell themselves and their services, as do many NDPBs (non-departmental public bodies). In talking with members of these organisations, it is clear that many of them find the new environment exciting, invigorating, and rejuvenating. Others find the whole idea of marketing, strategy and strict budgets quite unpleasant, even threatening.

❑ Marketing is a widespread activity

In any maelstrom of change there is a temptation to see oneself in a unique situation. The thought of having to master strategic marketing can strike some people as unfair. The truth is that one is not alone. Many other people face and have faced similar conditions in different countries, times and marketing areas:

- different countries
  - the privatisation of steel, car production, telecommunications, etc, is world-wide

- large parts of central and eastern Europe are adopting aspects of a market economy even where the previous communists/socialists have regained control.

- different times
  - for a long time, Rembrandt was thought of as being outstandingly good at marketing. He would undertake marketing tours, selling the output of himself and his studio. However, towards the end of his life, he failed to update his product line in step with market preferences
  - similarly, Michelangelo frequently found himself acting as an out-source. He had to submit a bid proposal in response to a bid specification, just like the rest of us. However, when he was cold selling with a direct mail shot, he would often submit ideas for siege engines
  - the Venetian ship-builders gained a reputation in the market for speed and cost. They attained high market share and competitive advantage. This was done by exploiting new technology, using contract labour and JIT (just-in-time), and being rigorous with all aspects of costs, cost control and book-keeping. They also had the advantage of a good home market on which to base exports.

- different marketing areas
  - your colleagues 'sell' themselves when submitting a curriculum vitae or sitting a Promotion Board
  - dance and theatre groups sell themselves to the Arts Council when seeking funds
  - beggars advertise their plight by having a notice around their neck
  - the British Council sells the English language in many countries. Since 40% of the world's trade is carried out in English, perhaps they would like to claim considerable success
  - religious cults have to sell their ideas to survive, and have a quiver full of techniques that can be used to that end.

In looking at successful religious cults, thoughts may fly first to certain American tele-evangelists. But this is merely a modern example of a very old marketing story. The Epidavros cult of Asklepios in Greece (c. 400–300 B.C.) was successful for a long time in holding its competitors at bay. Adherents maintained a strong domestic market base by claiming that they were the main drivers for tourism. They did this by claims that visitors could be cured of illness, claims that were backed up with some pretty impressive testimonials. This meant that income was received from thankful customer-invalids, a large hotel/restaurant complex, and from grateful local business people. This income was partly spent on new sumptuous buildings, all competitively-tendered and to strict budget limits, which helped bring even more customers.

However, they were careful not to become too chauvinistic and thence tied to just the local market. They exported franchise concessions to other city-states, even to Athens which some considered a difficult market to break into. Their main competitive advantage was that they could cure the sick. This in turn was based on the nature of their founder. He was the son of a god, had cured the sick and had raised the dead. This gave strong product characteristics and differentiated it from their competitors in an easily identified manner.

We can therefore see that marketing in management and strategy is not so very different, obscure or alien. Many other people do it and have done it for a long time.

❏ The new public sector in perspective

Some people are looking at the New Public Sector in a different way. Not just politicians or civil servants but management thinkers. One such is Professor James Quinn, so often in the past the originator of ways of thinking that have in time become received wisdom. In an interview (Kantrow, 1994) he says that he has been looking at 'intelligent enterprises':

> When we speak of education or health care or the environment, we speak of them largely as 'costs' . . . We even refer to them, in the economists' jargon, as 'public goods'. This is nonsense. They are not goods, but services. More to the point, they are important *markets*. And they are markets for services, not goods.

Quinn asks us not to think of health care, education and environmental improvements as costs but as public markets. And markets are good things. They allow choice. 'They create new jobs and new economic opportunities'.

References

Bridges, Sir E. (1950) *Portrait of a Profession* Rede Lecture, University of Cambridge, Cambridge University Press.

Cannon, T. (1990) *Basic Marketing*, London, Cassell.

Cravens, D.W. (1986) *Strategic Forces Affecting Marketing Strategy* Business Horizons, Vol. 29 No. 5, September – October.

Drucker, P. (1973) *Management – Tasks, Responsibilities, Practices* New York, Harper and Row.

Economist (1993) *Selling the State* 21 August.

Financial Times (1994) *Postman Pat and his E-mail cat* 29 June.

German, M. Donahue, D.A.Jr. and Schnaars, S.P. (1991) *A Chink in Marketing's Armor: Strategy above Tactics* Business Horizons, Vol. 34 No. 2, March – April.

Hennessy, P. (1989) *Whitehall* London, Martin Secker & Warburg.

Jain, S.C. (1986) *The Evolution of Strategic Marketing* in *Marketing Management: A Comprehensive Reader* Cincinnati, South-Western.

Kantrow, A.M. (1994) *Intelligent Enterprise and Public Markets* An interview with Professor J.B. Quinn, The McKinsey Quarterly, Number 2.

Morris, M.H. and Pitt, L.F. (1993) *The Contemporary Use of Strategy, Strategic Planning, and Planning Tools by Marketers: A Cross-national Comparison* European Journal of Marketing, Vol. 27 No. 9.

Ries, A. and Trout, J. (1986) *Marketing Warfare* New York, Plume Publishers.

Walker, O.C. and Reukert, R.W. (1987) *Marketing's Role in the Implementation of Business Strategies: A Critical Review and Conceptual Framework* Journal of Marketing, Vol. 51 No. 3, July.

Wright, P. Kroll, M. Chan, P. and Hamel, K. (1991) *Strategic Profiles and Performance: An Empirical Test of Select Key Propositions* Journal of the Academy of Marketing Science, Vol. 19 No. 3, Summer.

Yeskey, D. (1986) *Strategic Marketing* Management Review, Vol. 75 No. 4.

Chapter 2

Marketing services and the public sector

A reputation for good judgment, for fair dealing, for truth, and for rectitude, is itself a fortune.

H. W. Beecher, Proverbs from Plymouth Pulpit, 1887.

Knowing what
thou knowest not
Is in a sense
omniscience.

Piet Hein, Grooks, 1966.

There has been a tendency in the last two decades or so for the public sector to move out of manufacturing. This has certainly been true for Britain. This means that public sector marketing in Britain is now more concerned with selling services than goods. This is not universally true. Globally, the steel industry for example is still more public sector than private. A service can be defined as follows.

A service is any act that is offered or performed that is quintessentially intangible in nature, and does not of itself result in the transfer of the ownership of an object. Its production may or may not be linked to a physical object or product.

Most marketing has some element of service about it. Even purely physical products may have a service element bolted on to give an appearance of added-value and hence added price. Four categories can be observed.

- *purely physical objects* Examples in this category are a piece of wood or a packet of flour. A service is not essential for marketing such goods, though one can always be added to increase the price. If price is the over-riding selling consideration, then such items may be referred to as *commodities*

- *physical objects with reinforcing services* An example is an automobile, which is likely to be sold with an extended warranty; when supply exceeds demand this may be joined to free maintenance, interest-free loans, and a subscription to a break-down service

- *mainly service with reinforcing goods* An example of this category is a package holiday which is accompanied by a tote bag, a language dictionary and sunglasses

- *a pure service* Examples of this are a haircut, a massage and a computer dating service. Any service can, of course, have an added physical item - for example one hairdressing salon gives customers a free sample of its special shampoo. But such instances tend not to be part of the service but a form of institutional advertising.

This categorisation is really just a matter of convenience for marketers since the goods-and-services mix is a spectrum rather than a discrete division. A second type of categorisation that is used is the following.

- some services need the *customer's presence* (a haircut) while others are *presence independent* (refurbishing a wig)

- some services satisfy a *personal* need (psychotherapy) while others satisfy a *commercial* need (management consultancy)

- some services are *person based* (a plumber mending a leak) while others are *equipment based* (a weighing machine). Person-based services can be sub-divided into provision by unskilled, skilled or professional staff. Equipment-based services can be sub-divided into provision by fully automated machinery or that monitored by unskilled/skilled staff

- lastly, service provision can be differentiated by the organisation's *ownership* (public or private sectors) and by their financial *objectives* (profit or non-profit).

If one wished one could follow the example of some analysts and build up a large matrix by using the two sets of categories. This enables people to research certain areas of such a matrix, drawing out certain conclusions. However, since we are concentrating on specific aspects of marketing, such a diversion is contra-indicated.

Characteristics of services

It is generally agreed that marketing services is different from marketing goods. Indeed, some commentators hold that any argument about this being so is now over (Zeithaml, Parasuraman and Berry, 1985). This is because services are held to have certain unique characteristics.

Services are considered to be:

- intangible
- people-dependent
- inseparable from consumption
- normally unstandardised
- perishable
- subject to fluctuating demand.

❑ Services are intangible

Services cannot be sampled before being bought, (Bateson, 1977):

> They cannot be touched, tasted, smelt or seen ... In addition to their physical intangibility, services can also be difficult for the mind to grasp and thus can be mentally intangible.

Therefore they are bought on faith. Future benefits are uncertain. This places a premium on reputation, image and selling skills. Purchasers may demand proof of knowledge, suitability and experience before buying. This can be seen in the way Government departments buy services under out-sourcing rules. The specification given to a potential supplier can be lengthy. One Government department used a specification 17-pages long for suppliers to mount a one-week training course. Another department used over 20 pages in its specification for bids for $1\frac{1}{2}$ days of consultancy.

Some people consider that intangibility is the basic distinguishing characteristic of services (Bateson, 1979). Others have said that it is the one single feature common to all services (Klein and Lewis, 1985). One tactic to handle this difference is, oddly, to make the service more tangible, the opposite from that often suggested for selling products (Rushton and Carson, 1985). Ways of doing this include careful brand imaging:

- an outstanding brand name
- an unusual and easily identifiable sign or logo
- smart uniforms
- a memorable long-lasting slogan
- a recognised style of advertising.

In other words, give buyers a tangible object or message to associate with an intangible service. Public libraries may give users a 'membership card' rather than just a metal strip swipe card. Many British civil servants who deal with the public have name plates or badges. A hotel bedroom will have drinking glasses wrapped in plastic bags to show that the room has been cleaned especially for the guest to use. Promotional films and adverts will often show the people who will provide the service, and such people are obviously good people. They are people who can clearly be relied upon. One of the tools of marketing intangibles is to create a symbolic appearance of ability and believability. Customers have to be persuaded to have faith that what they expect is what they will get.

❏ Services are people-dependent

The persons offering the service have a more crucial role in customer satisfaction than is typically the case with physical goods. The contact person behind the counter in the Benefits Agency branch may be courteous, but this never compensates for a Giro cheque that has the wrong amount printed if the contact fails to be helpful in rectifying the error. The people-dependency aspect may also place a limit on the number of customers that can be handled. The NHS dentist can only treat so many patients; a Law Centre solicitor can only deal with so many cases.

❏ Services are inseparable from consumption

As Kotler (1991) puts it:

> Its [service] very act of being created requires the source ... to be present. In other words production and consumption occur simultaneously with services.

This feature gives rise to both problems and advantages in marketing. A service is often sold first, after which it is produced-and-consumed (e.g. help from Citizens' Advice Bureaux). Physical goods, on the other hand, tend to be produced first, then sold, then consumed (e.g. a packet of frozen peas). So ways may have to be found of selling a service without the buyer ever having had experience of it (e.g. DTI advice on office location). An advantage is that the consumer may also be involved in the production process, and then the consumer's presence may be integrated into the service (e.g. management consultancy advice).

A problem often associated with inseparability is the attitude of the providers of the service. These may see themselves as creators or skilled producers to such an extent that they ignore, even despise, the marketing aspects. They may become production-oriented rather than customer-oriented. As we have seen, services are often produced-and-consumed simultaneously. So the person giving the service is often marketing the next order. Doctors with a good bedside manner realise this fact instinctively. Others may not see the connection so clearly.

The marketing strategy in this situation will be that staff have to be convinced that the production process is a marketing activity. In some cases, such as the service provided by 'Exhaust-U-Like', this should be obvious to everybody. If customers argue bitterly with the exhaust fitter then they are unlikely to return for a battery or a tyre. In other cases, reliance is placed on training competent people in customer relations. The approach often used is known as 'Do-as-you-would-be-done-by' or '95/5'. This emphasises the fact that if a service provider is pleasant and helpful to customers, then the vast majority are pleasant in return (the 95% in 95/5). This approach has been found most useful in dealing with members of the general public.

❑ Services are usually unstandardised

Because services are people-dependent, the service they give will vary. Different people may have different ideas about what the service is meant to be. Moreover, the same individual will vary the service over a period of time, depending on mood, pressures and the relationships with individual customers. All this can lead to customers' regarding the resulting service as downright unpredictable. We have all had the experience of having eaten in the same canteen or restaurant more than once. Sometimes the experience is good, sometimes bad, even when run by a public sector organisation. The MacDonalds chain tries to reduce this variability by laying down precise behaviour patterns backed by extensive check-lists.

Variability is sometimes referred to as the problem of *heterogeneity*. This problem is particularly acute in labour-intensive services. Patients want to be confident that the quality of medical care will be the same irrespective of which doctor they consult. This affects product development, design, production, delivery, quality control, productivity and pricing. Ways of handling heterogeneity tend to go in two opposite directions. One way is customisation, which can be handled by increased responsibility and empowerment at the delivery sharp end. The other way is standardisation through, say, increased use of automation and information technology.

A customisation strategy involves modifying the service for individual customers so that they end up by feeling that they received a tailor-made service. The cheapest and easiest way of achieving this is to retain mass production for a series of modules and then assembling the modules in a personalised way. For example, distance-learning students may earn credits for their degrees by combining the subjects studied in the combination that they want.

A standardisation strategy may seem attractive for a mass market (though this is not always the best). Customers of a hotel chain or a Local Authority Housing Department may be more satisfied if they are confident that they will always get the same service. This type of standardisation can be effected through standardised systems and thorough staff training. In a number of situations, the increased use of machines to deliver service is an answer. Increased use of self-service can provide an answer in some situations. One provider used the slogan 'Service with a smile – serve yourself'. Self-service and machines can be combined as in the case of automatic car washes.

Both standardisation and customisation strategies have to be backed by on-going market research. This enables one to know both whether the service is what is wanted and if it lives up to people's expectations.

❏ Services tend to be perishable

Services cannot be stored and used later. Many services consist basically of selling skilled time. An NHS surgeon cannot regain lost time due to a patient not being ready and prepared. A planning enquiry has to hear a witness during a hearing. In many cases, the service has to be provided whether there are enough customers or not. One cannot run half a bus nor can one store half a bus for future use.

In some ways the problem is no different from providing perishable goods - the example often quoted is that of daily newspapers. One way of dealing with perishable services is the increasing impact of 'just-in-time' in offices, etc. Also, most service providers try to keep a backlog of ancillary tasks for those periods when they would otherwise be idle. But this does not solve the basic problem that time is not storable. So service organisations suffer more acutely from any incidence of fluctuating demand.

❏ Services tend to face fluctuating demand

People such as mail collectors and distributors can face peaks and troughs. So do many other services such as photocopying, ski lifts, hospital intensive care units. The Government broker sells bonds. Price is the main determinant but is not the only consideration. Demand can fluctuate due to factors such as uncertainty, market liquidity and the availability of other negotiable instruments, though some free-marketeers hold that price overcomes all. Ways of reducing the problems of perishability and fluctuating demand depend on the individual industry and market segment. They include peak pricing, encouraging off-peak usage, reservation systems, offering ancillary services, building in back-logs deliberately, employing casual staff or staff with more than one specialism. These characteristics mean that one adage is even more true for marketing services than for goods. Repeat sales are far cheaper than new sales. Always. Much.

Marketing and services

Historically, service providers lagged behind manufacturers in using marketing and even advertising. Reasons for this included:

- many service providers were small (e.g. a massage parlour) and drew their custom from a geographically compact area, while larger manufacturing units can cover a whole country
- many lacked an overall sales plan and did not use advanced management techniques
- the majority of professional advice groups (e.g. chartered accountants) felt that formal marketing was incompatible with their status as professionals
- many service providers had traditionally grown in size in response to a perceived increasing demand (e.g. hospitals) and so had no need to seek customers
- competitor service providers did not market, so the need was not obvious.

In addition, service providers did not see how the traditional techniques of marketing applied to their situation. In manufacturing, one fabricates an object first and then has to sell it. One does this by either *selling-in* (persuading retailers/wholesalers to stock your product) or by *selling-out* (persuading the ultimate user to go and look for your product on the shelves). As we have seen above, services differ from products in ways that make this approach seem inappropriate. Instead, one may be trying to build up trust, confidence and acceptance.

It has been cogently argued (Gronroos, 1984) that the answer to this problem is to reinforce the traditional product marketing approach with two additional marketing efforts, known as internal marketing and interactive marketing.

❏ Internal marketing

The marketing department has to train and motivate as a team the staff who come into contact with the customer. In many service organisations this can be most of the staff. The 'team' has both to sell at every opportunity and to ensure customer satisfaction. In other words (Berry, 1986), the marketing department should try to be exceptionally clever in getting everyone else in the organization to practice marketing.

At the Civil Service College, teams of lecturers and course support staff combine for each individual course. In addition, staff have targets for selling and delivering courses.

❏ Interactive marketing

This phrase is used to describe the abilities of the staff in dealing with customer contacts. The perceived quality of a service is an integral part of the service delivery which, as we have seen, is usually part of the service production. For example, a seminar has to be *technically* of a good quality. (Was it factually correct and informative?) It also has to be run to a *functionally* good quality. (Was it customer-friendly, were joining instructions and surroundings good, did it inspire confidence?) In marketing services (and especially in the case of professional services) one finds that there is a considerable overlap between people's perceptions of technical and functional quality. A well-known example of this halo effect is the bedside manner of doctors. Patients want a diagnosis to be accurate; they also want to be listened to and to feel confident that the treatment will work.

Nobody but the terminally optimistic among us will pretend that combining external/internal/interactive marketing is easy. However, if it avoids bankruptcy it seems worth trying. One firm of consultants (Harvard Consultants) begins its training of contact staff by inverting the considerations. It is pointed out that the majority of customers approach a service provider in either a neutral or positive frame of mind. Contact staff can push customers up the scale by being considerate. The result of this is that the entire contact is more pleasant. And this makes life more pleasant for the service provider. Thus good contact skills are not so much a duty, they bring a reward. The slogan used is:

> be selfish – be nice.

Many organisations have now introduced measurement and incentive systems to demonstrate improvements made and maintained. The Radford Community Hospital arranged a fund from which payments are made to reimburse patients with justifiable complaints about the service (Kotler, 1991). This covers aspects ranging from waiting too long in the emergency room to receiving cold food. The extra feature of this arrangement is that any money remaining in the fund at the end of the financial year is shared out between all the hospital staff. So people have a financial incentive as well, to give good service. This incentive seems to have worked well; in the first six months of the scheme, only £200 was paid out to dissatisfied patients.

The Civil Service College has a number of quality measurements in place. One is called 'Value for Money'. A questionnaire is completed on every course, assessing its functional quality (quality of joining instructions, hand-outs, accommodation, etc). This is converted to an index that is made available annually (among others) to the College's parent department, the Office of Public Service and Science. Quality scores are incorporated in a monetary incentive scheme. This is, however, somewhat complex and the maximum sums that can be paid out to staff are not large. So it is probably true that the quality scores in themselves act as the main incentive.

Managing services

There are three aspects of managing services (Kotler, 1991) that interact and which a service provider has to get right:

- service differentiation
- customer expectations
- productivity.

❏ Service differentiation

If one is in neither a monopoly position nor a cartel then one has to differentiate the service being provided, or risk a price war. The drift of current marketing opinion is against the desirability of all-out price wars (see Chapter 5). This leaves differentiation as a major management task. How is *our* service different, in the eyes of the customer, from that of our competitors so that they will want to buy from us rather than from them? The words, 'in the eyes of the customer' are important. Self-deception in this area is common and dangerous. People can too easily think that customers consider the Bloggs Agency to be superior when the only reason for thinking this is that they happen to be employed by the Bloggs Agency. A major firm of management consultants invited senior civil servants to a lunchtime presentation. One of the firm's directors said to one of the guests, 'In what ways do you think that we are the best consultants in the country?' The senior civil servant thought carefully while he looked out over the magnificent London park. 'Well', he said solemnly, 'I consider that your lunch-room has the best view out of the window of any consultancy'. This cut the conversation rather short.

Service differentiation has three components:

- service offer
- service delivery
- provider image.

Service offer

The service offer can also be considered as having two components:

- the basic offer
- the secondary features.

The basic offer is the heart of the service and tends to have a reasonable life span. When first introduced it may be innovatory in nature but, of itself, is always open to me-too copyists. The favoured ways of keeping a basic service offer differentiated are:

- trying to keep the cost-of-entry high to competitors
- gaining a large market share quickly
- gaining and maintaining a unique image, often through aggressive branding
- convincing the whole market segment that one has unique abilities or knowledge
- trying to enmesh the service offer with other attractive service offers.

When considering the question of secondary features, there are two temptations to be resisted as long as possible. The first is to use features that are attractive either because they can be obtained cheaply or because one finds them attractive oneself. The second is to use secondary features when one should be concentrating on the basic offer. A major U.K. airline held a series of meetings with business flyers (a profitable market segment). They said that the meetings were to discover what business flyers would like. The airline were thinking of items such as in-flight toilet bags, slippers, vouchers, paperbacks, gifts for a spouse. The meetings were not an unqualified success. Firstly, many customers felt that the presenters were trying to sell ideas thought up by senior management rather than gathering feedback. Secondly, business flyers (especially the most senior ones) did not put these freebies high on their list of requirements. What they really wanted above all else were:

- getting to their destination on time
- convenient flight times.

This strong message was not welcomed by the presenters. Indeed, some people attending were dubious if this message was ever truly reported back to the airline's top management.

Service delivery

Our second aspect (service delivery) can be differentiated in three main ways:

- people
- physical surroundings
- systems and procedures.

Since service is provided by people, their paramount importance can hardly be exaggerated. Staff need to be knowledgeable, helpful, pleasant and inspire confidence, qualities that are perceived by customers as being of a higher standard than that of the competition. A customer went into a high street bank to discuss with a designated 'business banker' the charges associated with Letters of Credit. Banks tend to lose money on letters of credit that are for small amounts; they tend to make money on charges for amendments and alterations. It soon became obvious that the business banker knew very little about commercial banking (a colleague had to be called in and a large book studied). Eventually the customer was told that there was no charge for amendments or alterations. If true, this would be a considerable surprise to the entire business community. The customer had years of knowledge of commerce, so left to find another bank. She wondered if she should offer to tutor the bank's staff about money.

The importance of physical surroundings may disappoint some people who think that the actual service is what should matter. But it is a fact of life. The Civil Service College spent millions of pounds in the 1990s refurbishing its accommodation, so that every attender has an en-suite bedroom. This was not an eleemosynary act but because customers expected this standard, and might not otherwise attend training courses, however good their technical quality.

Systems-and-procedures can often provide not only differentiation but also the appearance of good service. Rank Xerox introduced a sophisticated system of monitoring customers' usage of their photocopiers. This enabled them to telephone the customers with a suggested re-order time and quantity for paper supplies. Many customers came to rely on this system since they felt that it meant that they did not have to worry about stock levels.

The question of image is dealt with separately in this book. Image is frequently emphasised through branding and the use of distinctive logos and livery. Sometimes the name of the service provider becomes the brand name (e.g. The Royal Mint).

❑ Customer expectations

A major way of service differentiation is to emphasis the superiority of the service one will give over that of the competition. Success comes from meeting, then exceeding, the customers' expectations of service-quality. If perceived service falls short of expected service then the customer will sooner or later move on to a competitor. This presents organisations with a dilemma; promise too little and customers will not come, promise too much and customers will not return.

This leads to the importance of management taking a realistic view of the situation. What do customers want, how do they judge the service, are service-quality standards clear and realistic, are the standards delivered in line with expectations? Research suggests that customers use certain criteria when judging service-quality (Parasuraman, Zeithaml and Berry, 1985). These criteria appear to hold good irrespective of the service being judged:

- is the service easy to get (at a convenient time and place with little waiting)
- is the service described accurately and in plain language
- do staff have the required knowledge and skill
- are the staff trustworthy, and concerned with the customers' best interests
- are the staff friendly, respectful and considerate
- do the staff respond quickly and creatively to customers' problems and requests
- do the staff understand the customers' needs
- do the staff provide the service accurately and consistently
- is the service free from risk, danger and doubt
- do the service tangibles reflect the service-quality accurately?

The length of this list demonstrates again the importance of getting all the obvious matters right – or letting in the competition.

❏ Productivity

Productivity is another dichotomy – increase it too much or too obviously and customers may perceive it as being a reduction in the level of service provided. Ways of increasing productivity (Titman, 1990) include:

- reduce the amount or cost of non-labour inputs such as money (reduce the cost of capital), subsidiary services (use outsourcing), and materials (reduce the incidence of subsidiary gifts)
- increase the skill of those providing the service or improve their work rate (through training or work measurement). Alternatively, re-skill a total service into less skilled components and reduce the effect of peaks and troughs by smoothing out demand patterns

- specialise and/or standardise the service (e.g. clinics that provide treatment for just a single operation or disease, workshops that only do replacement of car exhausts)
- use a product or a machine to replace high labour content (e.g. antibiotics largely replaced TB sanatoria)
- reduce high service-quality standards (e.g. opticians providing spectacles in 24 hours instead of one hour)
- persuade the customers to carry out some of the work themselves (e.g. post office customers may save money by pre-sorting their mail).

Cynics may say that the most attractive way is to reduce the service while claiming it is helping society. Thus supermarkets reduced the thickness of their bags while claiming that this was not to increase profitability but to help the environment. It can be seen that a number of these might be interpreted as reductions in service, with an adverse effect on market demand for the service.

❏ The six pointers

In training people to sell a service, use is sometimes made of what is usually referred to as 'The Six Pointers'. These are pieces of home-spun philosophy which are repeated mantra-like to newcomers until they become second nature. They are:

- two ears, one mouth
- talk to mother
- idiot helpers
- the rat principle
- enemy interruptions
- out of uniform.

Two ears, one mouth

You have two ears but only one mouth. Why was this made the standard? So that you can listen to customers twice as much as you talk at them. In the public sector just as much as in the private sector, one must get feedback from the market-place. This is to discover both whether the service is right, and where the marketing is right or wrong.

Talk to mother

If your parent were thinking of buying something from you, what would you say? 'Hello Mum, nice to see you. You're thinking of buying a 586 computer? Do you really need that model? Would you like me to explain what else you could do?' In other words, treat customers as allies rather than as enemies.

Idiot helpers

When the marketing manager asked, 'Why am I always given idiots to work for me', the reply was, 'Ask them why they are such idiots'. In other words, talk to your colleagues and subordinates; find out what they do in their spare time, what special skills and knowledge they have. If you do, then magically they cease to be such idiots and it is possible to work together as a team.

The rat principle

'Remember – rats are as afraid of you, as you are of them'. It has to be confessed that we do not really like this particular pointer in this form. However, since it is used this may be because we fail to understand it properly. Instead, we prefer: 'to get to the other side, you have to jump in the pool some time'. This means that one cannot keep putting off committing oneself to real action.

Enemy interruptions

A notice in an office of an educational establishment proclaimed, 'Working here would be fine if it weren't for the students'. An immigration officer was heard to say in response to a mess-up, 'It doesn't matter, they're not even from the EC'. Both examples assume that customers are somehow an annoying interruption to what could be a pleasant existence. This is not so. The customer is the cause of the pleasant existence.

Out of uniform

When you are off-duty, you become somebody else's customer. How do you like to be treated then? As the old phrase puts it – do as you would be done by.

These six pointers are simple enough. However, they do encapsulate some basic truths in the marketing of services.

Public sector marketing

The idea that not-for-profit organisations should use marketing is now so widespread that it hardly warrants defence or comment. However the use of the phrase *not-for-profit marketing* does still cause difficulties. One reason for this is the problem of defining a not-for-profit organisation. Organisations that do not aim to make a profit in the normal sense of the word include charities, universities, state hospitals, tourist agencies, churches, civil services, and so on. All such lists are going to include a range of activities and organisations that are almost unbearably wide.

The phrase *public sector marketing* is more easily understood by the general public who generally take it to mean marketing by any organisation that is owned directly by the state. However, it is less liked by professionals and academics. This is because what is defined as the public sector differs from country to country, and from decade to decade within a single country. This makes comparisons hazardous if not meaningless. Most books (including this one) therefore use *public sector marketing* in a generalised, non-specific, short-hand manner. A third phrase that is encountered is *social marketing*. We consider that this phrase should be reserved for the selling (or 'acceptability enhancement') of social causes, ideas or desired behaviours. Even this phrase lacks complete precision. Perhaps for this reason, one can find authors who use the three phrases not-for-profit marketing/public sector marketing/social marketing as being completely interchangeable.

❏ Private v. public marketing

As already stated, there is a tendency for the public sector to market services rather than products, especially in the U.K. However, although there is considerable encouragement for the public sector to think in broad marketing terms, the truth is that there are certain characteristics of marketing in the public sector (Papadopoulos, Zikmund and d'Amico, 1988). These include:

- standards of behaviour
- mandates and constraints
- targeting market segments
- performance measurement.

Standards of behaviour

One of the strengths of the British civil service is the way it lives up to the high standards of behaviour expected of it by the British public. This is true of the public sector as a whole. If one wants a passport, one expects to be able to submit a form and get a passport in return. One does not expect to have to give a petty official a bottle of whisky to get the form accepted in the first place. This is not true in all countries of the world. This attitude spills over, naturally, into marketing. People demand that public sector marketing be fair, ethical, accountable and observe the proprieties.

Some marketing can blur the edges somewhat – indeed, people may actually enjoy a bit of exaggeration or hype. If, however, an advertisement by the Benefits Agency were less than straightforward and overtly honest then there would be an outcry. In a similar manner, the public sector has to be careful about over-spending on a new image or logo, especially when in a monopoly position. Another aspect of behaviour that warrants attention is the possible intrusion of what could be construed as support for a political party. There is a distinction between 'informative advertising' and 'persuasive advertising'. Indeed, one can imagine certain advertising that should not be paid for out of public funds.

Mandates and constraints

In a somewhat similar vein, public bodies do not have the same freedom of action as private firms in the areas of product and price. The Royal Mint can sell souvenirs but not china ornaments, unlike some private 'Mints'. Moreover, any hint of what competitors consider predatory pricing gives rise to complaints about a level playing field. The problem for the public sector is that constraints can be formal or informal, stated or understood. This can act as a strong brake on innovation and change. When training staff in marketing, emphasis has to be placed on considering changing the status quo rather than just accepting it as a given for all time.

Targeting market segments

Private for-profit firms typically define their main targets in terms of customer segments. Public organisations often find themselves having to target a large number of segments. Also, these segments can simultaneously include *up-stream* and *down-stream* segments. A charity concerned with the welfare of the blind has to use marketing to obtain money from the public, central and local government, capitalists and so on (up-stream). At the same time they have to use marketing to convince the public to allow equality of opportunity (down-stream). It is quite easy to aim a campaign in one direction that discomforts those in the other direction.

Performance measurement

It is a common problem in the public arena that it is even more difficult to quantify effectiveness than it is in the private sector. Over the past twenty years, this has slowly changed somewhat. The growing acceptance of marketing concepts has assisted this. So has the growing realisation that even a less-than-perfect measure is preferable to no measurement at all.

The Marketing Mix

The marketing of services and products is usually explained under a number of headings, collectively known as *The Marketing Mix*. This is referred to as 'The Six P's' (some people use 'The Four P's' or even 'The Eleven P's' but this difference can be ignored). The components of the Six P's or Marketing Mix are as follows.

Plan.	All aspects of planning in the marketing of services and goods.
Product.	What is being sold; product development; customer expectations.
Pricing.	Pricing strategies; types of price; pricing levels.
Promotion.	Advertising; selling; branding; image.
Place.	Channels of distribution; logistics; delivery.
People.	Segments; organisational structure and culture; staff selection and training.

These six aspects of marketing are discussed in turn in the next six chapters, that is, Chapters 3 to 8.

References

Bateson, J. (1977) *Do we need Service Marketing* in (Ed.) Eiglier, P., Langeard, E., Lovelock, C. and Bateson, J. *Marketing Services: New Insights* Cambridge, Marketing Science Institute.

Bateson, J. (1979) *Why we need Service Marketing* in (Ed.) Ferrell, O., Brown, S. and Lamb, C. *Conceptual and Theoretical Developments in Marketing* Chicago, American Marketing Association.

Berry, L. (1986) *Big Ideas in Service Marketing* Journal of Consumer Marketing, Spring.

Gronroos, C. (1984) *A Service Quality Model and its Marketing Implications* European Journal of Marketing, Vol. 18 No. 4.

Klein, D. and Lewis, R. (1985) *Personal Constructs Theory: A Foundation for Driving Tangible Surrogates in Services Marketing* in (Ed.) Bloch, T., Upah, G. and Zeithaml, V. *Service Marketing in a Changing Environment* Chicago, American Marketing Association.

Kotler, P. (1991) *Marketing Management* Englewood Cliffs, Prentice-Hall.

Papadopoulos, N. Zikmund, W. and d'Amico, M. (1988) *Marketing* Toronto, Wiley.

Parasuraman, A. Zeithaml, V. and Berry, L. (1985) *A Conceptual Model of Service Quality and its Implications for Future Research* Journal of Marketing, Autumn.

Rushton, A. and Carson, D. (1985) *The Marketing of Services: Managing the Intangibles* European Journal of Marketing, Vol. 19 No.3.

Titman, L. (1990) *The Effective Office* London, Cassell.

Zeithaml, V. Parasuraman, A. and Berry, L. (1985) *Problems and Strategies in Services Marketing* Journal of Marketing, Spring.

Chapter 3

Plan

It is beginning to be hinted that we are a nation of amateurs.

Lord Rosebery, Rectorial address,
Glasgow University, 16 November 1900.

Of course I'm doing something about my overdraft; I'm seeing my accountant.

Barry Fantoni, The Times, 22 June 1985.

There are a number of possible reactions to seeing the word 'plan' in print or hearing it said. There is the yawn, the grunt, the move-on. There is the objection, the refusal, the heightened blood pressure. Rarely do we notice the exultation, the rising expectation, the delighted grin. In terms of generating excitement, the prospect of discussing planning is not far ahead of watching synchronised stamp-licking. It has to be admitted that this even holds true among some marketing professionals. The writer was working at one time in an advertising agency which had a truly creative Creative Director. At a meeting, this person brandished aloft a new control document. The accountant was attempting to install this form to staunch losses on campaigns. The firm did not know until it was too late for action just how much they had spent on a client's campaign. In an industry where the margin is about 2 – 3% of spend, an over-run on a £1,000,000 campaign could get rather serious rather quickly.

The Creative Director looked on the edge of apoplexy. He was certainly having difficulty getting his words out. Eventually he managed it. 'This', he sneered, 'is the sort of thing I leave to the figure-pushers'. As insults go, it has to be admitted that this does not rank as the most telling. But at least everyone knew the score and where the planners stood in the pecking order.

On the other hand, the basic cussedness of humankind is shown by the fact that we are all vocal enough when we feel that a desired level of planning is absent or lacks robustness. We complain when the pavement is dug up and replaced in rapid succession by the electricity company, the local council and the cable television installers. Why, we wonder, cannot matters be better planned? We hate it if the annual leave rota is badly planned. We resent those marketing campaigns that advertise goods that we then find are not in the shops when we try to buy them. What sort of marketing professionals, we grumble, cannot plan a product launch properly?

In general parlance a 'product' can be a service, a physical object, a belief or an idea. All new products have to be 'launched'. Launching calls to mind the slow, graceful slide of a large ship into the water after which the builders turn their back on it and start on the next big ship. Some product launches can look rather the same to onlookers. These are the ones that lack decent planning.

The comments made about planning apply just as validly to project planning. We may not find it exciting or attractive, but we grumble when it is absent. Two hundred Britons descended on the town which they call St. Petersburg but which the local Russians still call Leningrad. Their objective was to refurbish and re-decorate part of the Komso children's hospital in a week. Many of them found the hard work enjoyable and worthwhile. But others agreed that it was one of the worst planned operations they had ever known. Some observers were alarmed at the deterioration of relationships between the volunteer workers and the television personnel who were making a film of the event.

Half-way through the week the television company sent a stills photographer over from Britain. Not having been warned about the situation, he wandered into a ward that was being worked on, whereupon one of the volunteers threat-ened to pour a 5-litre can of paint over the photographer, a threat accompanied by some ripe language. The work was eventually completed, but at the cost of some people working up to 23 hours at a stretch. At the end, one of the volun-teers said, 'I'll never come here again. Next time, I'll go to help in Bosnia'.

A more publicised event was the building of the British Library next to St. Pancras station. A construction programme that was budgeted for £164m had an even-tual anticipated cost of about three times as much. Due to be completed in the late 1980s, as late as 1994 a Departmental spokesperson said that it 'would not be sensible to announce an opening date'. The reasons for the mess are still unclear with everybody blaming one another, and with two commissioned stud-ies not being released (Independent, 1994). What is clear is that the British Li-brary is unlikely to become a textbook quoted example of outstandingly fine project control.

As we can see from the examples quoted, a lack of good planning brings in its train a number of disadvantages. The good news is the converse – that good planning brings with it several benefits (Smith, 1994):

- a sense of direction
- common purpose
- clear priorities
- conversion of aims into action
- coherence
- accurate allocation of resources involved
- better understanding of the work of the organisation
- guidance when dealing with uncertainty
- linkage between funding and the needs of the organisation.

Some people might feel that this list omits one of the most important benefits, namely that it helps preserve one's sanity when otherwise it might be severely threatened.

Approaches to planning

There is a range of planning approaches with which one can become involved. Exactly which ones are appropriate is dependent upon the circumstances. Every executive agency has to ponder its strategy when it is formed and at intervals afterwards. Prior to incorporation, a framework document has to be completed and agreed with the parent department and HM Treasury. The framework lays down the scope of the agency and also its aims and objectives. There have been instances when it also contains some specific lower-order targets expressed in arithmetic terms.

After the framework has been agreed, the new agency has to produce a corporate plan. This represents a strategy for the future. While the framework may effectively delineate the market segments to be operated within, the corporate plan demonstrates how they will be tackled. The thinking that goes into corporate plans becomes the basis for a bid for funding that is needed. A similar approach is used by many non-agency organisations such as NHS Trusts. A new plan has to be produced every few years so people have to consider strategy regularly.

It is at this stage that many organisations feel the impact of the market. Some will find themselves subject to market forces, including private sector competition and pricing. At one time, courses at the Civil Service College were 'free' to those attending them. Now, every course has to be sold to every course member. Anybody is free to spend their training budget where they wish and running training courses can look attractive to many commercial organisations.

❑ SWOT analysis

One of the best known components in preparing a strategy is the SWOT analysis:

S Strengths (what are our internal strengths, what are we good at)

W Weaknesses (what are our internal weaknesses, what are we poor at)

O Opportunities (what external opportunities might we exploit)

T Threats (what external minefields might we walk into).

There are a number of variations on the SWOT theme. Some people prefer a different order of working and call it a TOWS analysis. Some people use a 2x2 matrix. But however it is used and whatever it is called, this analysis remains a powerful and vital tool when building up a strategy. For a more detailed description see Smith (1994).

❑ Forward scanning

Parts of the SWOT analysis, and its associated discussions, inevitably concentrate on the present situation facing an organisation. However, we also need to think carefully about the future situation. What will the future be like? How must we prepare ourselves? The theme of forward scanning is to provide inputs for these decisions.

If one just asks people what they think the future holds, one difficulty soon becomes apparent. People have widely different views. This is true even for basic areas such as the country's economy. When will we have the next boom, the next slump? Will interest rates go up or down next year? The *Financial Times* and the *Economist* regularly publish tables showing the views of the experts in these areas, and there is usually little agreement among the resulting figures. There are two associated problems. Firstly, there is normally disagreement as to what trends are most important. Secondly, sales staff have the reputation of being enthusiastically optimistic unless they have just missed a sales target in which case there is much gloom.

Forward scanning reduces all these problems by imposing a structure and isolating the factors. The first step is to select those people who should participate; these tend to be those with special knowledge or who have demonstrated their scanning aptitude previously. The ideal group size is between 6 and 20. The best person to run the exercise is a facilitator from outside the organisation. This facilitator sends to each participant a form of questionnaire. This seeks their views on the future, when considered within a number of factors. The questionnaire asks participants to make statements (usually 4 to 6) about how they see the future. Here, 'the future' means four years' time. These statements can take the form of how people see the situation as being in four years' time, or the pressures then or the trends that will be apparent. In other words, what will the picture be in four years' time?

The reason for choosing four years is that it is far enough into the future to make people think deeply but not so far that they lack confidence in being able to predict. If a figure of five years is chosen, it has been found that it can encourage a far-away blue skies set of responses. If a ten years' horizon is selected, some of the responses will border on the science fiction type.

The questionnaire states the 4 to 6 factors with a set of explanatory questions for each one to assist responses. For example, if the factor 'political' is selected then the sample questions might be:

- what will the main political changes be
- will we be more in/out of favour
- will there be European Union changes
- will we have more/less control over our destiny?

It has been stated that it is usual to select 4 to 6 factors. These are usually selected from those shown in Figure 3.1.

The completed questionnaires are returned to the facilitator. One page for each factor is then prepared, e.g. information, financial. On to this page are typed all the statements that relate to that factor. This means that we now have on a single sheet up to 20 statements that people felt described the future situation about, say, information. Normally, there will be 4 to 6 such sheets. It is now necessary to use these sheets to arrive at a consensus.

The common approach in this position is to use the 'away-day' theme. The participants and the facilitator leave the office for a meeting in a hotel or similar centre, undistracted by interruptions. After an initial presentation by the facilitator and the chief executive, the participants are split into 4 to 6 syndicates, one syndicate per factor chosen. While in separate syndicate rooms, each syndicate reduces statements about their chosen factor to a consensus. This may be a repetition of a selection of the statements or it may be a completely new presentation of the consensus.

The syndicates re-convene into an entire group where the chair of each syndicate presents a mini-report. Some discussion may follow but care must be taken

---

FORWARD SCANNING

Possible factors

P – Political

- what changes?
- in/out of favour?
- EU impact?
- more/less control?

T – Technology

- impact?
- changes/directions?
- trend/revolution?
- implications? (finance, etc.)

F – Financial

- easier? harder?
- capital/cash flow?
- new types of finance?
- more/less autonomy?

E – Economic

- general economic situation?
- UK/Europe/world-wide?
- predictions/trends? (+ sources?)
- effect(s) on our organisation?

S – Social

- voters' expectations?
- image?
- pressure groups?
- green issues?

S – Stakeholders

- current stakeholders?
- possible changes?
- power and influence?
- 'architecture' approach?

M – Market

- competitive advantages still secure?
- new competitors?
- new market segments?
- product development?

I – Information

- what available in future?
- what information will competitors have?
- will sources of information change?
- what internal information in future?
- future management information system?

S – Science

- advances?
- technology?
- new emphasis?
- R & D?

I – Infrastructure

- changes in external logistics channels?
- changes in internal logistics channels?
- future organisation structure?
- parts of organisation contracted out?

K – Knowledge and skills

- new knowledge required?
- new skills required?

M – Management

- more/less/different?
- new skills, knowledge required?
- bring anybody in from outside?
- different style, culture for success?

Figure 3.1. Forward scanning factors.

that the whole process is not repeated merely in a larger forum. The group then discusses the implications of the consensuses on future strategy. Typically, the away-day conference will take one day of quite exhausting discussions. Those who have been on this type of conference usually praise it highly. Everybody has a chance to contribute, and the final result is thought to be a high quality piece of input to the way a group confidently prepares for the future.

❏ Mandate review plan

Many people in the public sector work for organisations that were set up by statute. Some staff in such organisations are constantly worried about performing any act that might be considered *ultra vires*. They are not alone in having this mind-set. To some, the simple mantra of 'mandates' represents the perfect defence against any intimation of change, a never-failing magic talisman.

This mind-set runs counter to the changes that have been seen throughout the world since 1980. The determined mandatists will often feel that they have right, history and seemliness on their side. This may cause their colleagues grief. But it does mean that a frontal assault may not be effective in getting change. In these and similar situations, the mandate review has been found to be most useful. Even in normal conditions, organisations can use it to re-position themselves or to uncover fresh product possibilities. It has been found that it can be of value at any stage of looking at marketing and/or strategy. This review has been used enthusiastically by groups varying from lawyers to librarians.

Some preparation work is needed. A facilitator will discuss with the chief executive and others possible marketing areas in a semi-brainstorming manner. Some facilitators will also talk to colleagues outside the client group. From these discussions, a list is prepared of products that might be sold. This list must include some or most of the products that are already sold. It also includes some products that are in the possible range as well as some that are close to being unthinkable (such as the Royal Artillery Office Block Demolition Service). An example of such a list is shown in Figure 3.2 (Smith, 1994).

The list is discussed by the participants. This is done either in syndicates and then the whole group or else just in the entire group, depending on numbers involved and time available. People are asked to say for each product:

- we **must** do this or must sell this product,
- we could get involved in this, or
- we must **not** get involved in this field.

People are also asked if their decision is backed by a mandate, and if so whether the mandate is a formal one or is an understanding. This can all be done on an away-day basis like the forward planning; indeed, they can be combined into one event. It has to be said that some people can find the discussion somewhat traumatic. They are being asked to consider change, to cast aside tradition, to move into a potentially threatening environment. Their colleagues may lose patience with them. The event therefore needs careful handling by the facilitator.

County Library Mandates analysis	Must	Could	Must not
Adult fiction	☐	☐	☐
Adult non-fiction	☐	☐	☐
Children's books	☐	☐	☐
Reference books	☐	☐	☐
Maps for reference	☐	☐	☐
Maps for loan	☐	☐	☐
Video recordings for loan	☐	☐	☐
Works of art for loan	☐	☐	☐
Special exhibitions relating to literature	☐	☐	☐
Special exhibitions not relating to literature	☐	☐	☐
Music concerts in library	☐	☐	☐
Arranging music concerts in other venues	☐	☐	☐
Opening on Sundays	☐	☐	☐
Advertising library services on television	☐	☐	☐
Contracting out the library service	☐	☐	☐
Close all but the central library	☐	☐	☐
Coffee shop in High Street	☐	☐	☐
Selling surplus books	☐	☐	☐
Selling new books in library	☐	☐	☐
Bookshop in High Street	☐	☐	☐

Please ✓ appropriate box

Figure 3.2. Mandate review.

It is possible that at this stage additional plans may have to be prepared or additional data obtained. This should be clear to those involved. The danger that has to be avoided is that of allowing the anti-change or anti-work brigades making suggestions that will only serve as delaying tactics. Pressure may have to be exerted to proceed now to the big issue, the marketing plan.

The marketing plan

Any strategy has to answer two basic questions:

- where are we going
- how do we get there?

The marketing plan answers both aspects. It has ten components:

- market assessment

- market segmentation
- product/service ranges
- aims, objectives and priorities
- the Marketing Mix sectors
- annual plan
- budgets
- monitoring, controls and reviews
- resources and the action plan
- action.

❏ Market assessment

There are examples around of an organisation stumbling into a market without knowing anything about it and being a giant success. This is usually achieved through the unwitting introduction of a new and revolutionary concept which catches the market's imagination. Those with this sort of story are almost always new entrepreneurs who have a good idea. More often, this is the route to failure in the market rather than success. It can hardly, therefore, be recommended to those in the public sector. The voters and the tabloid press are unlikely to be supportive of failure if this were due to ignorance. A market assessment looks at each of the areas listed below.

Past history

The history of a market can tell one a lot about it, giving one a 'feel' which can be valuable. On the other hand, there is an accompanying danger. Studying history too intently can prove inhibiting and act as a barrier against innovation.

Present situation

One can know too much history. But one can never know too much about what is going on right now. What is the competition doing? Are new competitors coming on to the scene; are old ones leaving it? What is new? What is happening to prices? Is demand up or down? What interesting rumours are there going the rounds? In the land of marketing, it is always ears-to-the-ground time.

Trends

There are some places where trends have to be watched and analysed continuously, e.g. university applications for specific faculties. In other places, one can be more affected by chaos and flip-flop theories of sudden movements, e.g. anything with an element of fashion. Accountancy Advice Division can find its market in accounting for inflation a matter of peaks and troughs rather than a gentle incline.

Pressures

A number of pressures can exist – some books suggest the technique of Force Field Analysis can be useful (McDonald and Leppard, 1991; Lewin, 1951). Public sector organisations are always subject to ministerial pressure which can suddenly open up a completely new market or make old ones more meaningful. Other pressures that can affect us include the results of newly released research findings and the activities of the accurately-named pressure groups.

Future expectations

These are an amalgam of the previous four factors. How formal and how arithmetic they are is a reflection of an organisation's general approach to strategy. Some organisations make use of scenario building (Wack, 1985). Others use a model. There is an econometric model for management consultancy based on the answers to the Confederation of British Industry's questionnaire on business expectations. Some prefer the wet finger approach, basing their expectations on personal knowledge and experience. Again, those in the public sector may not wish to be seen to be too enslaved by this method; there are particular dangers for the public servant if things go wrong and there is evidence that the situation was not properly thought through.

Market segmentation

Market segmentation is generally agreed to be one of the major drivers in marketing. It tries to specify what we are selling, where and to whom. It is possible to consider our market as consisting of a number of discrete products; the Department of Social Security and its predecessors thought for many years in terms of its different products. It is also possible to think of our market as being split by geographical areas (as multi-nationals may do) or type of outlet (National Savings Bonds). The commonest method of segmenting markets is by type of customer. Since market segmentation is an important subject, it is explored in greater depth in Chapter 6 ('people').

In the marketing plan, one collects data on and makes decisions about:

- *size and growth* The size of each segment has to be known as does the recent and anticipated increase or decrease of each

- *competition*   One has to assume that every segment either has competition or soon could have. In the public sector this could be direct competition (e.g. market testing) or indirect competition (e.g. radically new approaches to provision of the service). The relative strength and effectiveness of this competition, actual or potential, in our chosen segments can indicate possible opportunities or threats

- *market share*   Debate about the importance of size of one's share of a particular segment has been extensive in recent times. One can be a *market leader* with the lion's share of a segment, a *market follower* who would like to be market leader, a *market player* with a non-dominant share, or a *niche leader* who has happily identified a segment of a segment and is doing nicely in a smaller pond. The debate has centred on whether the advantage of market segment dominance is worth what can be the high cost of achievement. The jury is still out. In the public sector market share per se may not be so vital a consideration, except where there is direct competition, but identifying the specific niche or role for public sector provision is vital

- *opportunities and problems*   This is the amalgam of the previous three factors in helping one to make a good decision on the type of segment player one wishes to become.

❏ Product range

The range of products or services that one wishes to provide is something that needs thought. The temptation is not to let go of anything. The best defence against this type of thinking is a decent costing system which can show which products or services are of doubtful worth.

Before introducing a new product one must first realistically ask if it is likely to be a success. This can be a function of one's own internal resources and abilities as much as whether the 'market' will respond. A hospital may consider setting up or expanding an Organ Transplant Centre. Externally this may depend on whether the market is expanding and whether funds will be available. Internally, it will depend on space and trained staff availability. A marketing plan will consider:

- the current range of products offered and how well it is doing. The products may be grouped into *portfolios* if they have aspects in common

- the life cycles of individual products and/or the portfolios. No product lasts forever (e.g. the use of leeches by U.K. doctors is now quite rare). Most products have a sales pattern that follows a saddle-back curve when drawn on a graph. So marketing people watch for the appearance of the final downward curve, which in the public sector may appear in the form of declining public support rather than declining levels of activity

- the strengths and weaknesses of the products and the portfolios
- the planned development of new products.

The whole matter of products and product development is another major aspect and so is covered in Chapter 4 ('product').

❏ Aims, objectives and priorities

By this stage, a considerable amount of data and thought has accumulated. Now is the time to pull it together. This enables the first of our two basic questions to be answered:

where are we going?

As in all strategic thinking, it is necessary to stipulate:

- the aims and objectives
- the priorities.

Most textbooks state that these two items must be couched in numerical terms, and this is normally quite true. There are occasions, however, when a different approach is warranted. This is particularly true for the public sector, though even the private sector prefers a different emphasis at times (such as the famous Komatsu aim, 'Surround Caterpillar'). Since the public sector can be involved in changing opinions or spreading information, we may be satisfied with a softer aim such as increasing health, decreasing deaths, increasing awareness. In areas such as these objectives for market share are hardly appropriate. It should be hastily added that many analysts consider that arithmetic terms should *always* be used.

The Marketing Mix sectors

As already stated, we are taking the marketing mix as being the six P's with each 'P' being considered individually in Chapters 3 to 8:

- plan
- product
- price

- promotion
- place
- people.

Some textbooks use a different number of P aspects. A few reduce it to four Ps while one has as many as eleven. The number need not concern us unduly since all such schemes cover all the aspects but in a slightly different way. What we do have to concern ourselves with is the question of how we are going to blend the elements. How we do this depends on the circumstances. To explain how wide the list of ingredients in this blend can be, Figure 3.3 gives some examples of particular strategies which have emerged in different organisations.

It may initially be feared that mixing the elements into a robust and successful blend is a dauntingly skilled task that is not for the tyro. In practice this is not so. Most of the elements scream out for attention when they are relevant. By reading through the six chapters, confidence should be restored. The skill and experience is needed when actually carrying out each of the aspects. In this, there are plenty of experts around all eager to help. Using these experts effectively is a skill that does have to be acquired.

THE MARKETING MIX ELEMENTS

Examples of aspects

Element	Organisation	Example
Product development	Transport and Road Research Laboratory	New training for private sector personnel
Product modification	Department of Health	Change (after 40 years) in diets recommended for diabetics
Branding	Ordnance Survey	Ordnance Survey maps
Warranties	Agencies	Citizens' Charters
Distribution	Post Office Counters	Postage stamps availale in vending machines, retailers, post offices
Advertising	Health & Safety Executive	'Lighten the load' campaign
Promotion	HMSO	OECD Observer
Segmentation	BBC	Local radio
Prices	Hospital Trusts	Differential pricing for the private patient plans

Figure 3.3   Examples of Marketing Mix elements.

❏ Annual plan

The 'Aims, objectives and priorities' work enabled us to answer the question 'where are we going?'. The work on the 'Marketing Mix' got us closer to answering the question 'how are we going to get there?'. It is now necessary to apply the usual management thinking to the questions of a short-term plan, budgets, control, review and acting. In practice, these are all likely to be components of a seamless whole (Abratt, Beffon and Ford, 1994) but are shown separately here to stimulate consideration of each component.

Everybody in the public sector has an overall annual plan, or is keeping very quiet about it. The annual marketing plan is normally allied to, and is part of, the overall annual plan. However, the details of the marketing annual plan (like the details of the information technology annual plan and so on) will normally be a separate stand-alone document. Otherwise it could in many cases make the overall plan unwieldy and confusing.

❏ Budgets

Most people in the U.K. public sector have the marvellous benefit of an assured annual budget – annualisation. There are countries where this assurance is much less pronounced. Even in the U.K., discussions have revealed that some people in the public sector regard annualisation as a constraint rather than a blessing. It should be pointed out that many in the private sector would give an arm and a leg for annualisation. The whole of government spending is budgeted by the public expenditure survey or PES which reviews all public expenditure for the years ahead, and which was the brainchild of the controversial Sir Otto Clarke. This means that all public employees are fully aware of the basic nature of budgets.

As HM Treasury (1986) put it, budgeting is:

> a means of delivering value for money against a background of aims, objectives and targets. A fully articulated budgetary system must comprise control both of the costs of resources used (the input) and of the achievement of a planned level of activity (the output).

It is necessary to budget for each of the marketing components, the amount of detail being dictated by the size of the sums involved. The size of each component should, of course, be related back to the output and what is being aimed for. It has to be admitted that even the private sector will sometimes base the budgets on last year's actual rather than embrace any form of zero base budget. It is, alas, not uncommon to express next year's advertising budget as representing the same percentage of turnover as last year's. The excuses for this approach can include a lack of professionalism, a lack of confidence or a lack of intelligence.

❏ Monitoring, controls and review

Like budgets, there can be very few people in the public sector who are not intimately aware of these aspects. Normally, they will entail ensuring that the marketing activities become a part of the Management Information System that is in use. The extra dimension is that one has to install a reporting system for reviewing the turnover, activity or outcomes in the light of the marketing plan aspirations. This is sometimes known as 'Sell or Tell'. In the normal manner, the results of 'monitoring, control and review' become part of the input for taking corrective action now, and for the data for next year.

❏ Resources and the action plan

It is, as they say, a capital mistake to think that resourcing is only about money. Resource management asks:

- do we have enough of each resource for our needs
- is the standard of each resource high enough
- what are we going to do about any shortfall?

The action plan incorporates the answers to these questions in a series of actions. A mnemonic used in corporate strategy to help one remember each resource is *mesmerists*:

M Marketing

E Earnings and capital (this is the cash part)

S Staff (numbers, allocation)

M Making and distribution (of services, products or ideas)

E Effectiveness (quality of administration)

R Research and development

I Inhabitables (offices, warehouses, etc)

S Suppliers (and supplies)

T Technology

S Systems

The action plan should be kept simple. Just a one-sentence explanation of every action that has to be taken, the name of the person responsible for the action, and a date for completion.

❏ Action

Act. Just that. Act.

By now the marketing plan will be complete and utter success eagerly antici-pated. There is one slight caveat on the 'act' part. One may have to watch the Parliamentary time-table. There are a few occasions when one has to be careful not to jump the gun, not to act before Parliament has given approval. This rarely impacts on most of us so it should be regarded as a caveat, not an excuse for inaction.

References

Abratt, R., Beffon, M. and Ford, J. (1994) *Relationship between Marketing Planning and Annual Budgeting* Marketing Intelligence & Planning, Vol. 12 No.1.

HM Treasury (1986) *Multi-Departmental Review of Budgeting: Executive Summary* London, HM Treasury.

Independent (1994) *Library's Trilogy of Delay, Bills and Blame* 30 June.

Lewin, K. (1951) *Field Theory in Social Science* London, Harper.

McDonald, M. and Leppard, J. (1991) *The Marketing Audit* Oxford, Butterworth-Heinemann.

Smith, R. (1994) *Strategic Management and Corporate Planning in the Public Sector* Harlow, Longman.

Wack, P. (1985) *Scenarios: Shooting the Rapids* Harvard Business Review, November–December.

Chapter 4

Product

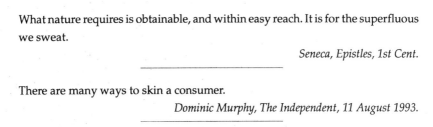

What nature requires is obtainable, and within easy reach. It is for the superfluous we sweat.

Seneca, Epistles, 1st Cent.

There are many ways to skin a consumer.

Dominic Murphy, The Independent, 11 August 1993.

A product is normally anything that you are selling. In the public sector, and in not-for-profit organisations more generally, 'selling' is not necessarily associated with 'buying', as the recipient does not always have to pay for the product. Nevertheless, someone does have to pay for the resources used, and there is a desire that people will accept the product and thereby justify that use of resources. So a product may be, for example:

- a solid, manufactured object (such as a paperweight from the Royal Mint)
- information (a local authority's newsletter with a notification and defence of its income and expenditure for the next twelve months)
- proselytisation (religion, politics, Departmental policy decisions)
- a service (personal car numbers from the Driver and Vehicle Licensing Agency)
- advice (on consultancies, from HM Treasury's Accountancy Advice Division)
- decisions (The Government Chemist is official referee analyst under various Acts)
- training (the horticulture diploma course from Royal Botanic Gardens, Kew)
- research (methods of disease control by the Public Health Laboratory Service)
- ideas and concepts (healthy eating habits from the Department of Health).

If nothing else, this list gives a flavour of just how widespread is the need for marketing in the public sector. Some analysts hold that the only distinction is between selling an object or selling a service. This list shows that though this split is acceptable for some purposes, there are times when we have to look beyond it.

The public sector is much more concerned than the private sector with the marketing of ideas in a pure form. The widget in a can of beer that produces nitrogen and hence froth can be thought of as an idea to be marketed. But this is not a truly basic change to people's behaviour. The public sector is often concerned with just such changes:

- Don't Drink and Drive
- Eat Less Fat
- Dig for Victory
- Equal Opportunities.

Such products need real marketing; some might consider that selling such changes is even more of a challenge than persuading people to change their brand of toothpaste. This challenge is the greater for three additional reasons:

- the amount of money spent is usually considerably less
- the results are often more difficult to quantify
- there are always critics around who are against any marketing of the idea, anyway.

All this means that we have to get the product right in the first place.

Product aspects

In the Marketing Mix, the P that is Product is normally thought to cover several aspects:

- product planning
- product mix and product portfolios
- product development
- product selection.

There can be a temptation among some people to feel that all this is hardly necessary. We already have a nice little product that has been chugging along quite satisfactorily for some years. So why change, especially if it entails a lot of effort and the possibility of failure if the new product is a flop? The answer is that fact of marketing – the product life cycle.

❏ The product life cycle

Every product has a finite life. Even staples and commodities can suffer in the same way though in a less pronounced form. In the 1940s, candles and silk stockings still constituted part of the then Retail Price Index. Their impact is now somewhat less than in the last century. The four distinct stages of a life cycle are usually considered as being:

- product development and launch (the impact starts, but costs are high compared with results)
- product growth (as the impact builds up)
- product maturity (impact tends to level out)
- product decline (when the product loses impact).

This is followed by product termination. Virtually every text book shows the life cycle in graphic terms (see Figure 4.1). There is a caveat to be made about the traditional curve, mainly of a defensive nature. The length of the curve can vary considerably. Bronze had a good innings while salt has done even better, only now being threatened by health fears; baking powder has been around for 150 years. Unless one thinks that one has a product to rival bronze, salt or baking powder then it is reasonable to ignore such abberations. Even branded products can have a long life. The examples usually given are Beecham's Powders, Gripe Water and Bass Red Triangle. The red triangle was the first trade mark registered in Britain, thanks to an employee who queued up all night outside the registration office.

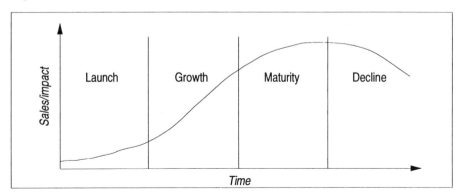

Figure 4.1. The product life cycle.

The product life cycle is important because each stage has to be actively managed. For example, it is often possible to extend the maturity stage by carefully introducing product modifications. This can be done by improving the product, re-launching, re-designing or attracting a new market segment.

Launch

Some people will try anything new, others will hold off for a long time. If we consider the totality of customers, it has been suggested (McDonald and Leppard, 1991) that the different types of customers fall into the following categories:

(a)	Innovators	(2.5%)
(b)	Early adopters	(13.5%)
(c)	Early majority	(34.0%)
(d)	Late majority	(34.0%)
(e)	Laggards	(16.0%)

At the launch stage, one wants not only to attract the innovators but to reach the early adopters as soon as possible. The launch of a book by HMSO will naturally be attractive to some of the innovators. The early adopters may wait for a review in the media before jumping in, so one has to arrange for the book reviews to appear as early as possible. Use is often made of signing sessions when the author may sign the book at retail outlets for any would-be purchasers. Signing sessions are thought to mop up many of the prospective early adopters, especially when accompanied by the usual appearances on local radio stations; they may even move some people into the 'early majority' segment.

Sometimes it is important to reach *critical mass*. This is the number of customers which, when reached, generates a growing impact. This can be because word-of-mouth recommendation starts to boost impact or because acquisition becomes socially acceptable or even socially necessary. Critical mass is particularly important for public service campaigns. Sometimes a shortfall in critical mass attainment practically guarantees failure. On the other hand, reaching it may be the single most important key to success. Examples of this are the don't-drink-and-drive and use-your-seatbelts type of campaign. Before reaching critical mass, both of these campaigns looked like failing because some sections (e.g. the macho brigade and the infringe-my-freedom brigade) were against them. Once a large enough percentage of the public accepted their validity, they were adopted by all but the most determined.

A launch may, in fact, be a re-launch. This is usually done because the product is going into the decline stage and the producer lacks a new product replacement. When this happens, it is normal to mount a different type of advertising campaign, re-design the packaging, distribute redemption coupons, and add some gimmicks. A re-launch may also be needed to counteract a major new player who has entered the market, or, particularly in the case of the public sector, another issue which has diverted attention.

Growth

It might be thought that the growth stage is so good that no management is needed. In fact, it is at the growth stage that competitors will move in and so these have to be taken care of. The traditional advice is to maintain competitive advantage, to stay differentiated and to make the cost of competitor entry as high as possible. Another way is to introduce *hooks*. A hook is something, anything, that promotes customer loyalty.

Hooks are popular at both the growth and the mature stages (if they are seen at the decline stage, other marketing folk may regard them as a sign of desperation). The 1930s saw many newspapers offering loyal readers special rewards. For example, the late News Chronicle offered an encyclopedia in return for a large quantity of 'edition numbers' cut from the masthead. The Daily Telegraph took a different route by cutting its price from twopence to a penny, which gave it an advantage over The Times. Some hooks have a blanket intention meant to promote loyalty and help growth. An example is National Savings Certificates. When a new issue is launched, the advertisements often emphasise the advantage of holders switching into the new issue instead of selling and moving into a competitive product. These advertisements are reinforced by public relations, with newspaper financial editors being sent press releases for their use in their columns.

The growth stage shows every competitor that here is a product or product line that seems to have a future and looks profitable. Competitor entry into the market is not always immediately a problem. At the growth stage, more competitors can enlarge the total market which is definitely not true in the decline stage. The competition will, however, add something to their product before entry. This may be lower costs, lower price, higher quality, use of an established attractive brand name, product enhancement. They will nearly always try to gain an advantage over you unless they are convinced that the market is so huge that it is largely untapped. You must therefore respond in kind (except by precipitating a price war) to try to create brand preference in your favour. In a non-competitive situation within the public sector, growth in demand may create a problem of resources. This may emerge as an issue of managing the expectations of the public. The competition may be from other areas of public expenditure rather than directly competing services.

Maturity

At any point in time, the majority of products and services are at the mature stage. This proves market acceptance and assumed profitability. It is also the stage when competition is at its fiercest. Not only do such services and products look like a sure seller, they will also attract the marginal organisations. These are organisations for whom the services and products are not core ones. During the 1990s' recession many public sector in-house training departments found that management consultancies were becoming competitors by intensifying their moves into what they clearly considered to be a mature market.

At this stage, defending the brand image and one's market share become a daily concern. Attacks on one's position are likely to be continuous. Two examples from the many available may demonstrate this. The analgesic Nurofen (manu-factured by a subsidiary of Boots) had competition from its generic component. The generic was obtainable from many independent pharmacists but not from Boots, except to special order, who normally only sold their own Nurofen. As the Consumers' Association (1994) pointed out this was not very useful if one had a headache.

The second example is that of cola drinks in cans. Coca-cola and Pepsi-cola were brand leaders and were thought to be very adept at defending their brands world-wide. Then a Canadian firm, Cott Corporation of Toronto, moved into the own-brand market. An own-brand is a brand that is unique to a particular retailing chain and usually bears their own brand name, such as Marks and Spencer with their own-brand St. Michael name. Cott-produced own-brand cola had 50 Ameri-can chains signed up before moving into Europe. These included the Wal-Mart chain who used the name 'Sam's American Choice Cola' and achieved sales higher than their sales of Coca-cola and Pepsi combined. Cott's sales rose from $36m in 1990 to $478m in 1993 (The European, 1994). The next year they signed an agreement with a British retailer (J. Sainsbury) to supply it with an own-brand drink, named 'Classic Cola'. The story was a repeat of Wal-Mart; within two months it had 60% of Sainsbury's cola sales.

Cott used methods which are not too unusual in such a situation. Firstly, they had very low advertising costs compared with, say, Coca-Cola who were spend-ing $4bn annually on world-wide advertising. Secondly, in the U.K. they con-tracted Cadbury Schweppes to bottle Cott cola in Europe for local own-brand customers. Thirdly they signed up Canadian Royal Crown Cola to supply Cotts with that most important ingredient, the concentrated cola syrup. Royal Crown had a taste that appealed to cola drinkers but it had avoided real success since the 1930s.

These are typical approaches used by a major new player. Find ways to hold costs down compared with the established players, and outsource services and products where possible to reduce exposure and capital needs. Only time will tell how well Cotts do and how Coca-cola and Pepsi will respond on a global scale. The Cott story shows another facet; a player in the mature stage of a product may not have been a leader at the launch stage. A leader in the launch of the concentrated detergent market was Colgate-Palmolive who in 1976 introduced Fresh Start. They were overtaken in 1990 when two new brands (Ultra Tide and Fab Ultra) were introduced. The lesson is clear – in marketing one has to keep looking over one's shoulder.

Some people may feel that an even better example than those of Boots and Cotts would be the building of hospitals by private medicine insurance organisations. Although this is a good example, we feel that this whole area is much more complex than merely that of the product life cycle. Often, within the public sector, the product is 'information'. In this case the strategy is to try to keep the product in the mature stage as long as possible. An example of this is Hansard ('The Official Report of the House of Commons'). Sales of the printed version went into decline as its price was increased. However, a version on CD-ROM was introduced. This had higher potential margins and increased the cost of entry to competitors. With other types of service, it may be necessary to prepare for what people will want next while watching carefully for signs of decline.

Decline

Even decline has to be managed, at a period when both turnover and profits are going down. It is a time when some of the players will get out of the market, and one has to decide if and when to follow suit. It is usually held that by this stage customers are fairly brand-loyal. Spending on promotion is therefore held down as is any major capital expenditure. At the same time, it may be necessary to switch resources into other areas and products.

Management must watch the situation carefully. They must decide if the market is really in a terminal state, or if it is just a temporary down-turn. The latter may be believed for longer than it should since marketing people are optimistic by nature. To avoid this myopia, one should try to find out exactly *why* the market is off. If a new substitute product is sweeping all before it, then it may be time to pack up and go home.

It is probably best to think of the product life cycle as a concept rather than as a precise mathematical tool – though one university press claimed that it could predict accurately the total sales of a book after just the first three weeks' sales. Others have cast a measure of doubt on the universal applicability of computer models based on life cycle curves. For example, one study looked at the 20-year record of 900 brands in 150 U.K. fast-moving consumer goods markets (Mercer, 1993, 1993a). The author of the study concluded that the life cycle is both more stable and much longer than previous theoretical models had assumed and that this was particularly true for brand leaders.

It is occasionally possible to re-launch a product or service even after near-death. This may be due to a new use being found or a new need or a new generation awaiting the pleasure of re-discovery (e.g. the yo-yo and the hula hoop). The precise timing of such re-launches is still a matter of some mystery, such as the re-launch in the mid-1990s of bicarbonate of soda for teeth cleaning after a dormant period of half a century.

Product decline and death can cause upsets. Most local authorities have now closed their communal wash-houses but the actual act of closure can result in considerable protests from the remaining users. Similar protests may greet the ending of a local dance or theatre group which fails to gain a continuation of its Arts Council grant due to falling demand.

❏ Product portfolio

The concept of the product portfolio is that of concentrating one's attention on the relationships between one's various products rather than concentrating on individual products. One aspect of this is looking at balance and gaps, rather like rich investors who may look at their investments to see if they are over-invested in some areas (high risk, high return) and under-invested in others (long-term gilts). The same investors might look at their portfolio of investments to see if there are any areas where they have no investments at all (Pacific rim). In the same way, marketing people will monitor their product mix to see if they are becoming too dependent on just a few products or if there are gaps in the organisation's offerings.

Another advantage of portfolio thinking is that it provides a surer basis for re-source allocation. An attractive case can often be made for capital expenditure on an individual item. The real need is usually to spread capital spend over a number of items such that overall strategy is maintained. The Ministry of Defence constantly finds itself subject to supporters of a large number of desirable projects – more battle tanks, more infantry, more large transporters. It tries to keep a balanced portfolio so that it can respond to a range of potential 'competitors'.

The best-known model of portfolio thinking concentrates on another aspect. This is the 2x2 portfolio matrix, sometimes referred to as the Boston matrix

(Henderson, 1979; Hambrick, MacMillan and Day, 1982). Although much less popular than it was, the concept seems to have entered most managers' consciousness. The first stage in product portfolio analysis when using the Boston matrix is to identify four types of offering:

- dogs
- cash cows
- problem children
- stars.

A 'dog' is a product without much future. It has relatively low sales in a market that is not growing. The tendency, therefore, is not to spend too much money on it since returns will be small. Eventually, one has to face the prospect of dropping it or trying to pass it to some-one. Many organisations hang on to their dogs for too long, either from misplaced emotional reasons or because they do at least bring in some activity which would need replacing somehow. A 'cash cow' is different. Although the demand is stagnant, one has a high share of that stagnant demand. Cash cows thus bring in a lot of cash without making too many demands on the organisation.

A 'problem child' classification is given when the demand is growing nicely but you only have a small piece of the action. Inevitably the need is to find out exactly why one is failing where others are doing well. A 'star' is that desirable creature, a product glowing with success in an expanding market, though maintaining success may need considerable cash injection.

One study suggested that chief executives with substantial sales/marketing experience and a willingness to take risks mark organisations with high performing star and problem child dominance. The same type of chief executive marked cases of underperformance in cash cow and dog categories (Gupta and Govindarjan, 1984). So perhaps one needs the entrepreneur type for high growth markets, and the administrative type for low growth markets. Certainly this sounds not unreasonable, and may be reflected in the widely-held notion that managers in the public sector are uncomfortable with rapid expansion.

It should be pointed out that over the years certain reservations have been expressed about portfolio management, especially the Boston brand:

- it is a simplification of real life
- it may lead the unwary or unskilled to feel unjustifiably secure
- it may lead to an inward looking attitude
- it may encourage one to take one's eyes off the competition.

The way to avoid these limitations is to use the concept in the proper manner. Categorising the product mix in the right boxes is not an answer. It is a means of describing the problem. Portfolio analysis will lead some public sector organisations to considerations of the variations in service offered. It will lead others (such as the Civil Service College and the Department for National Savings) to consider their product portfolios. The Department for National Savings has a wide range of products for personal savers. This includes Savings Certificates (fixed-interest and index-linked), Yearly Plan, Children's Bonus Bonds, Save As You Earn Share Option, Income Bonds, Investment Accounts, Capital Bonds, Premium Bonds, Ordinary Accounts as well as Gilts on the National Savings Stock Register. Managing this portfolio of products is quite a task, especially as it is necessary to watch sales and the price of sales (interest) as well as competitors' activities, such as the Building Societies. Much of the contents of this chapter apply to this portfolio. Portfolio analysis is also helpful if it leads one to consider the *product gaps.*

❏ Product gap

A product gap exists when one lacks a product in one's portfolio that one should have. One may need to meet the competition head on since otherwise the field of battle has been ceded without a fight. One may need to offer customers a wider choice of possible alternatives. One may want to have products in different price ranges or target different market segments.

It is common to demonstrate a product gap by means of a model. Traditionally this is based on a 2cm thick piece of polystyrene, about 20cms square. This polystyrene square soon acquires a grubby patina, apparently to prove that a number of people have seen and admired it before you did. The lower and left hand edges of the square represent two dimensions of a product. Taking cigarettes as an example, these might be price band and tar/nicotine strength. Long pins of various lengths are then stuck into the base, each pin representing a particular cigarette, with one's own brands of a distinctive colour. The height of the pins represents a third dimension, such as population segment aimed at. We thus have a 3-dimensional model. It is then easy to check visually where one has gaps compared with the competition. The same effect can be achieved on a computer screen, but creative advertising staff seem to prefer the grubby polystyrene. The advantage of the polystyrene is that it attracts the attention of clients better when produced at a meeting.

Another type of product gap is related directly back to the product life cycle as in Figure 4.1. As a product starts on its 'decline' stage, in an ideal situation one would have another product starting on its 'growth' stage. The two would overlap, leading (in theory) to a reasonably constant income. In a perfectly ideal life, one can imagine this continuing again and again to infinity.

A different type of product gap and probably a more common one in the public sector, is that associated with service expectations. This is so different that we much prefer the term *service gap*, to show clearly the difference. The service gap is that gap between service provision and customer expectation. There are four types of service gap:

- *producer perception / customer expectation gap* This exists where management do not understand or have failed to identify which aspects of service or quality are important to the customers. An example already given is an emphasis by an airline on free slippers and blindfolds when the customer is obsessed with departure and arrival times

- *producer perception / service specification gap* This exists when management know what the customer wants but then the specification laid down falls short. An advertiser claimed a '24-hour personalised service' though customers found themselves talking to an answering machine

- *service specification / service delivery gap* This occurs when front-line staff do not give the service as laid down by management. This gap is the one that we are all familiar with. The answer is better staff selection, better training, better supervision and in management spending more time at the coal face

- *service delivery / communications gap* This occurs when advertising, etc, promises more than the staff can hope to deliver. Some hotels claim that they offer ideal accommodation for holding meetings and seminars, but when you get there you find no flip charts, no overhead projectors, no coffee, and nobody earmarked to handle problems.

The Citizens' Charter, the other Charters and the Chartermark all aim to improve the service gaps. The way to handle product gaps and service quality gaps is:

- decide the strategy
- identify the gaps
- carry our research to discover which gaps really matter
- decide which ones to fill and which to leave
- fill the gaps you want to
- train the staff, the supervisors and the managers
- advertise truthfully
- monitor the result.

❑ Product development

As consumers, we are used to products developing all the time. Indeed, many of us would be disappointed if they failed to develop, if only because we may think of development as improvement. Universities have certainly changed their products since the Middle Ages. They have also changed them in the past 25 years. In the 1960s the Ministry of Pensions and National Insurance (as it then was called) issued leaflets for the public to understand their entitlement to benefits. These were and are barely comprehensible, and have now been replaced with something more user-friendly. We actually expect, even demand, that fire brigades, police forces and hospitals change their products in line with technological advances and our ideas of what a modern service provider should be like. At the same time, it has to be admitted that there are also many people who find any change unsettling. Any major changes to newspapers and radio schedules have to be introduced carefully and with planning, or resentment may boil over.

This same dichotomy can also be observed among the providers of services and goods. Some people dread changing a product, especially if it has been successful in the past. At the other extreme, some people seem to want change for the sake of it. The 'if it ain't broke, don't fix it' brigade are in conflict with the 'if it ain't fixed, it'll soon break' brigade. To overcome this difference of opinion, it is useful to consider the following four alternative approaches to growth or stabilisation:

Market penetration	–	Existing market; existing product.
Market development	–	New market; existing product.
Product development	–	Existing market; new product.
Diversification	–	New market; new product.

Reasons for development

The reasons and drives for development include:

- *growth*   A wish or need for growth in turnover
- *gap*   A gap in one's product mix which offers an attractive opportunity if filled
- *competitor activity*   This may spur one to defensive or offensive actions
- *life cycle implications*   Which may indicate a need for change before moving too far along the curve
- *novelty*   The danger of a service or product becoming ordinary, boring or taken for granted is that a new competitor may find it easy to make rapid inroads

- *new target market segment* Identification of a new segment may come through published research, own market research, observation or its becoming received wisdom. Whatever its source, the new target may indicate a need for product development
- *improving mix* It may be desirable for the product mix to be improved for reasons other than seeing an actual gap in the line. These reasons can include the availability of resources, distribution, over-reliance on too few products
- *me-tooism* A competitor may make a change that forces a me-too response
- *other countries* These may introduce a change which looks attractive
- *building on a loyal customer base* Changes which may not be sufficient to bring in new customers may nevertheless tie in existing customers more closely and/or increase sales. Organisations have mostly learnt not to express this as exploiting the loyal customer base. There are plenty of euphemisms around such as 'offering greater choice' or even 'rewarding loyal/regular customers'.

The filing cabinet example

Open any office furniture catalogue and there will be a section devoted to the filing cabinet, unscathed apparently by the advent of the computer hard disk. This omnipresent piece of equipment expresses the options open to product developers. Firstly, there are certain types of filing cabinet:

- 2-drawer, 3-drawer, 4-drawer, 5-drawer reduced height
- made of wood, veneered chipboard or steel
- made of thin steel to reduce cost
- antique reproduction
- fire-resistant cabinets
- security cabinets like safes
- coloured (other than grey or beige)
- circular, carousel, sideways
- powered cabinets up to 3-storeys high
- niche cabinets such as those for microforms, computer print-outs.

Even with this abbreviated list, there are few if any manufacturers that cover the whole product mix. Most have made the decision to restrict their range. The whole time, manufacturers have to look at the market. Should one spend on research and development (R & D) in the hope of inventing a completely new type of cabinet? Should one's range be extended? Should one use new materials, such as fibreboard? Should one move into new products such as desk-top single-drawer cabinets or desk-top cradles? Should one me-too such as having the inside of the folders a lighter colour than the outside to reduce mis-filing in the gaps? Should one go into services such as refurbishment or colour spraying? Similar considerations affect every provider of services and products. In the public as well as the private sector, the emphasis is on meeting customer expectations/ needs.

❏ New product development

No definition of a 'new product' is offered. A producer may consider that adding lemon juice to a detergent, or changing the rate of interest on a National Savings account is making a 'new product'. At the other extreme is the *new-to-the-world* product such as the heart pace-maker, the Premium Bond, the television. About a quarter of new products belong to the new-to-the-world category. There are two main drives for new products:

- R & D, where a group of people make something possible through invention
- the market, where it is realised that people want or need something that is then produced, or where it is thought that people could be persuaded to want a dreamt-up product.

Stages of development

Of course, there will always be the occasional amateur inventor working in the garage who arrives at a new product unknown to the market producers, such as Bell and the telephone. But these are the exceptions just as there is an exception to just about everything one can say about marketing and management. The stages of new product development can be stated as seen by Booz Allen & Hamilton (Particelli and Killips, 1986) thus:

(a) *Business strategy.*

 New product strategy.

 These strategies lay down the ground rules and delineate the areas for researching. In practice, it has to be said, this is rarely an actual stage that is seen operating since the strategies and their implications are widely known by all concerned.

(b) *Idea-concept generation.*

The search for new ideas and concepts that meet the organisation's objectives. This will often involve forms of brainstorming, mapping and similar techniques.

(c) *Screening and evaluation.*

An initial analysis to decide which ideas are worthy of further consideration. It is the constant worry of innovators that they may personally throw an idea out at this stage that later proves to be a world-beater. Procter & Gamble ask three questions at this stage:

- will there be a real consumer need or want for this
- do we have the abilities and knowledge to develop this
- is the potential attractive enough to offer potential profit?

(d) *Market analysis.*

It is at this stage that an idea comes up against the rigorous application of facts and figures. Detailed quantitative data about likely market demand, capital requirements, cost implications, effects on existing products, competitive activities, market research, forecasts, break-even analysis, risk analysis, probabilities. All of these and more may be used in pursuit of a right choice.

(e) *Development.*

The new product idea is now transformed into a prototype. This enables better prognostications to be made about costs, production methods and difficulties, likely materials, quality needs. It is also normal at this stage to formulate the packaging, the logistics, brand name, market segments, and selling tactics. It is not uncommon at this time to use *concept testing*. This is a test of a new product idea by gauging the reactions of consumers and dealers.

(f) *Testing.*

This is commercial experimentation to test the earlier business judgements. The most common form is *test marketing*. In this an individual town or area of a country is subject to what is in effect a mini-launch of the product. Depending on the results, it is then possible to decide to abandon the product, to modify it, or to go national and launch the product. As will be realised, the cost of a test marketing exercise is high, rarely less than £1 million, but this is still less than a product failure.

(g)   *Commercialisation.*

If the new product has passed all the other filters, then it is ready for the final push to full-scale production, distribution and selling. It has to be said that products can still fail. For example, Liquid Tyre Chain was a mixture of resins and methyl alcohol. It was sprayed on to tyres to improve traction on icy roads. Motorists kept the pressurised cans in their car boots, where the product solidified in the cold weather, making it unusable. The tests that Dow Chemical had made had somehow failed to disclose this feature.

In discussing new product development, what has changed over the past quarter century has been the stages that have in turn received most attention at different times. During the 1970s it was the idea-concept stage that worried management. Nowadays this is not thought to be too difficult. There are always plenty of new ideas around and, anyway, inspiring creativity is now considered a pleasant activity except in the most determinedly bureaucratic or hidebound organisations. What is considered important nowadays is innovation.

There is a difference between creativity and innovation. Creativity is the ability of individuals or groups to think of new ideas. Innovation is the ability to produce a new product physically. This distinction has led some writers to think of creativity as being a concern for the individual while innovation was a corporate concern. While there may be some merit in this boundary-setting it should not be followed too slavishly. This is because one wants both individuals and the organisation to feel a responsibility and a full involvement in both creativity and innovation. Both are important in the public sector, from policy creation to social service benefits innovation.

Reducing time for development

In the 1980s the emphasis moved to speeding up the whole process of new product development. This was probably inspired by the JIT (Just-In-Time) movement. The two main approaches used to reduce the total time for new product development are:

- involvement of potential, preferred or selected suppliers at an early stage
- overlapping some of the stages through improved project control.

Traditionally, external suppliers would be involved right at the end of the development process. They would be given a specification of the final product at the end of the test market stage and invited to tender as a supplier. This was a reasonable approach when producers tended to keep responsibility for production mainly in-house. That situation has changed. More and more organisations buy in part or even whole products. Out-sourcing has become the norm throughout the public and private sectors. It was not unusual in Japan for first-tier suppliers (or *primary suppliers*) to be involved at the concept stage, that is before the product design. This probably owes much to the network of producers and suppliers that has long been a feature of Japan (Asanuma, 1975). In the West, a slightly different approach has been observed (Bonaccorsi and Turnbull, 1989) in high-tech areas such as aircraft. Selected preferred suppliers may be involved well before the product specifications. They may be asked to help in the development stage or even in suggesting innovations. Who pays for this work is subject to negotiation, as usual. The advantages (Bonaccorsi and Lipparini, 1994) of 'partnering' can include:

- earlier availability of prototypes
- more and better target price contracts
- earlier identification of problems
- consistency between design requirements and suppliers' abilities.

The second main approach (overlapping stages) should be approached with a modicum of circumspection. There are times when it is a vital tool. On the other hand, it can push up costs and introduce another couple of layers of bureaucracy. Enthusiasts for overlapping point to the success stories. The mobile phone company Cellnet had to launch a new service in ten months (Towner, 1994) to catch the Christmas market; otherwise, it was felt, their main competitor Vodaphone would launch a similar service thus reducing the Cellnet return on investment. When Kodak introduced the 'Funsaver' camera (Hammer and Champy, 1993), it used parallel stages to reduce the TTM (*time-to-market*) to 38 weeks, a reduction of 50%.

The other side of this particular coin is the danger of increasing costs without just cause. It is easy, and by no means uncommon, to start to produce prototypes before the design stage is complete only to find a design problem arising. The prototypes are then either thrown away or, more usually, subjected to a rushed 'lash-up' manoeuvre. This, in turn, may lead to problems at the production stage. There are some who would say (Mark and Carver, 1987) that the *Challenger* shuttle disaster was partly because of overlapping stages and poor co-ordination (the official report into the disaster indicates that it was due to a number of interlocking causes).

The other danger of overlapping stages is that it can lead to more not less bureaucracy in the structure. When overlapping the stages it is quite common to introduce a Product Steering Committee to oversee the project. A *product champion* will probably be appointed to push the product through and to try to overcome problems. At this stage it may be realised that a Programme Office with a power computer is needed to draw up and observe the really detailed planning needed. This will naturally lead every function to introduce its own project officer even if only for sound defensive reasons. It may now be realised that a matrix is attractive and so matrix managers will be brought in.

By now there are so many people involved, that one clearly needs an internal news-letter (which will inevitably be called 'Impact' because it always is). If anybody should feel like denying the impact of office politics, they should watch the relation-ships between product steering committee, product champion, programme officer, project officers, and matrix managers. So – overlapping stages can be vital, they can be a cost-saver, and they can also become hopelessly bureaucratic. It has to be said that, overall, the Office of Public Service and Science in the Cabinet Office has used product champions in a manner superior to that pictured above. These have in-cluded, among others, the Citizen's Charter Unit, the Next Steps Project Team, the Efficiency Unit and the Top Management Programme.

Success or failure

Given a good level of efficiency and productivity within an organisation, one of the most surprising facts is what separates the successes from the failures. *NewProd* is a series of research studies into new product activities, concentrating on what differentiates the winners from the losers. NewProd started in the 1970s and now contains over 1,000 case studies. It may be discouraging to realise that what separates the winners from the losers has not changed much over the past quarter century. However, it may be encouraging to realise that the causes are both terribly obvious and very easy to deal with (or so one would think).

The key success factors (Cooper and Kleinschmidt, 1990; 1993) are the following:

- the number one success factor is to create a *unique superior product*. This is a product that offers features not available on competing products. It will meet customer needs better than others, solve customers' problems and/or reduce customers' costs, or be of better quality
- the second factor is the proper undertaking of the pre-development stages. Those organisations rated among the best 20% at doing this were 75% successful in their new products. Those rated poor at this work attained only 30% success. The winners spent 70% more person-days on these activities than did the losers

- the odds of winning were increased markedly by *sharp and early product definition.* This means defining the target market segment, describing the product concept and its benefits, and listing the product's features and attributes. This definition gets everybody concentrating on the right priorities
- the product must be *market-oriented.* In other words, it must be customer focused and market-driven
- finally, the technology and production activities must be of high quality.

As already stated, there is nothing revolutionary or esoteric here. It is all straight-forward and obvious. So straightforward and obvious, it is a pity that more or-ganisations do not try it. Lest it be thought that this is an isolated area of re-search, it has been shown (Barclay, 1992) that similar results have been observed since 1956. The SAPPHO project (Rothwell et al, 1974) showed the importance of understanding customers' needs and performing development work more efficiently (though not necessarily more quickly) than the failures managed. The PII, Project Industriele Innovatie (Buijs, 1984), emphasised the need for a staged innovation process and strong external orientation. A Booz Allen & Hamilton (1982) study showed that the factors for success included products that fitted market needs, product superiority and a staged process. So it goes on up to the present day. The research is there, the conclusions are there, the only thing miss-ing is the action.

References

Asanuma, B. (1975) *Manufacturer-supplier relationships in Japan and the concept of relation-specific skill* Journal of the Japanese and International Economies, No. 3.

Barclay, I. (1992) *The New Product Development Process: Past Evidence and Future Practical Application* R & D Management, Vol. 22 No.3.

Bonaccorsi, A. and Turnbull, P. (1989) *The Use of Procurement Networks for Strategic Competitive Advantage in the Civil Aircraft Industry* in Wilson, D. et al (Eds.) *Research in Marketing: An International Perspective* Proceedings of the 5th I.M.P. Conference, Pennsylvania State University, September.

Bonaccorsi, A. and Lipparini, A. (1994) *Strategic Partnerships in New Product Development* Journal of Product Innovation Management, No. 11.

Booz Allen and Hamilton (1982) *New Product Development in the 1980s* New York, Booz Allen and Hamilton.

Buijs, J. (1984) *Stimulating Innovation: the Dutch Experience* Creativity and Innovation Network, Vol. 10 No. 4.

Consumers Association (1994) *Which?* July.

Cooper, R. and Kleinschmidt, E. (1990) *New Products: The Key Factors in Success* Chicago, American Marketing Association.

Cooper, R. and Kleinschmidt, E. (1993) *Screening New Products for Potential Winners* Long Range Planning Vol. 26 No. 6.

European (1994) *Cott Set to Take the Fizz out of Coca-Cola*, 8 July.

Gupta, A. and Govindarjan, V. (1984) *Business Unit Strategy, Managerial Characteristics and Business Unit Effectiveness at Strategy Implementation* Academy of Management Journal, March.

Hambrick, D., MacMillan, I. and Day, D. (1982) *Strategic Attributes and Performance in the BCG Matrix – A PIMS-based Analysis of Industrial Product Businesses* Academy of Management Journal, September.

Hammer, M. and Champy, J. (1993) *Re-engineering the Corporation – A Manifesto for Business Revolution* New York, Harper Collins.

Henderson, B. (1979) *Henderson on Corporate Strategy* Cambridge, Abt Books.

Mark, H. and Carver, L. (1987) *Challenger and Chernobyl* Interdisciplinary Science Review, Vol. 12 No.3, September.

McDonald, M. and Leppard, J. (1991) *The Marketing Audit* Oxford, Butterworth-Heinemann.

Mercer, D. (1993) *Death of the Product Life Cycle?* Admap, September.

Mercer, D. (1993a) *A Two-decade Test of Product Life-Cycle Theory* British Journal of Management, December.

Particelli, M. and Killips, C. (1986) *Successful New Product Development* in Buell, V. (Ed.), *Handbook of Modern Marketing* New York, McGraw-Hill.

Rothwell, R., Freeman, C., Horsley, A., Jervis, V., Robertson, A. and Townsend, J. (1974) *SAPPHO Updated: Project SAPPHO Phase II* Research Policy, 3.

Towner, S. (1994) *Four Ways to Accelerate New Product Development* Long Range Planning, Vol. 27 No. 2.

Chapter 5

Pricing

One person's price is another person's income.

> *W. H. Heller, American Economic Review, March 1975.*

We didn't actually overspend our budget. The Health Commission allocation simply fell short of our expenditure.

> *K. Davis (Chairman, Wollongong Hospital),*
> *Sydney Morning Herald, 14 November 1981.*

Organisations in the public sector have a special constraint in the matter of pricing. This is particularly true of those organisations that have customers in both the private and public sectors. Public-to-public sales are carefully regulated by HM Treasury rules; these are widely referred to as the *Fees and Charges* regimen. At the same time, the public sector may sell to the private sector. Public-to-private sales will be subject to the rules of the market-place though, at the same time, they still remain regulated by the Treasury rules.

Those organisations that sell to both segments will thus find themselves having to handle and understand two different types of pricing. An example is the Royal Mint who sell U. K. coins to 'the Government' but who also sell commemorative medals and limited editions to private collectors. Another set of problems arises when an organisation has to compare outsourcing with in-house and intra-departmental prices and costs.

Discussing both sides of this duality is necessary but can prove confusing. This chapter is therefore split into two parts. For convenience, this can be thought of as being:

- non-commercial pricing ('Fees and Charges')
- commercial pricing (the 'marketplace').

Since it is more germane for more public sector managers, the first area to be covered is the non-commercial pricing.

Fees and charges in the Public Sector

The past fifteen years or so have seen a substantial growth in the importance of fees and charges, and the related issue of pricing of services, in the public sector. To understand this development we need to see it in the context of changes in the culture of public service in recent years.

The Government's general attitude to the public services has been conditioned by three main factors. Firstly the state of the public finances over the past twenty years (and arguably going back further) has forced the Government to look at public expenditure and to try to bear down heavily on that spending. Secondly, Government's view over the last decade or so has been that the operation of free market forces is the best way of obtaining a productive and healthy economy. Lastly, Government has felt that the non-market economy would benefit from an injection of the commercial disciplines which operate in the private sector. As we shall see, these three factors have produced an environment in which fees and charges form an increasingly important revenue raising option in the public sector.

Falling out of Government's broad perspective on where the boundary between the market and the non-market economies should properly lie have come several initiatives which have increased the number and volume of services which are provided on a fees and charges basis. There has been a movement away from general taxation as a means of financing public services toward, wherever possible, charging for those services. If the benefit of a service can be identified as exclusively accruing to an individual or individuals, it may be argued, in economic theory, that those individuals should pay directly for the service rather than expect it to be provided at the expense of all taxpayers, many of whom may not wish to use it at all. This movement towards charging has been particularly prevalent in local authorities, whose two main sources of finance, central Government grants and local taxation (council tax), have been severely restricted. It may also have manifested itself in policies of increasing prescription charges and fees for dental work on the NHS and in suggestions for introducing motorway tolls.

The economic argument for charging goes further. Price can be used as a signal to markets as to the value of resources tied up in providing the service. Hence, in a competitive market, the operation of the mechanisms of supply and demand in establishing an equilibrium price will, under certain assumptions, ensure the best possible allocation of scarce resources. If a good or service, say the use of a motorway, is provided 'free of charge' then people will use more of that good or service than the balance of benefits and costs really justifies. Classical economists argue that any intervention by Government in the operation of markets by employing subsidies or tariffs, (or by providing 'free goods' which the market would provide if left to its own devices), distorts the market mechanism and leads to the inefficient distribution of resources.

Government's adherence to such market principles in recent times has influenced its attitude to the public sector. The presumption is firmly that commercial or quasi-commercial activities should preferably be in the private sector where commercial disciplines will ensure greater efficiency and quality. This belief has given rise to a privatisation programme which has now extended beyond the traditional national-ised industries and is now entering the administrative and regulatory areas of gov-ernment. The privatisation of the information technology functions of driver and vehicle licensing (DVOIT) in December 1993 may be followed by other Govern-ment activities which currently are established as executive agencies. Privatisation is only part of the story, however. Within the functions that remain within the public sector Government has in many areas created semi-autonomous, self-accounting units such as executive agencies (sometimes referred to as Next Steps agencies), and Trading Funds. It has also encouraged central Government departments to separate out core activities from more service-orientated activities and to put the service ac-tivities into a quasi or even fully contractual relationship with the core department. These relationships are often controlled and regulated by Supply and Service Agree-ments which lay down the terms and conditions of business between the 'service' and the 'core' in the same way as a formal contract between supplier and customer. Such agreements are relatively new in central Government whereas local govern-ment has been employing similar arrangements, styled Service Level Agreements, for many years.

This creation of internal markets, replacing the old bureaucratic relationships with contractual ones, is seen as a means to increased efficiency from public services. As the White Paper 'Competing for Quality' (HM Treasury, 1991) says:

Competition is the best guarantee of quality and value for money.

The White Paper goes on to point out that the idea of breaking down monolithic bureaucracies into smaller units which 'trade' with each other is not new:

In recent years, private sector businesses have increasingly chosen to concentrate on their core business. They stick with what they know best. And they buy in specialist contractors to provide new ideas, more flexibility, and a higher level of expertise than could exist in a purely in-house operation. Public sector bodies are increasingly doing the same

It is against this background that we must set the subject of fees and charges in central Government. Much of the detailed guidance on setting fees and charges reflects the context described above. Some of the guidance also derives from other principles about the role of the public sector, such as fairness and equity. In the following sections we shall see how these principles are translated into guidance and applied in practice.

❏ Categories of service for which fees and charges are levied

Guidance on setting fees and charges in central government and the National Health Service is set out in *The Fees and Charges Guide* (HM Treasury, 1992). The Guide identifies four categories of service for which a fee or charge may be levied:

- statutory services
- inter-departmental services
- intra-departmental services
- commercial services.

Statutory services

There are some situations in which a minister, department, agency, non-departmental public body (NDPB) or NHS body is responsible *under statute* for recovering a fee for a service. In general, and as a matter of policy, fees and charges are set in order to recover the full cost of providing a service, (a more detailed explanation of the breakdown of full cost is given below). It is also an important constitutional consideration, particularly with statutory services, that fees are not set purposely in order to achieve a surplus. To do so would in effect be levying extra taxation. The prerogative of levying taxation is jealously guarded by Parliament. Fees for statutory services should therefore be set to recover the full cost of the service (including a reasonable proportion of indirect costs) but no more than the full cost, although some degree of flexibility is obviously allowed in the interests of feasibility. Section 102 of the Finance (No. 2) Act 1987 allows the responsible Minister to make a Statutory Instrument which defines or increases the scope of costs which may be recovered by a fee. The Statutory Instrument, (when approved by the House of Commons by affirmative resolution), also allows the Minister to set a fee which is designed to cover ex-post deficits in the provision of the particular service.

Inter-departmental services

The levying of fees and charges by central Government departments on other departments, agencies, trading funds, NDPBs and NHS bodies and vice versa has grown considerably in recent years. Previously services provided by one department to another were dealt with on 'allied service' terms. In essence, the attitude was that, providing that both customer and supplier were within the government 'family' and that the net cost to the Exchequer was zero, there was little point in setting up systems to enable departments to charge for services provided. However, as we have seen above, the prevailing argument is that pricing is an important signal in the allocation of resources and it is now felt that 'allied service' terms mask the true picture of which departments are responsible for controlling what spending. Nowadays there are very few inter-departmental services that are provided without cash charging. The only justification for using allied service terms is provided by Government Accounting (HM Treasury, 1989 – as amended):

> Goods and services should . . . only be provided on allied service terms if the cost
> of payment transactions (e.g. raising invoices and paying bills) would outweigh
> the benefits of payment or if there are other exceptional considerations

Even if allied service terms exist the supplying department is obliged to inform the receiving department of the costs of the service and the receiving department is obliged to include the relevant elements of the costs in any charges which it makes on other bodies. The general policy is therefore that inter-departmental services should be charged for in cash and that charges should reflect the full cost of providing the service. The Fees and Charges Guide (HM Treasury, 1992) justifies this policy in the following terms:

> The general policy is that inter-departmental services should be charged for in cash.
> Payment provides the customer department with a greater incentive to use goods
> and services efficiently and economically, and results in more accurate presentation
> of costs to assist managers in making decisions. Payment also encourages the
> supplying department to provide goods and services which represent value for
> money. Customer departments should be free to buy services from whatever source
> provides best value for money.

Intra-departmental services

Again the development of 'hard charging' regimes between different sections of the same department has been a growing trend in recent years. The rationale for charging for intra-departmental services is much the same as that for inter-departmental charging; budgets are in the hands of customers who are free to choose between different suppliers, one of which may be the in-house supplier. The in-house supplier has to compete for funding to maintain the service and hence has a real interest in quality, customer service and a competitive pricing structure. Tight control of costs is therefore encouraged. The financial objective of an intra-departmental service is a matter for management to decide. Normally the policy should be to recover the full cost of providing the service.

Commercial services

With departments being increasingly encouraged to adopt a more commercial approach to service provision it is not surprising to find that there is nowadays a much wider range of services provided by Government to the wider public sector and the private sector for which discretionary fees are levied (as opposed to statutory fee services dealt with above). The Meterological Office sells detailed regional weather forecasts to a supermarket chain which uses the information to plan what type of sandwiches will be in demand. The Driver and Vehicle Licensing Agency sells and transfers cherished number plates to drivers. However, this is one area where Government's objective of encouraging a more commercial approach may come into conflict with one of its other objectives, that of reducing the size of the public sector. Treasury guidance entitled *Selling Government Services into Wider Markets* (HM Treasury, September 1991) highlights the potential conflict:

> The Government's policy is to restrict the size of the public sector and in general the presumption is that services should wherever possible be provided by the private sector rather than by the public sector, with the public sector buying in the services as necessary. This presumption applies in particular where a public body would be competing with the private sector. The fact that a public body can provide a service as well and as cheaply as any outside supplier is not in itself a reason for extending public sector activity.

As with the other categories of service outlined above the general rule is that commercial services will be priced with the objective of recovering the full cost of provision of the service, with due allowance made for the cost of capital, (for a fuller explanation of the concept of full cost see below). Charging at full cost is particularly important for commercial services since competition with private sector providers needs to be fair. A level playing field has to be maintained to ensure against accusations of unfair subsidies which may breach Articles 85 and 86 of the Treaty of Rome (the competition rules). As we have seen above in all categories of service, whether to internal or external customers or whether of a statutory or discretionary service, the general presumption is that charges will be based on full cost. It is now necessary to explore the idea of full cost in more detail, since traditional accounting methods in central Government do not easily arrive at accurate and reliable figures which reflect the full cost of resources consumed.

❏ The concept of full cost in central Government

In his budget speech in November 1993, the Chancellor of the Exchequer, Kenneth Clarke, said:

Government accounting for public spending has become archaic. In my view, the time has come to move to a system of accounting which identifies more clearly the cost of resources. This will put departments onto a similar accounting basis to commercial organisations and many other parts of the public sector

One of the main complaints about traditional Government accounting is that costing information for the purposes of setting fees and charges and designing performance indicators does not easily fall out of the existing system. A number of subtle and at first confusing adjustments have to be made to the bald figures produced in the appropriation accounts, (the main method by which departments present financial results to Parliament), to arrive at a measure of the resources consumed by a particular activity or service.

The chief reason for this incongruity is that appropriation accounts and the accounting systems that produce them are designed to capture only the *cash* costs of a department's operations, a system known not surprisingly as 'cash accounting'. Under cash accounting only the *payments made* by the end of financial year (usually 31 March) and the *receipts actually received* are recorded in the financial accounts. This contrasts with the commercial practice whereby expenditure is recorded as it is incurred and income is recorded as it is earned. This method is known as accruals accounting or the matching concept, since income is matched with the expenditure incurred in earning it with a view to presenting a fairer picture of financial performance, (Archibald, 1994).

Cash accounting also falls short of a true measure of resource consumption in the way in which it deals with capital expenditure. In commercial accounts relevant proportions of capital expenditure are charged to the operating account over a number of years broadly reflecting the consumption of the asset over time. Under cash accounting the purchase of an asset (which may have an expected life of say 10 years) is charged in full in the year of purchase. No account is taken of the utility of the asset over the remaining nine years of its life despite the fact that it may be contributing towards earning revenue in future years.

There are proposals to change the way in which Government (HM Treasury, July 1994) accounts for its spending to bring the system more in line with commercial-style accounts. However, in the meantime, in order to derive realistic figures about the full cost of resources consumed from the existing cash accounting systems a number of adjustments have to be made. These adjustments fall into three broad categories (although there is some overlap between the categories):

- timing differences
- non-cash costs
- notional costs.

Timing differences

Treasury guidance requires that, for the purpose of setting a fee or charge, costs should be calculated on an accruals basis. Briefly the main difference between the cash and accruals bases of accounting relates to how and when transactions are recorded in the accounts. Under cash accounting, sometimes referred to as receipts and payments accounting, payments are recorded when made and receipts when received. Under accruals accounting expenditure is recorded as and when it is incurred; similarly income is recorded as it is earned not when it is received. Because most Government departments account for expenditure on a cash basis, informal accruals-based accounts have to be prepared as part of the management accounting system. These accounts are known as Memorandum Trading Accounts (MTAs). MTAs are not published nor audited by the Government's external auditor, the Comptroller and Auditor General. MTAs record transactions on an income and expenditure basis (accruals) and also seek to measure the actual consumption of, rather than the cash paid for, items such as stock and fixed assets.

Non-cash costs

This is a slightly misleading use of terminology since many of the costs in this category are ultimately paid for in cash. However they do not necessarily fall directly on the budget of the department or section of the department which is providing the service to which the costs relate. Hence adjustments and apportionments need to be made which may not necessarily reflect actual cash paid in the relevant accounting period. The principal items under this category are overheads or indirect costs. These should include a relevant and fair proportion of the costs of management and of support services and inspection which relate to the activity being costed. Usually overheads are apportioned to activities by use of a proxy measure, e.g. the costs of the personnel department might be apportioned to activities on the basis of the number of employees working on the activity.

The other major item under this heading is depreciation. As mentioned above, central Government departments do not account for the consumption of capital assets. Depreciation is the mechanism by which this consumption is measured and matched with the income derived from the assets employed. Briefly, a proportion of the value of a capital asset is charged to a particular accounting period, the remainder being carried over to be charged to future years approximating to the useful life of the asset. As well as according with the 'matching concept' described above, this has the effect of smoothing expenditure patterns over a number of years. Given that most fees and charges are set to recover full

cost on a year-on-year basis this method of accounting for capital avoids fluc-
tuations in the level of the fee from year to year. Examples of other costs under
this heading are:

- development costs which may under certain circumstances be
  amortised over a period of more than one year in a similar way to
  capital assets
- relocation and redundancy costs
- the costs of allied services (see above)
- superannuation costs which may not be borne directly by the activity
  providing the service.

Notional costs

The idea of a 'notional cost' is an odd one and is difficult to describe generically.
The two main costs in government which are usually referred to as notional
costs are:

- insurance
- the cost of capital.

Government departments generally work on the principle that 'the Crown bears
its own risks'. Departments do not therefore pay a premium for insurance against
public liability, damage to property and so on. Any losses from such events have
to be made good through the normal procedures of Parliament voting cash for
specified purposes. However, Treasury guidance says that in order to reflect the
true cost of resources consumed notional premia should be charged in the build-
up of full cost for charging purposes. Treasury issues guidance on premium rates
for the main types of risk likely to be encountered. As an example, employer's
liability for clerical and office staff is to be charged at 0.1% of payroll. Another
reason for charging notional insurance is the 'level playing field' argument. A
potential private sector supplier of a particular service would have to bear a real
cost of insurance, therefore a Government department should reflect this in its
costings to ensure fair competition.

The inclusion of a charge to reflect the cost of capital tied up in a particular
service is also a reflection of the need for a level playing field for competition
between public and private provision. The Government raises its funding principally through taxation; the private sector raises money through borrowing at
commercial rates of interest. A private sector company will require a return on
capital employed at least equal to or in excess of the rate it is paying to borrow

money, (or the opportunity cost of holding its assets in buildings, machinery and so on rather than in interest-bearing deposits). In order to level the playing field Treasury requires that fees and charges should be set to recover full cost including the cost of capital. Given that there is no real interest cost attached to capital raised through taxation the Treasury sets a notional rate for the cost of capital of 6% in circumstances where there is little competition from the private sector. In instances where there is competition or the private sector might be thought to be bearing a higher risk (thus requiring higher returns) a cost of capital of 8% or higher may be appropriate.

❏ Other pricing considerations

As already explained, the presumption in establishing a price for a service in central Government is that the price should reflect the full cost of providing that service, including an appropriate charge for the cost of capital employed. The arguments behind this approach are that it promotes accountability, transparency and provides a level playing field between public and private provision.

However, as described below, full cost is not the only basis used for setting prices. This is particularly true in the private sector where considerations other than the recovery of full costs may prevail. The establishment of, or increase in, market share may lead companies to set prices below full cost in the short or medium term, the 'loss leader' concept. Equally where market conditions indicate that there is excess demand companies may price on the basis of what they believe the market is prepared to pay for their products or services. This may be well above full cost plus a normal profit margin. So far we have concentrated on the concept of full cost as being the basis of setting fees and charges in central Government. Treasury guidance (HM Treasury, 1989) is in fact slightly less prescriptive on this matter than the earlier discussion might imply:

> Fees and charges for goods and services should reflect the appropriate costs. They should normally be set to recover the value of the resources used to produce them. This is the economic concept of 'opportunity cost', which values resources in the use to which they would otherwise be put were they not used in producing the service in question.

The guidance goes on to stress that in the majority of cases opportunity cost will equate to full cost and that full cost should be the basis for setting fees for inter- and intra-departmental charges. However, in setting fees for discretionary services to the wider public sector and the private sector it may be appropriate to reflect the fact that in special cases the opportunity cost may be above or below full cost. The main instance in which opportunity cost is less than full cost is where a department has planned or unplanned spare capacity. Frequently this arises because departments have obligations to maintain spare capacity to cope with emergencies. In this case the opportunity cost of using the spare capacity to provide services is zero and the real cost is limited to the extra cost of resources which do have alternative uses such as staff and materials, a concept known as 'marginal cost'. Departments are permitted in such cases to charge to recover their marginal costs only (but in no circumstances should fees be set to recover less than marginal cost).

Any decision to charge less than full cost needs to be considered very carefully since there is a danger that accusations of unfair competition may be levelled at departments by the private sector. Several tests need to be satisfied which are detailed in Treasury guidelines (HM Treasury, 1991) entitled *Selling Government Services into Wider Markets*. Briefly the activity must be justified in terms of its contribution to the department's core objectives and the pricing must be seen to be fair so that the private sector would have no reasonable cause for complaint.

Instances in Government where opportunity cost is greater than full cost are very rare. In essence opportunity cost is greater than full cost when more is demanded of a service than can be supplied at current levels of capacity. In such instances it may be appropriate to charge the price that the market will bear, since this is the best measure of opportunity cost. Again care needs to be exercised in such cases because Government could be accused of levying extra taxation or of abusing its monopoly position in the provision of certain services. An interesting, if highly untypical, example of Government charging the market rate for providing a service in conditions where excess demand exists is the sale of cherished number plates by the Driver and Vehicle Licensing Agency. In 1992–3 the DVLA collected £23. 2 million from the sale of 75,000 cherished marks against costs of £4. 4 million. This represents a rate of return which would be the envy of any private sector business.

The issue of the pricing of goods and services provided by Government is a complex one and is growing in importance as the public sector is encouraged to adopt a more commercial approach to its operations. These complexities tend to arise where Government occupies the middle ground between the provision of pure public and pure private goods and services.

Current Government thinking suggests that the public sector should as far as possible withdraw from that middle ground and allow the market economy to occupy it. Where this is not possible or feasible Government is keen to ensure that commercial disciplines operate and that wherever possible and sensible the costs of public services are financed by consumers rather than tax payers. Road charging and charging for the use of Government tradeable information are but two developments under active consideration. The setting of appropriate and equitable fees and charges seems likely to be an issue which grows rather than diminishes in importance in the future.

Commercial pricing

The idea of price in the market place holds a fascination for many people. This may be because of a basic dichotomy that faces us all. We often have an idea of what the price of something *ought* to be but find that this is different from what we are asked to pay. Why, we wonder, does the price of water in the U.K. depend so much on where we live? Then, some prices appear fixed while others are variable. We will pay the price asked for petrol but expect to haggle over a second-hand car. We accept the National Insurance amounts as immutable but will argue with the Inland Revenue. At auctions, nothing is certain. Even some academics lean to pragmatism rather than dogmatism. Tim Ambler (1994) of the London Business School said:

> Pricing in the real world has more variables than the mind can consider . . . throw away your economic text books, it's all garbage.

During the early 1990s, a drug known as GHB enjoyed a spell as an aphrodisiac. The cost of production was 5p a tablet while the price on the street was £15 each, a profit margin to satisfy the most devoted free-marketeer. If an NHS hospital tried to charge for private beds at a similar profit margin it is unlikely that the event would have passed without comment from the press. At the same time as the GHB bonanza, a restaurant chain was selling an orange drink to its customers at a price that was 60 times the raw material cost. At the time, the customers seemed happy with both the product and the price.

There are many pressures and factors that can affect price, and price can vary widely with time, place and other variables. The person dying of thirst in the Sahara would pay a higher price per litre for water than would somebody accustomed to getting it from a tap in Eastbourne. During the tulipmania craze, the price of a rare tulip bulb was equivalent to twenty years' average wages because it was thought that the price the next day could be twenty-two or twenty-four years' wages.

Clearly then, the concept of price can be complicated, even bizarre. What is less complicated, however, is that customers tend to expect that purchases from the public sector should in some way be 'fair'. The public sector is not protected when it is in mirror mode. It often has to make its purchases in the marketplace where the concept of fairness does not apply. It is important, therefore, for everybody in the public sector to understand about prices in the free market economy. Such an understanding will also be relevant in those situations pointed out earlier where full cost and opportunity cost are not necessarily the same.

❏ Prices and strategy

The policy that is adopted for pricing is at the heart of almost every organisa-tional strategy. Income is the product of price and quantity sold, and quantity sold will normally be a function of price, so this year's results depend on price. A well-known firm of management consultants pointed out (in a privately dis-tributed paper) that, even more fundamentally, today's pricing determines who your customers and competitors will be in the future.

The approach to pricing and its strategic importance will depend (Zikmund and d'Amico, 1993) on which objectives are uppermost in an organisation's strategy. Objectives could embrace any or more than one of the following:

Income:	attain a target Return on Investment, maximise profits, raise shareholder added value, optimise cash flow, keep the concern going, survive.
Sales:	maintain/increase market share, maintain/increase actual sales, discourage sales.
Competition:	meet/beat competition, undercut competition, avoid/prevent competition.
Social concerns:	behave ethically, support green concerns, maintain employment.

If the primary objective is to maximise sales, then it may be acceptable to take small margins and so to price low. If the primary objective is to maximise income, then it is necessary to take account of elasticity of demand in setting price. If the over-riding objective is 'to survive' then a range of discounts may be used. If the objective is stated baldly as being to maximise profits, then there is the possibility that managers will take a too short-term attitude to pricing. They may price very high, 'whatever the market will bear'. This is a particular temptation for the unskilled product-monopolist. If the price is so high that people feel that they are being cheated then the advantage may prove short lived. In the extreme, such actions may attract countering actions by a Government or super-governmental body.

❏ Target market expectations

Every sales director has to ask the question:

> Who are the customers we are aiming at, and how much do they expect to pay?

It will be noted that this is a very different question from the accountant's one:

> How much does it cost to make and how much mark-up do we add?

It is also different from the sales rep who asks:

> How much is my competitor charging and why isn't my list price 15% less?

The consumers, of course, always want to buy at the cheapest possible price – is that not true? No, it is not true. Consumers will often choose services and goods that are far from being the cheapest around. This is because of belief in the principle that 'price confers quality and value'. People often boast that they bought a personal computer at a knock-down price; the same people would not dream of claiming that the whisky being offered to guests was the cheapest around. It is a favourite exercise at business schools to get a street trader to divide their apples into three piles with three different prices. The students are gratifyingly impressed to watch how many people ignore the cheapest pile and go for the middle price, believing that this represents best value.

The bad news about target market expectations is that they are not entirely amenable to market research. Before launching a new product, it is possible to show a picture or a mock-up to people and to ask them whether they would propose to buy it if it became available. This is normally done while suggesting a wide range of prices that the item could cost. In theory it should then be possible to build up an idea of probable sales as well as to get an indication of the elasticity of demand. Price elasticity measures the effect of a change in price on the demand for a product; it indicates the price sensitivity. It is clearly useful to know what the price sensitivity of a service or good is since that enables one to calculate the price at which profitability is maximised. Some products, such as insulin, are not sensitive to price changes. Diabetics need a certain quantity of insulin and would not increase their consumption if the price were reduced. On the other hand, it appears that the sales of red roses are much more dependent on price.

The problem with asking people if they would buy, say, a green dye that would make their lawn look absolutely perfect is that many of them would reply positively. Too many, in fact, since it would be more than would actually buy the product when it hit the shops. The expectation would be yes, the reality would be no, for a large number of respondents.

Another type of problem with target market expectations occurs when people get used to a particular price level and show great resistance to paying more. It is not always easy to predict when this is going to happen. Two examples from America may illustrate this. In 1992, competition forced the price of a return air ticket between New York and Los Angeles to $199. This price became stuck in people's minds as the 'right' price. In 1993 the price went back to a more commercial level and was promptly met with very weak flight demand. The other example is Arby's roast beef fast food chain. Looking for new products they introduced barbecued ribs at $2. 59 and $3. 99. The ribs were popular with customers. Since Arby's were not making any money on the ribs they tried to raise the price four times in a year but the customers just did not want to pay the higher price. The product was good, the customers liked it but the price was inconsistent with what people expected it to be. These are two examples of consumers apparently being strong enough to resist price increases.

On the other hand, customers readily accept the high margins and hence high price of fragrances and do not go on strike when the price rises. Similarly, the retail price of instant coffee during the 1980s and 1990s did not precisely reflect the price of raw coffee. It might be expected that people would be driven to tea as a substitute (as they are for the butter/margarine market) when instant coffee rose in price, but this did not happen. Economists will say that this is just a matter of elasticity of demand. The practical problem is being able to predict with certainty what the elasticity will be, and whether and when it will change.

The public sector has exactly the same problems as the following four examples demonstrate.

- *museum admission charges* Britons on foreign holidays accept that they will have to pay to get into museums, but are resistant to paying the same amount at home. This causes difficulties for British museums when setting a price. Some have used the 'voluntary donation' route to escape the problem. Most marketers consider that this problem will reduce with the passage of time
- *passports* There seems to be a widespread acceptance of the fee that has to be paid for a passport. Though people that we have spoken to also feel that there should be no element of profit over and above the cost of production
- *charges for NHS prescriptions* Most people accept (albeit grudgingly) the fact of a charge for NHS prescriptions, except for a few who consider that they should be free. Moreover, most people accept the

idea of dual pricing based on a system of exceptions. However, the thought of trying to decide what the charge 'ought' to be is somewhat daunting

- *Royal Mint prices* The Royal Mint charges customers much more than the cost of production for many of its items, such as limited editions and proof coinage. The customers accept this. If the Mint sold at cost price then customers would buy for onward selling at a profit to themselves. This would create a climate of uncertainty that collectors do not want.

❏ Types of price

We can define price as follows:

The price of an item represents the point of agreement between a seller and a buyer. It can also be considered a point of conflict between buyer and seller.

Accepting this definition, it is not surprising that the literature puts forward a large number of different types of price. Some of these types are common, others much less so.

Cost pricing

One of the commonest ways of setting price is *economic price* which is also known as 'standard cost' price. This is the level at which the seller covers the fixed and variable costs plus a percentage (or unit add-on) as a profit margin. Since in most cases it would be difficult to allocate the actual fixed and variable costs for individual items, it is usual to use a standard figure for costs based on standard conditions and volume. This method looks reasonable to many people, and to many cost accountants looks the most reliable. It is therefore worth considering some of its disadvantages, which are as follows:

- in practice it is difficult to allocate joint costs to specific products. There are some organisations that still allocate joint costs on the basis of the labour hours for each product. The growing use of equipment, machinery and automation make this type of approach progressively less accurate as capital expenditure rises
- it ignores elasticity of demand, profit optimisation, and market share aims
- it also ignores competition, capital needs, replacement costs and return on investment questions

- it shies away from the fact that costs vary with volume – and volume varies with price.

Economic or standard-cost pricing should not be confused with *cost-plus* pricing. Under cost-plus pricing a buyer agrees to pay what the seller says are its costs plus an amount for profit. Put like this, some of the disadvantages should be immediately obvious. However, there are some very big contracts when it is accepted that a cost-plus-profit formula is desirable. When the navy wants a new type of submarine built, it knows the difficulties facing a ship-yard in forecasting accurately a price, especially if technical problems and mind-changing are expected. So a cost-plus formula may be used. Other contracts may also use a formula. For example, IBM had such a contract with a hotel chain for executives on visits, and Marks and Spencer had a contract with a Welsh firm to produce fruit cake. But in both cases the buyer had access to all accounts and could even suggest cost savings. The disadvantages of a cost-plus system are the same as the ones for economic price given above with some extra ones as follows:

- checking the costs is a pretty tortuous affair, especially if semi-variable costs loom large (e. g. repairs, specialised equipment, delivery)
- without the type of rights exercised by IBM and Marks and Spencer, inefficiency is encouraged
- without a high measure of goodwill, accuracy and honesty, the buyer may become stuck with another customer's costs. No leading film producer or actor would accept a deal based on a percentage of the profits of a film; instead they would insist on a percentage of gross takings.

Another questionable approach is *average cost* price. Here all the costs are added up together, allocated to the various services or goods and a profit added. If a competitor is using average cost pricing, then one knows one is on to a winner. An extreme example may show the futility of this approach. A hospital could calculate its total costs for a year and than divide this by the number of operations carried out in the year. This would mean that the charge for a tonsillectomy would be the same as for a major organ transplant. An organisation using average cost pricing across a range of services or products inevitably over-charges for part of its offerings and under-charges for most of the rest. This is a reasonably assured path to ultimate bankruptcy, in a competitive situation, because competitors will undercut where one is over-charging, leaving one with large volumes of business where one is under-charging.

There is another path to bankruptcy that is even more assured. That is the one known as *marginal pricing*. The 'marginal cost' is the increase in total costs when just one more unit is produced. The marginal revenue is the increase in total revenues when one more unit is sold. (Professional economists might prefer a longer explanation but this will suffice for our purposes). There is a temptation among sales staff to use this to justify selling at almost any price. One has to watch particularly for phrases like, 'it's a contribution to overheads and profits'. The marginal cost for an extra guest in a hotel is often less than £1. Would you expect to be able to go along to a hotel, offer £2 for the night and expect to be greeted with open arms? The problem is that marginal cost prices do not recover overheads, sufficient products must be sold at above marginal cost to allow those overheads to be recovered.

There are a few, most rare, occasions when a marginal price is allowable. When this is done, one must be careful never, never, to commit any of the following heinous sins (Winkler, 1984):

- using it across national boundaries, or else a court action for dumping or unfair competition is quite likely to ensue
- allowing it to set a precedent for the future or for other customers
- allowing just a few selected costs to be included in the 'marginal' category
- allowing the volumes sold at marginal cost prices to commit you to extra capital expenditure
- allowing it to take away resources from other sales
- allowing responsibility for the decision to use marginal price to be delegated (or perhaps to be given to anybody in the marketing or sales division).

In the public sector there is a risk that marginal cost pricing could be interpreted by the private sector as unfair competition.

Having been unkind to prices based on costs, it has to be strongly emphasised that we are in no way suggesting that cost information is less than important. In fact, it is vital. Costs remain one of the foremost pieces of information to guide management in its decision making. It is just that it is a poor instrument as a single drive to deciding price. Not only must costs be known, they must be constantly pushed downwards to remain competitive and/or to improve value for money.

Market-related prices

Some textbooks define *market price* as being the price that the market is willing to pay. If asked, many sales directors will cheerfully give one a figure that reflects this definition. Strictly speaking, one should not talk of market price in the singular since there are lots of market prices. If there is any validity in the concepts of supply and demand and elasticity then market prices have to reflect this. A market price is the market price at a particular level of volume. The lower the price, the more that people will buy; the higher the price, the less that people will buy. Salespeople may riposte that market price is the price that maximises sales or profits. This forces one to make the decision usually expressed as going for either high margin-low volume or low margin-high volume – or, of course, anywhere along the spectrum in between. The market price will depend upon the volumes of sales or the market share which you wish to achieve.

We have already seen that it is not usually possible to get a market price by asking people what they would be willing to pay. They do not know until they are faced with the actual buying decision. Therefore, one tries to narrow the range by employing a range of techniques:

(a) *Market survey research*   This is asking people to their face certain questions about likely buying patterns. As just stated, this is an uncertain method. When used it is usually advisable to employ independent researchers, and to ask questions about price in an oblique way. It is also vital to ensure that the sample is representative of the relevant market. All of this is likely to require professional advice.

(b) *Market trials*   The service or good is test sold in different areas or segments at different prices. It is not easy, though, to isolate the effect that just the price alone is having. Remember that unless the competition is exceptionally dozy they will know what you are doing.

(c) *Statistical analysis*   Taking great care with the methodology and the resulting information, it is possible to get statisticians to build up from past and present data a correlation between price and volume. This has to be interpreted using one's own specialised knowledge. For example, were there special factors around, are there large inventories in the system which imply that volumes distributed are not actually being sold? Obviously, this approach is useless for new services and goods.

(d) *Market and competitor data*   This, in the real world, is the basis of much marketprice setting. What are the prices of the same and similar products in the market place right now? Do we wish to get up or down of that, and by how much? What are the competition doing that could affect the picture?

(e) *Other information*   This includes data from one's own sales force, market reports, trade journals, trade associations, newspapers, annual reports, price lists, and so on.

None of these guarantees success but they all help to reduce the odds and all could be relevant to pricing services in the public sector for assessing, for example, the impact of changes in prescription charges, of new entrance charges, or of different charges for internal consultancy services. The use of the first four does require support from those with particular professional skills, especially statisticians, economists or operational researchers.

There are some forecasting graveyards around. One of the best known is the special offers to readers made by magazines and newspapers. In spite of much mathematical effort, these remain very difficult to predict.

The following are some of the many market-related pricing approaches.

(a) *Skim price*   This is a very high price that is intended to 'skim off' the top tranche of demand. Collectors in general are likely to find themselves subjected to skimming, and being unable psychologically to do much about it. It is also commonly used at the introductory stage of a new and highly unusual product. The 'innovators' and 'early adopters' will pay a high price. Importantly, when this happens the later reduction in price does not cause resentment.

(b) *Prestige price*   This is also a high price but one which is meant to bring prestige to the purchaser. Products such as fragrances, furs, and diamonds all infer quality if the price is kept high. Some luxury cars have a certain cachet because they are expensive; a cheap Ferrari would become much less exciting to buy. It is possible, but difficult, to maintain a prestige profile in one segment only. The management consultants McKinsey had for a while a far higher reputation in the U.K. than in America. The Vidal Sassoon name was used in up-market hair salons while being affixed to mid-market hair products in supermarkets. What is almost impossible is to sell grossly inferior products at a prestige price for long. Prestige prices may be felt to be inapplicable in the public sector, but there can be cases where a high price could be acceptable for a special service, for example, driving tests at the weekend. Even there, people may accept the higher price only because they recognise that costs are higher, they may not accept the idea of a high level of profit for the special service.

(c) *Moral price*   A moral price is based on a notion of fairness which is somewhat hazy but which is understood by most people. It is used most by local and central Government and by charities. Sometimes this is because a true cost is difficult or time-consuming to prepare, but more usually because of social or political sensibilities. A charity will sell goods at their retail shops very cheaply but charge high prices for a gala evening at the Royal Opera House. The idea of 'green' prices would be put into this category. A town in Hungary wished to encourage the use of public transport so ran trams to the largest employer at 2p a time. The take-up remained low except for single-parents and the 'physicals' as they were known. There was even a measure of resentment and ridicule from the Party officials and senior management who felt that they were paying for the subsidy through higher taxes. This highlights a problem for moral prices. If they are low relative to costs, someone has to pay for them maybe without their agreement. The notion of fairness is likely to play a particularly important role in setting prices for public services.

(d) *Charm price* (also known as 'pricing points' and 'odd-and-even pricing') A car may be priced at £9,999 rather than £10,000 because it feels much less; that is the theory and it certainly seems to work. Even large-scale contracts in the £millions have been seen with charm pricing. There are times when a charm price does not work. First, when it means that change has to come into the transaction (coin-op machines, daily newspapers), second, when the sale is of professional services or a prestige purchase. A lawyer would not charge £999 instead of £1,000, a diamond tiara would not be priced at £149,995 though a house might be.

(e) *Promotion pricing* This may seem to be an imprecise term but people in marketing recognise it as being distinct. Promotion pricing is often used to take up slack demand or to dispose of end-of-season stock. It is meant to dispose of something you have that would otherwise stick. Thus telephone charges are lower during off-peak times. Airlines offer stand-by tickets and theatres offer on-the-night reduced seat prices. Promotion prices are often connected with special discounts and other help to coal-face sellers (the Monopolies and Mergers Commission spent four years looking at discounts in the 1980s). Promotion pricing should be thought of as being short term in operation. Otherwise the seller may lose profits. For example, many people send fax messages overnight during the off-peak rate thus saving money. This may be acceptable if the shift to the off-peak price saves costs by allowing peak capacity to be lower than it otherwise would be. Airline passengers may buy a regular-priced ticket and then turn up at the airport to try to buy a stand-by. If they buy one, they cash the regular priced ticket and so save money and if none are available they use the normal ticket and lose nothing. This loss of revenue would have no compensating cost saving. Off-peak pricing has been a common feature of nationalised industries over the last twenty years or so. It is likely to be more easily accepted where it is recognised that it helps to reduce costs, by reducing the need for expensive peak capacity.

(f) *Penetration price* This is a price set so low that it is difficult for the competition to follow. It is therefore often used at the launch of a new product or a move into a new market segment to make the 'cost of entry' high for the competition. It is particularly useful if any of the following situations apply:

- demand for the product is very price-sensitive
- substantial cost savings are possible at high volumes
- imitation is easy and the costs of entry low
- market segmentation is weak since there is mass market acceptance.

Penetration prices have to be truly well below what would otherwise be the case. The odd few percentage points are not enough, 40% or more may be required. At one time, ball-point pens were actually prestige objects. Baron Bic gambled on bringing the price down so much that they would become a mass market. In this case, the gamble paid off but it does not always; penetration prices are strictly for those with strong nerves. A penetration price is designed to secure a degree of competitive advantage which would not normally be acceptable in the public sector.

(g) *Variable prices*   In the western industrial countries there is a tendency to think of most prices as being fixed. A tube of toothpaste from Boots in Sheffield should be the same price as one from Boots in Solihull. This can lead to the consumer being less vigilant than is warranted. A stallholder in a market is quite likely to charge customers different prices depending on their appearance. Even a supermarket may change its prices in one store to meet local competition. A certain mail order company selling office equipment and stationery products sends out catalogues to potential customers with tempting prices. If an organisation sends in an order then it will later get another catalogue, but some of the prices will be higher. The company concerned claims that people will buy initially because of the prices but will continue to buy because of the level of service offered. Variable prices might be thought to be wholly inappropriate in the public sector but in practice there are cases where the price paid depends upon an individual's circumstances, (for example, eye-tests and school trips). The notion of 'fairness' has to come into play here. What would people regard as fair for this particular service?

❏ Price wars

There are people around who would really enjoy the prospect of a price war. It can look to some people as though it holds out the possibility of finally beating the opposition for once and all. Various sorts of military images and metaphors spring to mind, 'blitzkrieg', 'gaining the high ground', 'a pre-emptive strike', and so on. In a price war, two or more competitors keep reducing their prices to gain market share or to drive the competition out of business.

Attractive though this may seem, the advice of marketing consultants nowadays is that price wars should be avoided except in the most rare and specialised of circumstances. This advice is often ignored; price wars can become rather emotional affairs and too much ego can drive out arithmetic. It is arithmetic that provides the first reason for avoiding a price war unless one has unusually high profit margins. Figure 5. 1 shows the extra amount that has to be sold just to stand still in terms of profit if one cuts prices. The extra volume required depends on the price cut percentage and the gross profit margin percentage. As can be seen, this table implies an elasticity of demand that is higher than is usually found.

Volumes required to maintain profit as prices are reduced			
	Profit Margin *(percentage)*		
	10%	20%	30%
1	+11%	+5%	+3%
2	+25%	+11%	+7%
3	+43%	+18%	+11%
4	+67%	+25%	+15%
5	+100%	+33%	+20%
10	∞	+100%	+50%

(left axis label: Price Cut (percentage))

Figure 5. 1. Increasing volumes and price cuts.

The second reason for avoiding a price war is that the table assumes that the competition will stand idly by and not retaliate to the price cut. In real life, a price cut is one of the competitive tools that is easiest to imitate. Anybody can follow suit. If there is a market share gain from price cutting, then the competition will normally do it as well. The third reason for avoiding a price war is that it is likely to change customers' expectations in two ways. They think that the new lower price is normal, and will start to think much more in terms of price alone when making a buying decision. Finally, the industry shake-outs that are expected from all-out wars sometimes do not occur. Two airlines (PanAm and Eastern) went under but their capacity did not entirely disappear. New entrants (Kiwi and Reno) bought up parts of the two failed airlines at 25% of value which meant that their costs were that much lower than the players who stayed in the game.

There is anecdotal evidence (Serwer, 1994) that organisations that fight on price alone may find it difficult to fight their way out. In America, Heinz had to reduce their price to retailers of the pet-food '9-Lives' by 22% over a period of time. Eventually, they decided to stop the reductions and in 1991 they increased the price. Not one of the competitors followed suit and Heinz' market share dropped from 23% to 15%. Heinz then decided that they would have to re-figure or re-design their product since customers' expectations had changed. They now expected a $5\frac{1}{2}$ oz can of pet-food to cost 25 – 35 cents. Heinz realised that they had to bring their cost of production down so that they could live with this situation. The process re-design was major. It included closing eight plants, centralisation, vertical integration, and reducing operating costs by 30%. There is also anecdotal evidence (Garda and Marn, 1993) that more organisations get into a price war through accident rather than as deliberate policy. This is often through misreading a competitor's intentions, or jumping to (incorrect) conclusions.

Wars are particularly likely to break out when there is excess capacity in an industry, when deflation occurs, where brand-name products cost a lot more than unbranded or private label, where gross margins are very high, where a market has a high percentage of products with low profit margins and where entrepreneurs run an organisation as a private fiefdom.

The results of a price war can take years to overcome. In 1983, Reemtsma Cigarettenfabriken cut the cost of its 'West' cigarettes in Germany from DM 3. 80 to DM 3. 30. It saw its market share shoot up in four months from less than 1% to 10%. Naturally, the competition responded, upsetting the previously stable price structures. It was four years before stability returned. In 1993, just ten years later, Philip Morris cut the price of Marlborough cigarettes in America from $2. 20 to $1. 80. This was because the spread of own-label cigarettes was hurting. RJR followed suit with its Winston brand. Marlborough's market share increased from 22% to 27%; domestic operating profits from Philip Morris's tobacco business fell 25% (from $1 billion to $769 million per quarter).

When considering price wars, one is reminded of the battle of Edgehill in 1642 between the Royalists and the Parliamentarians. When night fell on 23 October, both sides thought that they had lost but neither considered itself entirely defeated. However, at nightfall both sides knew that a bloody war had become inevitable, and so it proved.

Price wars are most likely to occur where there is a strongly competitive market, a situation where the public sector is unlikely to be involved as a major supplier. If a public sector organisation were to be caught up in a price war it would raise some very difficult questions, because the price reductions might well fall foul of the requirement for competition from public sector suppliers to be fair at all times.

Price is increasing in importance. Moreover (Simon, 1992):

> Virtually no segment of the market is immune from price attacks, not even

premium categories ... Often, aggressive pricing is the only choice for newcomers. Such entries induce a collapse of hitherto stable price systems.

This implies that organisations must think long and hard about their pricing strategy and relate this to their overall strategy. This is not a universal approach, by any means. Let us hope that we can all avoid the extreme picture painted by David Ogilvy. He once said (1988):

> Pricing is guesswork. It is usually assumed that marketers use scientific methods to determine the price of their products. Nothing could be further from the truth. In almost every case, the process of decision is one of guesswork.

References

Ambler, T. (1994) *Pricing's Powerful Punch* Marketing, 4 August.

Archibald, V. (1994) *Accruals Accounting in the Public Sector* Harlow, Longman.

Garda, R. and Marn, M. (1993) *Price Wars* The McKinsey Quarterly, No. 3.

HM Treasury (1991) *Competing for Quality: Buying Better Public Services* (Cm 1730) London HMSO.

HM Treasury (1992) *The Fees and Charges Guide* London HMSO.

HM Treasury (1994) *Better Accounting for the Taxpayer's Money: Resource Accounting and Budgeting in Government* (Cm 2626) London HMSO.

HM Treasury (1989 – as amended) *Government Accounting* London HMSO.

HM Treasury (1991) *Selling Government Services into Wider Markets* (unpublished).

Ogilvy, D. (1988) *Ogilvy on Advertising* New York, Vintage Books.

Serwer, A. (1994) *How to Escape a Price War* Fortune, 13 June.

Simon, H. (1992) *Pricing Opportunities – and How to Exploit Them* Sloan Management Review, Winter.

Winkler, J. (1984) *Pricing for Results* Bicester, Facts on File Publications.

Zikmund, W. and d'Amico, M. (1993) *Marketing* St. Paul, West Publishing.

Chapter 6

Promotion

'All publicity is good publicity'. This famous piece of advice has been ascribed to so many different people that it is now difficult to know whom to blame. It will therefore have to suffice to say that it is not true. The past is littered with examples of promotion ideas, publicity and advertising that manifestly harmed rather than helped. One of the most oft-quoted examples is Strand cigarettes. These were launched in 1960 using mood photographs of a young man in a raincoat mooching around in lonely locations. This picture was accompanied by the famous slogan, 'You're never alone with a Strand'. The figure was, it has been claimed, supposed to be reminiscent of the late James Dean as well as Frank Sinatra (the theme tune became a hit). The idea of the advertisement was to highlight the user-friendly nature of the new cigarette. You could rely on a Strand to be your friend. The impact was not that intended. The target segment rejected the picture and slogan emphatically. The youth was not a romantic figure to them. Why was he alone late at night, was he a loner, a loser? Virtually nobody wanted to identify with the figure. Strand cigarettes soon disappeared from the market.

Another famous gaffe was that of the chief of Ratners, a jewellery chain, who announced in a speech that his shops sold 'crap' and that the life of some of their products was 'less than a Marks and Spencer sandwich'. This was meant to be a light-hearted moment in the speech but the fates decreed otherwise. Sales dropped off very sharply. The chief had to resign and the chain changed its name.

But our favourite riposte to the above epigram concerned the building of a magnificent new staff canteen by the U.S. Department of Agriculture in 1977. This was named to commemorate a nineteenth-century Colorado pioneer. Amidst a blaze of publicity the Agriculture Secretary declared open the Alfred Packer Memorial Dining Facility. He said, 'Alfred Packer exemplifies the spirit and fare this agriculture department cafeteria will provide'. A few months later the cafeteria was re-named with rather less publicity. An historian had pointed out that, in 1874, Alfred Packer had been convicted of murdering and eating five prospectors.

The promotion mix

The promotion mix is the name given to the various types of promotion that may be used; strategy is the way that these are used and how they are used. The types of promotion are usually described as being the following.

(a) *Publicity*   This is information about an organisation, an event or a product that is normally carried by a third party such as radio, newspapers or magazines without payment or control by the organisation itself. The lack of payment is attractive but the lack of control is less so. A journalist visited the Civil Service College to collect material for an article. One of the first questions asked was, 'Is it true that on the creative thinking course you get all the men and women to feel one another all over?' Visions of potential headlines were worrying but unfounded. *Public relations* are efforts to try to manage the type of publicity that arises.

(b) *Advertising*   This is the best known method of promotion and the one with which most people are familiar. Advertising is a message that persuades (or that informs) people with the aim of increasing the likelihood of an action being taken. It is directed through various media such as film, posters, radio, newspapers, journals, and television. It is paid for by the relevant sponsor, who also keeps almost complete control over the content of the message. The intriguing part of advertising is that there is no control over the impact of the message. As with all communication, the key phrase is, 'I know what I said but I don't know what you heard'.

(c) *Personal selling,* also known as face-to-face selling   This is a meeting between seller and potential buyer where the seller is trying to persuade the potential buyer to buy something, to do something, to accept a proposition or point of view, or to develop an improved relationship with the seller. This is the situation where somebody comes to your house and tries to persuade you to buy double-glazing, an encyclopedia or life insurance. It also covers the times that a caller tries to get you to vote for a particular candidate or agree with a particular religious viewpoint, as well as when a representative of a drug firm tries to persuade a doctor to start prescribing a specific medicine.

(d) *Sales promotion*   These are all the various activities that are not in the other three main categories that are aimed at stimulating a buyer to purchase or a dealer to raise its efforts or effectiveness on the sponsor's behalf. Sales promotions are usually maintained for a specific and comparatively short time span.

These categories are explored later and are the ones most often used by analysts and researchers. In normal conversation, however, there tends to be a degree of flexibility in their usage, even among marketing people. For example, take a plastic carrier bag with a logo and the slogan, 'Buy your artichokes from Bloggs emporium for quality at lower cost'. Is this publicity? In the vernacular it would be, but not to the pedantically minded. They would probably classify the bags as being a form of sales promotion.

Publicity and public relations

Publicity can be aimed at the public, the voters, users, buyers, opinion formers, segments, own staff, politicians, Government officials, stakeholders, competitors, and so on. It has three main purposes:

- to enhance institutional visibility and/or image (e.g. the Child Support Agency may wish to tell people about the work that they were set up to do). In general terms, one may wish people to know about progress made, successes achieved, failures overcome, financial results, policy changes, news about personnel changes, forthcoming special events

- to disseminate product information (e.g. new pension arrangements for the over-80s). Items that are covered include cost and pricechanges (new NHS prescription charges), new products (formation of a new regulatory body), product usage information (dangers of over-dosages of an analgesic), product improvements (formation of educational trusts)

- to reinforce advertising campaigns (e.g. sending newspapers copies of the Black Widow picture in the road safety campaign). Sometimes publicity may seem to supplant advertising, as in the use made of publicity by the U.S. Surgeon General to inform the public about the dangers of silicon breast implants.

It achieves these purposes through a number of vehicles:

(a) *News releases*   Professionals spent much time and effort on crafting their output. A good one will be newsworthy (the media are the judge of this), in a form that the media can utilise easily and quickly, one to two pages long, and written in clear language. They may be accompanied by photographs, films or videotapes. Some news releases are supernaturally boring. These tend not to get used. On the other hand, one analysis suggested that 70% of the City page of one newspaper came from news releases.

(b) *News conferences*   These should only be used if there is something of genuine interest to be stated, or an organisation may find itself ignored later at what could be an inconvenient point. Speakers should know their brief, know the message, know the no-go areas. If possible they should be good speakers and rehearsed, and a news release should be ready for the end of the meeting. News conferences are considered useful by the police, politicians, company chairmen and aspirant pop singers.

(c) *Annual report*   As the name clearly states, an annual report is an overall report on the previous year. It should be fairly obvious therefore that by its very nature an annual report is unlikely to set the Thames afire. Public relations staff have learnt over the years that this simple logic does not appeal to clients. So they may decide to aim to make the annual report a thing of beauty and then distribute it to as many people as possible.

(d) *Lobbying*   Lobbyists deal with legislators, regulators and Government officials hoping to promote, defeat or amend legislation and regulation. This activity has become so professional and intricate that some people would no longer call it public relations but instead call it 'personal selling'.

(e) *Counselling*   This involves telling one's own staff about organisational and Government policy (with reasons and justification), public interest issues, and the activities and propaganda of pressure groups. It will also normally extend to training the staff in dealing with the media.

(f) *Joint ventures*   An organisation may be able to convince a television company that a film should be made about the organisation. An example would be a film about the chief executive working in the Third World or an inner city deprived area. Joint ventures are particularly employed when an organisation has (or wants to attain) an unusual image, when an organisation wants to become more lovable, when it is at the cutting edge of technology, when it is greatly affected by recent legislation, and as an addition to lobbying.

(g) *Special events*   This is the phrase used to accommodate all those unusual activities that public relations (PR) people delight in arranging in the hope of getting some mention. One of the most popular with politicians, chief executives and pressure groups is the *photo opportunity*. This is when the media is told that Lord or Lady X will be doing something unusual (even silly) next Tuesday and would the media like to record it for posterity? A rather more solid example was the picture of the Chancellor and the Governor of the Bank of England holding aloft a one metre model of a £2 coin produced to commemorate the Bank's tercentenary of 1694. This picture was later used by the Royal Mint for marketing purposes.

Other examples of special events are benefit evenings, charity dinners, anniversary celebrations, art exhibitions, contests, speeches, people dressing in funny clothes, the involvement of famous personalities, and so on. Strictly speaking, sponsorship is sales promotion not publicity since one has to pay for it. Such semantic judgements may not be too important. If you persuade a member of the staff to ride a bicycle over Niagara Falls then it is publicity. If you employ a stunt person to do it then it becomes sales promotion and if you show a film of it then it could be called advertising. Since the effect is going to be much the same, the different terminology can hardly matter except to a budget holder.

❏ Advantages of publicity

The main advantage for publicity that is usually advanced is that it is 'free'. When one looks at the budget for public relations in some organisations this is hardly accurate. Indeed some organisations deliberately put more of their promotion spend into PR than advertising. The real advantage is that publicity, when well handled, can appear more socially acceptable, even ethical. It is this aspect that can make good PR so cost-effective. A film on BBC television showing how an organisation is paying for the education of orphans in Rio de Janeiro may help sales more than a slogan along the lines of, 'we really, truly, honestly care for our customers'.

❏ Disadvantages of publicity

There are disadvantages to publicity, mainly the fact that it cannot usually be controlled and that it has the potential for going wrong at any time (hence the archetype PR manager who is supposed to wear a permanently haggard expression). The retail chain Body Shop preferred PR to advertising but ran into difficulties on this front with the Royal Society for the Prevention of Cruelty to Animals and an American magazine. Not all comment was favourable (Kellaway, 1994):

> The Roddicks are suffering as a result of their own PR. Anyone who shouts so loud about being perfect is bound to be attacked when the slightest thing goes wrong.

When the PR is for internal consumption, it can be even more difficult to get it just right. One organisation wished to reduce costs and produced a magazine and a professionally-made video that everyone was supposed to view. The magazine gave examples of costs including the cost of toilet paper and string. The video showed the top man pointing out the sacrifice that he had made by making visits to Canada, Australia and South Africa to increase efficiency. The comments of the staff can be imagined.

❑ Some questions of ethics

It is important that the new public sector learns to utilise public relations while at the same time maintaining a responsible and ethical role. Particularly important is to recognise the distinction between publicity which can be regarded as falling in the normal course of business, that which seeks to explain the decisions and policies of Ministers, and that which could be regarded as party political. This last category has to be left to the political parties to deal with. Issues of responsibility and ethics also arise when deciding how much to spend. There are times when those in the public sector have to resist the temptation to reinforce or even replace publicity by expensive institutional advertising. One internal civil service letter put the situation very well:

- is it necessary to have a publicity proposal which goes beyond what can be achieved in the normal way
- if so, what is the precise goal, and precise target audience
- what means of publicity is best suited to achieve this goal and target
- what is affordable
- in the light of these considerations, is the publicity course chosen the most economical, efficient and effective in the circumstances?

It would be difficult to better this list of appropriate questions.

Advertising

Advertising is the most obvious form of promotion, and the most glamorous. Every marketer daydreams of producing an advertisement so perfect that it achieves its objectives overnight (and which garners in lots of awards). Some commentators have tried dating advertising to ancient Greek and Roman times (the famous slogan at Pompeii concerning a young lady's sexual activities may have been the young lady's advertisement but it was more likely to have been a social commentary, in our opinion). Coming closer to our own times, Caxton's hand press was not fully exploited because of the then low level of literacy. During the 17th and 18th centuries, the Government found it hard to accept what it regarded as the gutter press and generally made life difficult. From 1620, there were a number of free sheets and Gazettes but their life span tended to be short. The *Tatler* and the *Spectator* carried an increasing volume of advertising until 1712. That year a tax of 12d. per advertisement was introduced, as well as a tax of $\frac{1}{2}$d. per copy on all journals.

The result of the tax was almost immediate. Many newspapers went under, and many business people reduced advertising drastically. Ironically, those least affected were those selling useless medicines and dodgy financial deals, because their profit margins were so much higher. These people could also use handbills and posters (generally thought to be too expensive hitherto). This led to a general lowering of advertising standards. The tax on advertisements was not abandoned until 1853 which was just the right time for the mass merchandising and selling that we still have today. Also since then, we have at least three sets of people involved in advertising:

- the advertiser
- the advertising agent
- the media organisation.

❏ The advertiser

The advertiser must know the objectives of the advertisement and these must be actually written down. This may seem boring, but then so is waiting at the traffic lights for them to turn green. The advertiser also has a duty to itself to understand the nature of the target market (e.g. car driving 18 – 24 year-olds), the nature of the product (a change in driving patterns), and the nature of the channels of communication (cinema films, fanzine magazines). This is not so that the agency can be kept in line but so that the advertiser can give a robust brief to the agency and can decide on the work mix. The work mix will often be a combination of in-house work, input from the agency, bought-in creative services and employing a media buying specialist. Alternatively, one can rely completely on a *full-service agency* to do practically everything.

❏ The advertising agent

The advertising agent is basically in business to sell space to advertisers on behalf of the media, in return for which commission is earned. Thus if an advertiser places an advertisement for £1 million, the agency will receive 10 – 15% in commission in the form of a rebate, i.e. £100,000 – £150,000. It is out of this sum that the agency has to pay for all its services such as making a television commercial. In general terms, the agency will be able to make 0.8 – 2.5% profit on the original £1 million. This system is used by the main media only (television, cinema, press, radio and posters) and expenditure for these is often referred to as being *above-the-line*. Advertising in other media involves paying a specific fee for work done, and is known as *below-the-line*.

This arrangement is the basic, unadorned system though there are some additional facts that should be borne in mind. First, if the agency has to buy in extra services such as market research then this will have to be paid for separately at cost + 17.65% (arithmetically equivalent to the 15% commission). Second, if one wants a very fancy and expensive TV commercial then one will have to pay an additional fee. Third, in 1978 the Office of Fair Trading decided that fixed commissions were a restrictive trade practice though the immediate and obvious impact was somewhat muted. Fourth, EC regulations mean that the advertiser should either negotiate the commission level with the media (how about 15%?) or agree a fee with the agency.

❏ The media

The media wants to sell 'space', space or room in its transmission or publication. Every media owner considers that they are just the right vehicle for your advertisement and so one has to learn the differences between them. The agency knows the profile of every medium (e.g. how many 25 – 34 year-olds of social class AB go to the cinema more than once a month). The agency will also know the current costs and will normally use a computer programme to help maximise impact if more than one medium is considered. The media for placing advertisements are usually thought to comprise:

- television (terrestrial, satellite, cable)
- commercial radio
- newspapers (national, Sunday, regional, free-sheets)
- magazines (general, segmented, specialist, technical, trade)
- outdoor (posters, transportation, kiosk, illuminated, bins, parking meters)
- indoor (hotel TV, video in Post Offices/pubs/clubs, electronic displays).

Direct mail and sample distribution can be considered advertising though it is below-the-line and many people would consider them as being sales promotion.

❏ A good advertisement

What is a good advertisement? One that works – without upsetting the stakeholders too radically. Most of us keep a dossier of examples of advertisements that were effective in the past. This must be used not as copy-cat material but as inspiration. It also has to be admitted that some of the most successful advertising was a surprise to many when it did succeed, as three examples show. Boddington's Bitter was a beer that had never had a large share of the bitter market and was also suffering from a general swing to lager. It decided to increase its spend considerably, a gamble especially as it also decided to use humour, an approach that may increase awareness but not necessarily sales. The slogan used was, 'The cream of Manchester' and the press campaign was largely based on use of the word 'cream'. For example a glass of beer was shown providing the cream in a cream bun. At the same time, a television campaign was mounted that consisted of an apparently exotic location that turned out to be, say, Manchester ship canal. The campaigns gained not only high awareness but also a satisfyingly increased market share.

A second example was when the food retailer Sainsbury's showed a series of recipes on television in which the food was actually prepared. These recipes were based on ingredients that could be purchased at Sainsbury's stores. This increased the sales of the ingredients not by just the odd percentage amount but by up to seven times their previous sales' figures. The third success story comes from Russia. A finance company, MMM, advertised its investment fund shares in what looked to Western eyes something akin to a pyramid scheme, known as a 'Ponzi' scheme. MMM advertised massively on television, up to five times an hour. The advertisements showed an ordinary Muscovite family (the Golubkovs) who had invested in MMM shares. The father, Lyonya Golubkov, proudly showed the result – a house in Paris, holidays in the U.S.A. and so on. It has been estimated that MMM spent up to £60 million a year. The result was that many (millions?) of Russians bought the MMM shares. Eventually the Russian government banned the company from advertising on all state-run media (Wall Street Journal Europe, 1994). By this time the share price had collapsed but people were so enamoured of the scheme that they blamed the Government, not MMM, for the collapse.

These examples show two things. First, it pays to advertise. Second, some campaigns can surprise one by their sheer effectiveness. So if an agency comes up with an idea that seems different from the brief that they were given, do not dismiss it out of hand as it may be a winner. Even in the public sector, the unconventional may well be acceptable. Indeed, drink-driving campaigns have in the past deliberately set out to shock, to maximise impact. However, it is probably doubly important in the public sector to ensure that nothing in an advertisement could be misinterpreted, be potentially misleading or be seen as extravagant. The best way to guard against this is probably to share the ideas and the finished advertisement with some independent observers before going public.

Personal selling

The definition of personal selling already given is face-to-face selling. People in the public sector do this every day, though they will frequently call it by one of a number of other names. These include:

- customer care
- dealing with clients
- presentations
- giving expert evidence
- mounting briefings.

The occasions when personal selling takes place include persuading an elderly person to have meals-on-wheels, persuading a youth to go on a training scheme, selling the advantages to a foreign manufacturer of locating a new factory in Britain, promoting an in-house competitive service bid, the police introducing a neighbourhood watch scheme, Embassy staff helping exporters, local authority staff dealing with housing problems, departmental staff giving evidence at a public enquiry. So public sector staff are not only deeply involved in personal selling, they are involved in a wide range of selling situations.

❑ Categories of personal selling

It is generally agreed that personal selling can be categorised as follows.

- *deliverers* Staff whose primary function is delivering a product, and whose selling input is occasional, incidental or subsidiary (e.g. Benefits Agency counter staff)
- *order takers* People who do not normally have to persuade a customer but who wait for the customer to come forward. Order takers are either inside order takers (e.g. Citizens' Advice Bureaux) or outside order takers (e.g. meals-on-wheels)
- *missionaries* Do not normally accept sales orders, oddly enough. Instead they help to build up goodwill or to educate potential users (e.g. the telephone enquiry sections on the railways)

- *technical sales staff*   Are found in situations where the service or goods need considerable technical know-how; sometimes they will be involved in helping to solve customers' problems (e.g. MAFF food scientists)
- *demand creators*   Are the people who actually have to find customers and persuade them to buy a tangible good or an intangible service (e.g. Civil Service College lecturers selling courses to corporate clients).

Who makes the best sales creator? From the past forty years, many books and much research are available. The problem is that it is not very conclusive nor are there many common themes. The archetype (extrovert, brash, uncaring, bombastic) is not supported by research. There is no significant correlation between selling success and intelligence, age, personality traits, character traits, or level of education. Sales people (whether successful or not) are different from other staff in four main ways. They are:

- intuitive rather than logical
- persuasive rather than critical
- have higher energy levels
- are strongly motivated by a need for prestige, power or money instead of security or a sense of idealism.

Some research suggests that sales staff are successful when they resemble the customer, even in such things as weight, age, educational level, class, speech, political outlook and religion. It should be pointed out that the resemblance can be apparent as well as real, hence the jibe about salespersons being all things to all people.

❏ Stages of personal selling

The stages of selling face-to-face are:

- prospecting
- qualifying prospects
- pre-approach
- approach
- presentation
- handling objections
- the close
- the trial close
- the follow-up.

Prospecting

Prospecting means locating potential customers. This can be done by asking current customers for suggested names ('leads'), selling anew or extensions to existing customers, trawling trade associations or similar groupings, asking non-competitors for leads (suppliers, banks, dealers), joining organizations (golf clubs), giving speeches and seminars, writing articles, examining lists and databanks, or just approaching potentials ('cold selling' – the most expensive).

Qualifying prospects

Qualifying prospects is the process of deciding if the prospect should be pursued. Can the prospect make or strongly influence the buying decision? Can the organisation pay? Is the likely sales' size sufficient to warrant further effort? It may be that even if a personal discussion is not felt to be warranted, it may be worth holding for the future (for fresh products) or sending a direct mail shot instead.

Pre-approach

Pre-approach has two alternative meanings. It can be another word for 'qualifying prospects'. More usually, it is the stage of finding out as much as possible about the prospect. Do we know their buying style? Is the buying decision centralised? What can we discover about them (organisation chart, credit rating, people)?

Approach

The approach involves making the initial contact, persuading the prospect to see the presentation and establishing an early rapport. It is usually necessary to gain 'attention' to get a presentation agreed but not always. A long-term relationship will help greatly in arranging a presentation. The approach is often via telephone or mail, and for this reason no attempt is made actually to sell or persuade at this stage. A 'yes' is frankly very unusual at this time, a 'no' would be before you have presented your arguments and effectively shuts the door, possibly for a long time.

Presentation

The presentation is the face-to-face part of the sale. It is widely believed that one has about 30 seconds to make an impact. This belief has led most marketers to develop an immediate sound-bite.

These are phrases such as:

- I'm here to show you how to avoid prosecution by the Inland Revenue next week
- is bankruptcy staring you in the face without you knowing it?

Full-time professional buyers have now become so used to this approach that it has become little more than a social lubricant. Some sales staff still use the old careworn phrases which should be reserved for particular segments. Three oldies which have all been used on the writer recently are:

- you've got a lovely home here
- the world's in a terrible state, isn't it
- we're here to save your soul from eternal damnation.

Certainly, the opening moments are very important to the establishment of a rapport. Presentations should always, without fail, be carefully prepared and practised beforehand, so that the presenter is on top of the material throughout.

Handling objections

Experience tells us that it is extremely rare for prospects to be so overcome by the sheer genius of our product that they instantly shout, 'how many can I have?'. Most sellers know that a dialogue is better than a monologue, so it will be natural for the buyer to pronounce some point of resistance at some stage. Objections are either *psychological resistance* (e.g. a current supplier is an amusing companion) or *logical resistance* (e.g. uncertainty about delivery schedules). The seller may respond by maintaining an upbeat approach, asking for clarification of the objection, denying the objection, brushing it aside as irrelevant, claiming that the objection is trivial compared with quoted advantages, turning the objection into a reason for buying, repeating the presentation in another way, and 'yes-butting'. A yes-but to an objection that the price is higher than the competition would be, 'Yes, but our quality is higher'. Some sellers (such as management consultancies) will prepare beforehand their responses to what are known as 'awkward questions' such as, 'how long have you been a consultant?'

The close

The close is the final point of the presentation, when one asks for an order or confirms that a purchase has been made. Just as there are many books on handling objections so there are just as many on making the close. Some of these claim that there are certain non-verbal moves that signal a sale is imminent, as well as certain statements or questions (e.g. 'when can you deliver?'). The seller can make the close in a number of ways such as 'I'll just make a note in my diary of when we will start' or by pushing the contract across the desk for a signature. The important feature about the close is timing. A premature or over-hard final push may result in a fast and definite loss of sale. On the other hand, once a buyer has agreed to purchase there is no point in going on since all that one can then do is to unsell. Management consultants and others call this stage 'finish and out'. Once the sale is finished, get out of the room.

The trial close

The *trial close* is a move designed to discover whether a sale is near or not. Some of the techniques that can be used at this stage are:

- the *direct* approach ('I think we're just about there, aren't we?')
- the *choice* ('Do you want the seminar on your own premises or at a hotel?')
- the *assumptive close* (draw a piece of paper close and ask 'How many people will you send to us?')
- the *standing room only* close ('Our facilities are severely limited and are in strong demand so I'll need your answer today')
- the *summary* approach – go through the benefits once more, show how the disadvantages have been overcome, and ask for the order.

The follow-up

The *follow-up* is the final stage and is intended to ensure customer satisfaction and, of course, repeat business. The seller visits or telephones the buyer to ensure that delivery was satisfactory, and if not to iron out any problems. More than that, rapport is further established and trust increased. In time, another presentation can be arranged.

The plethora of books on personal selling include a number of other ideas on overcoming objections and sale closing. Not all of them will have wide appeal to the public sector (nor the private sector, come to that). For example, one suggested close is to offer to toss a coin with the buyer to decide the price – 'You can be sure that quite a lot of people will toss for the sake of the challenge' (Ellis, 1992). Within the public sector it is important to be aware of the techniques, particularly as a buyer, but when selling there are certain values which people will expect to see maintained. Generally, they would not expect to see a brash approach, or attempts to ride rough-shod over objections. An emphasis on factual and objective information would be expected.

❏ Sales promotion

While advertising tends to provide a *reason* for doing something, sales promotions tend to offer an *incentive* to do something. The usual advantages of sales promotions are the rapid response, more precise targeting, easier-to-measure results and faster acceptance of new and changed products. On the other hand, they tend not to gain new, long-term buyers in mature markets and tend not to affect greatly loyal brand buyers. There are three main types of promotion:

- consumer promotion (aimed at the ultimate user)
- trade promotion (aimed at those in the distribution channels)
- salesforce promotion.

Examples of sales promotion are limited only by one's imagination but types of consumer promotion include:

- samples such as small bars of soap (in America Surf once spent $43 million delivering samples to 80% of households)
- coupons offering money off a purchase (newspaper coupons have about a 2% redemption rate)
- cash refunds for a 'proof of purchase' after a purchase has been made
- price packs, such as two-for-one offers; 'banded packs' may join two products together (such as shampoo and hair spray)
- premiums are items offered free or at low cost
- prizes for contests, sweepstakes or games; young people in Britain like 'instant gratification' prizes such as instant wins inside confectionery wrappers
- patronage awards such as frequent-flyer plans or air-miles
- free trials such as free car test drives.

The money spent on sales promotions has increased greatly over the past twenty years but are more of a feature in the private rather than the public sector.

Communication and response

Promotion is often expressed by analysts as a process of communication between a *sender* (the seller) and a *receiver* or *target* (the potential buyer or person to be influenced). This process is shown by the following stages (Evans, 1978):

1 The sender *conceives* the message to be sent.

2 The sender *encodes* or *modulates* the message into a symbolic format.

3 The sender selects the *medium* to be used to send the message.

4 The message goes from the sender to the receiver or target.

5 The receiver *decodes* or de-modulates the message that has been received.

6 The receiver *interprets* what the message was thought to be.

7 The receiver *responds* or ignores the message.

8 The receiver's action (or not) sends *feedback* to the sender.

This picture of what happens when a message goes from a sender to a receiver has been used and referred to in textbooks for the past thirty years. It has been illustrated by a number of different diagrams all aiming to explain the same concept. However, over the same thirty years there have been many competing extensions of the basic thought. Clearly, if we could only understand what happens when somebody sees a slogan such as 'don't drink and drive' (and obeys it), then all our promotion ideas would become highly effective almost overnight. Careful observers will have noticed that this has not happened.

Marshall McLuhan (1965) famously said that *the medium is the message* (once a target or receiver has been identified, the primary decision is which channel of communication should be used). Another writer (Schramm, 1955) defined communication as *the process of establishing a commonness or oneness of thought between a sender and receiver*. A slightly wider view (McCarthy and Perreault, 1984) is that marketing communications consist of advertising, publicity and sales promotion. A still wider view (DeLozier, 1976) is that communications embrace all the marketing-mix components as well as every non-internal activity. There is little point in exploring fully the differences between the various concepts of communications, though one should be aware that there is a considerable body of literature on the matter.

An aspect of communications that has received much attention over the years is the question of *dissonance*. Dissonance occurs when a message (or visual stimulus) is seen as being in conflict with one's knowledge, beliefs or attitudes. This can be of great importance in the public sector which is often trying to promote a message that many people do not want to hear (e.g. 'only 21 units of alcohol a week'). People have such a wide mix of knowledge, beliefs and attitudes, some in the political arena strongly held, that it is well-nigh impossible for any Government slogan and campaign not to offend somebody, which does not mean that we do not have to go ahead.

A widely-accepted theory (Festinger, 1957) is that we may handle dissonance in several ways.

- *Avoidance*   We carefully screen out the conflict between a message or stimulus and our own subconscious. This can occur both before or after a decision. So a Government campaign aimed at computer hackers would have to contend with those hackers with a subconscious need to hack.

- *Rationalisation*   We interpret the message to suit ourselves (the referee gave a penalty because of poor eyesight).

- *Additional information*   We seek out other information or research findings that support our point of view and can then safely disregard the original message. This extra information may be nothing more than the opinion of a friend.

- *Forget* or *suppress*   the 'inconsistent' information after we have received it.

Dissonance may force us, in the public sector, to keep repeating the same message, to express it in different ways, and to bombard the receivers with a simple but strong statistic (e.g. the campaign for measles' vaccination).

A second important aspect of communication is the matter of the stages of the purchasing decision, the best known model of which is AIDA, standing for:

A   Attention

I   Interest

D   Desire

A   Action.

It is far from being the sole model for these stages. The confusion between the various models was neatly solved by Kotler (1991) by taking the four best-known models and linking their different stages to three standard stages:

- *cognitive stage*   when the sender wishes to plant something in the receiver's mind such as a message or a symbol to be recognised again later

- *affective stage*   at which the marketer hopes to be able to alter the consumer's attitude or belief

- *behaviour stage*   the final stage during which it is hoped to get the receiver or customer to act in a particular way (such as making a purchase).

The four models considered by Kotler are AIDA (Strong, 1925), the hierarchy-of-effects model (Lavidge and Steiner, 1961), the innovation-adoption model

(Rogers, 1962), and the various communications models. The comparison of the first two is shown in Figure 6.1. Such models are sometimes known as *response hierarchy models* and the hierarchy-of-effects model in particular is sometimes referred to as the *learn-feel-do* model.

In the plethora of communications, responses and models there is one final aspect that must not be allowed to escape attention. It is important that organisations have co-ordination of their communications, firstly, to ensure equitable spend between competing channels (e.g. advertising, publicity and sales reps.), secondly, to ensure that competing or contradictory messages are not being sent out. A health warning that North Korean peasants have a poor life expectancy which may be because they are the heaviest garlic users in the world would lose its impact if people were also told that it is possible that garlic may reduce heart disease.

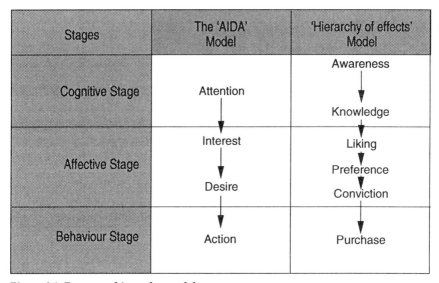

Figure 6.1. Response hierarchy models.

Slogans

A slogan was originally (1513) a Highland or native Irish war-cry or battle-cry. This undertone persisted into the nineteenth century, e.g. the religious slogan in 1880 of 'Duty, God, immortality'. But even by then its use by advertisers had started to gather pace. Now, a slogan is a short phrase (up to ten words) intended to stimulate interest, encourage action or support, or to state a position. It can be used by political parties, pressure groups, commercial interests, and religious factions. It is also very widely used by Government departments in campaigns, initiatives and advertising.

A good slogan can enter the language as a catch phrase for a long time; a poor slogan can kill a campaign dead, as we saw with 'You're never alone with a Strand' in 1960. Some slogans have enjoyed a long life. Kellogg's Rice Crispies' 'Snap! Crackle! Pop!' dates from 1928 while Kit Kat's 'Have a Break, have a Kit Kat' started in 1955. Other slogans have a short life. Coca-Cola have used almost one new slogan a year over the past 100 years, although many of them have some similarity. Just as many new Executive Agencies see a need for a logo, so most Government campaigns nowadays utilise a slogan. Such slogans impart information in a pithy format, and are therefore above all a method of communication. Some examples will show the impact, or lack of it, achieved by Government slogans over the years.

'Your country needs you' is an impressive example of a slogan that reinforced, and was reinforced by, a visual, a picture of Lord Kitchener pointing straight at you. It first appeared on the cover of the magazine *London Opinion* in September 1914 and appeared on posters a week later. It was copied in America, with a stylised Uncle Sam in place of Lord Kitchener. With various additions and alterations it has been the basis for many posters ever since. Who it was that got the idea through the system is not known. This is a pity since it replaced a less dramatic approach. This was the royal coat of arms with the slogan 'Your King and Country need you'. The phrase entered the language in an odd way. The infantry would use it in response to being given any particularly unpleasant task.

'Is your journey really necessary?' started life in 1939 when it was intended to discourage evacuated civil servants from going home in large numbers when others could not do so. From 1941 it was widely used on the whole population. It then became one of our examples of being part of a campaign *instead* of passing a law (to ban all travel over more than 50 miles without a permit).

'Dig for Victory' was the first of several slogans on the same theme, all intended to encourage people to grow their own fruit and vegetables, thus reducing imports. First quoted by the Minister of Agriculture in October 1939, it later became allied to another effective visual, a booted foot pushing a spade into the ground. This was part of a campaign that saw the number of allotments increase from 800,000 in 1939 to 1,400,000 by 1943. In the 1980s the poster was resurrected by green supporters.

'Keep death off the road' was another Government slogan that used a powerful visual. This was a poster (1946) that became known as the 'Black Widow', a skull clothed in a black shroud. This aroused much controversy, as Benneton's advertisements did in the 1990s.

'Keep Britain Tidy' is one of the longest-lasting Government slogans, even

threatening to outlive the Rice Crispies one. This is in spite of the fact that over the years it has been badly served from a visual impact aspect. It probably originates from around 1949. In 1952 the Central Office of Information produced a sticker with the slogan, on behalf of the Ministry of Housing and Local Government.

'Dull it isn't' was intended to be a short life slogan for recruitment to the Metropolitan Police. It caught on in the vernacular like a comedian's catch phrase. The story is told (Lavidge and Steiner, 1961) of a policeman trying to break up a fight at Tottenham Hotspur's football ground. He dived into the crowd, emerging later successfully holding a young miscreant but looking decidedly dishevelled from his efforts. Whereupon a cockney voice from the crowd shouted:

'Dull it * * * * isn't, eh?'

Much effort is expended on thinking up Government slogans, though it often seems that the best come from an anonymous individual rather than a committee. A first try at a slogan is usually followed by a period of digestion, incubation and polishing. During this period, the originator can feel rather disenfranchised, even cheated. Some rules to be followed are:

- a slogan should concentrate on just one thought. Two thoughts means an immediate and inevitable loss of impact, more than two thoughts means that you have a speech, not a slogan
- keep it short. Ten words is the absolute maximum, five is better, three are better still if it can be managed. The impact is stronger (e.g. Keep Britain Tidy), and it should have a longer life
- use simple words that are in the target's normal vocabulary. The exception to this rule is where there is an element of humour in the slogan or where an unusual word is or can become one of the points of the campaign. An example (1994) of the latter is 'Pfandbriefe – Solid value from the ground up' where the aim was to get people to look at Pfandbrief bonds as investments
- use a visual where possible. A visual can dramatically increase impact and effectiveness, especially when the two components (slogan + visual) reinforce one another. It is not always easy to predict when a visual will become memorable. It is worth spending as much time on the visual as on the slogan (see Chapter 13 for an example)
- do not use a slogan that has *dissonance* unless it is inescapable. The Sicilian authorities used the slogan 'Tourism is Culture'. This has three stages of premise that people go through before getting to the message

'holiday in Sicily'. There are times when it is impossible to avoid dissonance in Government campaigns –where one is trying to change attitudes, for example

- try to get a phrase that has a natural rhythm to it. This is not always easy, but someone on the team with experience of writing poetry may help.

A presentational point is not to get too messy. A slogan in an exotic typeface on a cluttered background may momentarily get the Attention in AIDA but will not get to Interest if the target has any difficulty at all in reading the slogan itself. One final point. Never fall in love with your own slogan if others are dubious about it, or if tests show that it is not working.

Communications development

In developing a campaign, the first step is to identify the target audience, to establish their current perceptions and how these need to change. The survey work necessary for this will also suggest actual changes which need to be made to the service. We are effectively asking ourselves three questions:

- have people heard our message
- do they understand it
- what is their reaction?

❏ Identify the target

There has to be a clear picture of who the target audience is. For the DSS this may be all over 80 year-olds, sole parents or even the whole general public. For Health it might be people going to certain foreign countries, all diabetics or parents of 4 year-olds. For Education it might be all schools, people taking examinations or certain ethnic minorities. To help identify the target, it is usual to ask respondents, in a survey, to position themselves on two scales showing *familiarity* and *favourability*. Normally the two are studied at the same time.

On the first scale, people are asked how familiar they are with something under investigation. For example, this might be the availability of mobile X-ray centres, smear testing, or blood donor centres. Respondents are offered a five-point scale of responses, varying from 'Never heard of it' to 'Know it very well' (a 7-point scale now seems to have been largely dropped in favour of the 5-point scale).

On the second scale, people are asked how they feel about something, usually the same object or idea as was used on the first scale. Again, respondents are offered a 5-point scale, varying this time from 'Very unfavourable' to 'Very favourable'. An alternative that is sometimes appropriate is a 5-point scale from 'Would never use it' to 'Would always use it'.

This approach is usually referred to as positioning through *semantic differential* (Hartley, 1989). Originally developed to measure the inference that a subject (a political issue, a work of art) had for people, it looks at different dimensions of words. Thus originally a seven-point scale was used running from Bad to Good, on which people could give both an opinion and a value. This was refined for many other dimensions such as, for example:

- reliable – unreliable
- modern – old-fashioned
- unusual – ordinary.

It is now used to compare two or more objects or ideas (such as hospitals) on a number of dimensions at the same interview or questionnaire. Comparison between objects is then possible, in relation to the others. Thus Hospital A might be seen as helpful, old-fashioned, lacking facilities, and difficult to get to, in comparison with several other hospitals. This enables one to know what aspects have to be concentrated upon, both in terms of the actual service and in promotion of the service.

A refinement of semantic differential that has been developed by the writer is the use of *open-ended adjectives*. This was developed from an Organisation Development approach. In use, one asks a target population to suggest some words that describe a service (or object). For example, patients were asked to describe an NHS practice. They used words such as supercilious, unhelpful, inefficient, untruthful. This response highlights several aspects of this approach:

- the researcher will have to translate words and slang into normal adjectives
- the technique often shows where operational improvements are required rather than merely aiding the marketing effort
- it is better to ask individuals or very small groups rather than large groups or else the whole study can degenerate into a peon of praise or a flow of venom
- a method is needed to assemble the adjectives into groupings of similar words to accentuate the overall reactions.

The way the last is tackled is for all of the research team to use copies of the same thesaurus. They can then use the head word in the thesaurus as a means of grouping the words. As a further stage, it has been found a time-saver to use the reference numbers of the head words during the study (in extreme cases, this may also serve to defend the sensibilities of an over-sensitive client). As an example, both 'supercilious' and 'pompous' could be collated under '878 – Pride' prior to analysis.

References

DeLozier, M. (1976) *The Marketing Communications Process* Tokyo, McGraw-Hill.

Ellis, P. (1992) *Who Dares Sells: The Ultimate Guide to Selling Anything to Anyone* London, Thorsons.

Evans, D. (1978) *People and Communications* London, Pitman Publishing.

Festinger, L. (1957) *A Theory of Cognitive Dissonance* London, Row and Peterson.

Hartley, R. (1989) *Marketing Mistakes* New York, John Wiley.

Kellaway, L. (1994) *Tired of the Sweet Smell of Success* Financial Times 5 September.

Kotler, P. (1991) *Marketing Management* Englewood Cliffs, Prentice Hall.

Lavidge, R. and Steiner, G. (1961) *A Model for Predictive Measurements of Advertising Effectiveness* Journal of Marketing, October.

McCarthy, E. and Perreault, W. (1984) *Basic Marketing* Homewood, Irwin.

McLuhan, M. (1965) *Understanding Media: The Extension of Man* New York, McGraw-Hill.

Rees, N. (1990) *Dictionary of Popular Phrases* London, Bloomsbury Publishing.

Rogers, E. (1962) *Diffusion of Innovations* New York, Free Press.

Schramm, W. (1955) *The Process and Effects of Mass Communications* Chicago, University of Illinois Press.

Strong, E. (1925) *The Psychology of Selling* New York, McGraw-Hill.

Wall Street Journal Europe (1994) *MMM Investment Fund* 5 September

Chapter 7

Place

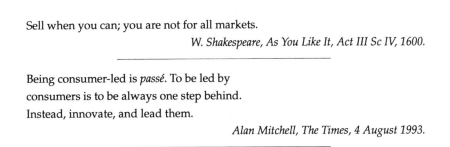

The fifth of the six 'Ps' is place. This may seem to some an odd word to use in this context. Presumably it originated in the idea of 'placing' ones product with distributors, placing one's offering in front of the public or even in placing an advertisement in one of the selected media. Whatever the origination, we are stuck with it now. 'Place' includes such aspects as:

- channels of distribution, logistics, mixing the channels to optimum effect
- alternative methods of service delivery
- centralisation v. decentralisation, the place and use of branches
- identification of exactly what is being delivered.

In the public sector a number of politically contentious issues could arise under these headings, privatisation v. public ownership, one-stop shops, agency formation and autonomy, municipalisation, and joint ventures. Since many of these contentious aspects are not an integral part of marketing as such, they will be largely ignored here, and left principally for political authorities to resolve.

In general, it is advisable to use several channels of distribution for both ideas and services but especially for ideas. A campaign for healthy eating will use publicity, pamphlets (through doctors' surgeries, schools, retail shops), advertisements in many outlets, give-aways (badges, calorie counters), influence (school lunches) and the law (against adulteration and noxious substances). The need to use multiple channels is not new. In the last century, Abbé Migne built up one of the world's great publishing houses. He published 1,095 volumes in thirty years which is equivalent to one book every ten days. Migne saw himself as keeping the barbarians at bay by promulgating a 'science of Catholicism', even though he was often in conflict with the church. Migne sold what he claimed was a superior product, achieving low costs through mass production, plagiarisation, very low wages, standardisation and mass marketing. He sold direct, cutting out the middleman which caused the Parisian booksellers to ask the archbishop to close him down. Migne used other channels, pamphlets, brochures, a society and magazines that he founded.

Migne also used a number of channels for marketing. He bribed reviewers for favourable comments, paid priests commission, printed handbills and pseudo-posters, and used what has been called 'ventriloquistic salesmanship' (Bloch, 1994). In this, Migne would make some statement, contrive to get somebody else to paraphrase him and then quote the paraphrase, so that there (Johnson, 1994) appeared to be a:

> chorus of voices where there was in reality only one

Migne was not a nice person but he knew how to distribute ideas; his enterprise came to an end in a mysterious fire in 1868 but by then he had completed the 168 volumes of his *Encyclopédie Théologique*. This priest turned entrepreneur is little read nowadays, he has been described as 'a forgotten continent', but then nowadays one does not often see posters entreating one to 'Dig for Victory' either.

Politics and Government

A Government has four main types of channel to put forward its ideas, wherever these may be on a spectrum from reducing cholesterol levels to reducing immigration.

- *Coercion.* Truly draconian measures have been the exception in western Europe this century though elsewhere regulations by a dictator are common. Of course, people adversely affected will claim that a measure is draconian (such as the fate of pit-bulls under the Dangerous Dogs Act) but such moves are regulated through parliaments.

- *Legal measures.* In the United Kingdom such measures have normally had to go through a parliamentary system before adoption. The advantage of a law is that it introduces a sense of certainty and enables people to decide whether they wish to obey or pay the price of noncompliance. The disadvantage is that, unless crafted with care, a law is inflexible and may cease to reflect the current situation over time.

- *Pressure and publicity.* These include ministerial pronouncements, lobbying newspapers and other media, networking, distributing or retaining information, and so on. Any method that does not involve direct payments would be allocated to this channel.
- *Propaganda and advertising.* These embrace channels which have to be paid for.

Ignoring coercion, a decision has to be made as to which main channel(s) will be employed and then which of the approaches within those channels. Decisions at this level will need a political involvement, as they could be politically controversial. An example of this would be birth control. A Government may wish to see the population increase quickly or gradually, decrease or stay roughly static. The first contradiction that a Government has to face is between those who regard increasing population as either economically advisable or a civil right on the one hand, as against those who fear a 'population explosion'.

The argument between people favouring *collaboration* (individual choice) and those wanting *over-ride* (the law or economic sanctions) is not always amenable to reason and statistics on either side. In these circumstances, political backing for any campaign would be essential, and this situation will arise in most cases where the product or service being marketed is 'ideas' or 'attitudes'.

The channels

The scope of decisions which need to be taken about channels can best be described by looking at examples of the range of channels actually employed. The public sector continues to be involved in the distribution of manufactured goods, sometimes in quite complex ways. For example, the House of Commons Official Report, 'Hansard', is published by Her Majesty's Stationery Office (HMSO) who distribute the printed version either directly, through its own shops, through wholesalers and retailers, or through agents. The compact disc version, however, is published as a joint venture. One may buy it from HMSO in Norwich, or from Chadwyck-Healey. If you live in the U.S.A., Canada, France or Spain you buy it from the national subsidiary of Chadwyck-Healey.

HMSO is an interesting example of the complexity of distribution in other ways. It is a publisher of, among other things, calendars, greetings cards and books which it sells like any private sector publisher. It sells consultancy services direct (e.g. advising the Russian Federation on administration). It gives direct assistance (part of the administration and promotion of the Duke of Edinburgh's Award scheme). It sells printing both in-house and as an agent (23 million copies of the *Citizen's Charter*), using as one of the marketing channels a print-buyers' catalogue called Blueprint.

Another HMSO activity that is well known is its selling of furniture, business machinery and supplies with a turnover of about £200 million. This is sold through regionally-based selling teams, selective direct marketing and a telephone-sales group. This is backed up with a number of full-colour catalogues, a showroom at Millwall Dock, a fleet of delivery lorries and electronic trading. At the opposite end of the spectrum, HMSO acts as an agent for the sales of other organisations' products such as the OECD 'Observer' magazine. It can thus be seen that HMSO uses and/or is active within many of the marketing channels.

F. W. Woolworth is supposed to have said:

> I am the world's worst salesman, therefore I must make it easy for people to buy.

Originators of services and ideas have exactly the same problems to overcome as manufacturers and sellers of industrial and consumer goods, how to make their products *available* and *accessible*. Hospitals, schools, Benefits Agency offices and churches have to be built (like supermarkets) so that they are convenient for use by the consumers.

The marketing channels used change over time. This may be due to technology (interactive TV, HMSO electronic selling), changing conventions (private sector sales literature in doctors' surgeries), management theories (decentralisation), customer-orientation (one-stop shopping) and political pressures (less-regulated market forces). One area affected by several of these factors is the local authority. Traditionally, local government distributed its services through separate departments that were each centralised. Neighbourhood offices for social services and housing are now common, Westminster City Council being among the first to adopt one-stop shopping across departmental boundaries, and system planning is now widespread for planning, housing, transport, social services and education.

❑ The main channels summarised

A lot of mystique is built up about the marketing channels, and many people produce complex charts showing all the possible variations that exist for reaching the consumer. This is not necessary. The main channels can be expressed quite simply (Baker, 1990) as being:

- direct from originator to ultimate consumer
- direct to a 'retailer' for onward distribution to the ultimate consumer
- indirectly through an agent, a 'wholesaler' or other intermediary
- some combination of these.

Direct from originator to ultimate consumer

Examples of this are the Inland Revenue, a self-employed plumber, Social Security benefits, a window cleaner, a Law Centre. A degree of buying-in would not disqualify one from staying in this category. Direct selling is usually achieved by:

- setting up a chain of dedicated outlets (Benefits Agency, Sainsbury's)
- direct targeting (electronic trading, mail order, TV selling, catalogues)
- face-to-face, especially door-to-door (double glazing, Jehovah's Witnesses).

An advantage of direct approaches is the greater control that it gives over the whole process. Other advantages and disadvantages vary with the type of channel:

- *own chain*   Advantages are economies of scale, co-ordination of all promotional activities, and better feedback from customers' wants, preferences and perceptions; disadvantages are the higher capital requirements, the taking on of all risks and the possibility of reduced access to the total market
- *direct targeting*   Advantages are access to the whole target market, economies of scale are available, consumer convenience and ability to switch products fast; disadvantages are high costs of delivery and promotion, cost of getting and maintaining good listings and the cost of financing credit (where applicable)
- *face-to-face*   Advantages are the facility of selective targeting and the fact that this may be the best way of demonstrating complex products (financial services) or very simple products needing the personal touch (Boy Scouts' jobs); disadvantages are consumer resistance if unsolicited or inconvenient, the difficulty of recruitment and control of good staff, and the high labour cost.

Through a 'retailer'

Most household purchases are made this way and so it has become a common method for much of the public sector to use. Postage stamps can be bought at a newsagents while many main post offices are now located in a private retail shop so that one can get one's pension along with the potatoes and red wine. Other examples are grant maintained schools and paying a general practitioner to do cervical smears and diphtheria inoculations. The advantages of this channel are reduced costs, reduced management time and involvement, and downward distribution (passing some of the time, cost and inconvenience down to the ultimate consumer). The disadvantages are a loss of control and information, the risk of stock getting out of date, and the possibility that the 'retailers' may be able to change the service in ways to suit themselves against the wishes of the originator or the consumer.

Through an intermediary

An intermediary is a third party, such as an agent or wholesaler, who would not be regarded as a retailer. Examples of this are the London Metal Exchange (almost a market), a Hospital Trust (the Department of Health being the ultimate provider), some Training and Enterprise Council activities and the OECD-HMSO arrangement for distributing OECD journals in the UK. The advantages of an indirect channel are the reduction of selling effort, the reduction of involvement and the potential for allowing those nearer the final customer to react to and reflect the customers' needs. The disadvantages are the almost complete lack of control, the difficulty of promotion to end-users and the increased costs which may be difficult to analyse. An example that includes many of these pros and cons is a software house that offers a computer manufacturer a menu of its products that the manufacturer offers to a retailer who can then arrange different bundles for different retail market segments.

❑ Channel design and logistics

There is an inevitable overlap, even confusion, between marketing channels and logistics, where logistics can be defined as getting the product to the consumer. This is because quite often the two are to all intents and purposes the same. Getting a pension into the hands of a pensioner *is* the service. In the public sector, there are many situations when OTD (On-Time Delivery) is so much a part of the service delivery that it should dominate the delivery chain. This can also be true in the private sector. Dell computers decided that their marketing aim should be customer satisfaction, and carried out market surveys. These showed that OTD was the second highest concern of customers, coming behind only the product attributes. This was an area where Dell had already put in efforts and a further improvement involved revamping the entire production system. This major effort paid off. Within two years the surveys showed that Dell had the best OTD record in the industry, that Dell ranked first in customer satisfaction, and that sales increased by 70% (Kumar and Sharman, 1992).

The steps in designing the marketing channels are straightforward. However, they are frequently not driven by the customer. Instead they are driven by history, administrative convenience and the internal organisation structure of the management (local authorities suffered from this last point for many years). There is often therefore a gap between what the customers want and what management think they should get. Channel design, adapted from Stern, Sturdivant and Getz (1993), aims to overcome this gap. It has eight steps.

The first step is to survey the end-users to find out what their expectations are, levels of service, frequency of delivery, length of time for delivery, variety, convenience. The end-users are rarely homogenous (some people want their pensions as cash while others are happy to have them paid into a bank account). It is therefore necessary to find out the distribution benefits perceived by users, the relative importance of these benefits, the perceived performance of the channels (e.g. Directory Enquiries), the channels used by most end-users (e.g. the local post office) and the type of desired-attributes segments. These segments are defined as being:

- *price-sensitive users* will sacrifice other benefits if they can have a lower price; people may prefer to use second class mail for their letters although they may use first class for a child's birthday card to ensure better delivery speed

- *systems buyers* expect suppliers to supply different products through one channel to provide what is known as a 'systems solution' (this is likely to be particularly true if the product is types of information). Thus a patient may prefer a general practitioner to tell them the results of an X-ray rather than the hospital that did the actual work

- *component buyers* use different products to create their own final product, such as a person who has an industrial pension, a top-up pension as well as payments from the state

- *relationship seekers* value on-going personal service above other benefits. Most local authority housing departments have customers who only like to deal with the one same person each time

- *variety seekers* want a variety of brands or products to choose from each time. A person sending large letters overseas may like to have all the alternatives explained to them each time so that they can choose the most appropriate for a specific package.

These differences can often be exploited, either to improve service or even to reduce costs. For example, employers have sometimes made payments to staff who agree to changing from wage packets to being paid through a bank or building society; if one were feeling brave, one might suggest making a charge for paying state pensions at a post office instead of into a bank account.

The second step is to build up an 'ideal' channel or system that is wholly customer-driven. If this is completely new it is referred to as the *greenfields* solution. It is always possible that management will throw up their hands in horror at this system. So the third step is to obtain their input. Rather than ask for a third system in addition to the existing and ideal systems already to hand, it is better to ask management to stipulate and defend any constraints or no-go areas. For example, they may say that any system must not venture outside Departmental boundaries, or that redundancies must be minimal, or that some constraints are political and impossible to change.

It is always possible that management raise so many constraints and boundaries that one is left feeling that the existing system is the only one possible. But this is a problem that is known and understood by every experienced system worker there is. The fourth stage is to examine the gaps and shortcomings in the current system, the ideal system, and the constraints. Within the public sector arguments that might be used in closing the gaps include recent ministerial pronouncements, past policies, marketing needs, cost structures, new management theories, quality needs, customer preferences that might be turned into votes, what is done in other countries, and plain logic.

The fifth step is to create an optimal solution. This is rarely the same as the 'ideal' solution, no matter how lovingly this was crafted. It is also common for one to have to create more than one solution at this stage. Options give people a feeling of security. Moreover, even at this stage, it is possible that a drawback may be spotted in a single optimal scheme.

The sixth step is to agree this optimal system with all concerned. The seventh step is to prepare for the system introduction. This will include:

- talking to everybody in the delivery chain again
- designing, printing and distributing all forms and control documentation
- checking again the information technology ramifications
- probably arranging an effective campaign to inform the public.

The eighth step is the actual introduction of the new arrangements which, if all the previous steps have been carried out properly, should be plain sailing. It is not always plain sailing. Porsche managers were threatened with physical violence when they tried to install a new distribution system (Tinnin, 1984). The dealers then threatened joint action through the courts whereupon Porsche made a quick retreat.

Research (Batchelor, 1994) suggests that logistics is a poor relation in many organisations. A study by Arthur Andersen and the Institute of Purchasing and Supply said that less than half of large U.K. companies know their logistics costs as such or had an overall strategy. Moreover, a survey by PE Consulting and the Institute of Logistics found that 40% of people who had contracted out their logistics were not satisfied with the way things were handled and that there was a lack of controls. If the originators were dissatisfied, one wonders how the end-users felt.

❑ Channel conflict

The interests of different channel providers do not always coincide and so there is the possibility of conflict. The types of conflict that arise are:

- *vertical channel conflict*   when there is argument between different levels in the same channel. Examples are Coca-Cola and those bottlers who wanted to bottle Dr. Pepper as well, and those disagreements observed between hospitals and local GPs
- *horizontal channel conflict*   between members at the same level within a channel. Examples might be Hospital Trusts competing for fund-holders' attention outside their 'normal' geographical area, Pizza chain franchisees complaining that others were cutting ingredients, and Employment Service offices' feelings about staffing levels at their office compared with elsewhere
- *multi-channel conflict*   between competing channels within the same market or with the same product range. Examples are the wish of post offices to sell National Lottery tickets in competition with retail shops, when Levi Straus started to sell their jeans through ordinary retail outlets instead of just speciality-store outlets, and when general practitioners dispense medicines in competition with pharmacists.

A main reason for channel conflict may be *change*, with each person in the chain imagining that a change will act against their interest, security or income. Moreover, every change in the chain will involve some cost to those in a channel even if it is only re-training staff. A second cause is *goal incompatibility*. This can certainly arise if an originator wishes to go from high margin-low volume to low margin-high volume. Conflict can also be due to *uncertain roles* and 'rights'. Examples are hospitals who use facilities for private and public patients, software firms who sell through agents and also direct to large customers, and departments and executive agencies as these latter move into new areas. Similarly, conflict can arise through the *umbilical cord* problems faced by people who felt that they had exclusivity in a field and think this is being removed. Recent examples of this are DTI laboratories, tied public houses and in-house training sections.

The potential for conflict should be taken into account when channels are designed and designed out as far as possible. Once conflict has arisen, resolution must come about through the usual management approaches of diplomacy, arbitration and mediation. Aids to this may be the adoption of *superordinate goals* such as the public good or customer satisfaction, or by appealing to what is known as the *channel captain*. The channel captain is the dominant member of a channel, such as a senior civil servant or even the Minister.

In considering marketing channels, four facts have to be remembered. First, they can be complex (extreme simplicity usually means that somebody somewhere is getting poor service). Second, they cost (frequently 10 – 20% of total costs, so 5% is exceptional). Third, they keep changing (if only because of new technology). Fourth, we never get it quite right first time, so we must not delude ourselves.

References

Baker, M. (1990) *Marketing: An Introductory Text* Basingstoke, Macmillan Education.

Batchelor, C. (1994) *Relentless Drive to Reduce Costs* Financial Times, Logistics Supplement, 21 September.

Bloch, R. (1994) *God's Plagiarist: Being an Account of the Fabulous Industry and Irregular Commerce of the Abbé Migne* London, University of Chicago Press.

Johnson, D. (1994) *The Tycoon Priest* The New York Review of Books, Vol. XLI No. 15, 22 September.

Kumar, A. and Sharman, G. (1992) *We Love your Product, but Where is it?* Sloan Management Review, Winter.

Stern, L., Sturdivant, F. and Getz, G. (1993) *Accomplished Marketing Channel Change* European Management Journal, Vol. 11 No.1, March.

Tinnin, D. (1984) *Porsche's Civil War with its Dealers* Fortune, 16 April.

Chapter 8

People

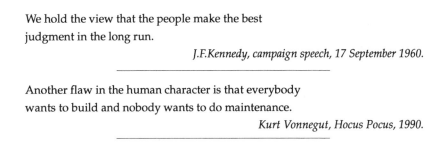

We hold the view that the people make the best
judgment in the long run.

J.F.Kennedy, campaign speech, 17 September 1960.

Another flaw in the human character is that everybody
wants to build and nobody wants to do maintenance.

Kurt Vonnegut, Hocus Pocus, 1990.

The sixth and final 'P' in our mix is people. We have already seen how the new
public sector has to look two ways at once when considering pricing. The same
is true of the people aspects. We have to look outwards – whom are we trying to
influence, to whom should we be talking, who needs our information? We also
have to look inwards – at our own staff. It is a cliché (and therefore self-evi-
dently true) that it is the quality of our staff that decides our marketing skills
and effectiveness. This chapter looks at both aspects – the market segments we
are trying to reach, and (briefly) our staff who are doing the reaching.

Market segmentation

Classical economic theory held that supply and demand were homogeneous,
until the 1930s saw the introduction of imperfect competition theories suggesting that they could be heterogeneous. It was not until the 1950s that it was realised that heterogeneity could lead to two deliberate marketing strategies – product differentiation and market segmentation (Smith, 1956). The idea of market
segmentation is based on three propositions:

- customers are different, even unique
- customer differences are related to differences in demand
- groups ('segments') of customers can be separated out from the total
  market.

Segmentation is not the universal panacea that some people imagine. There is little point is using segmentation:

- if the market is so small that going after just parts of it is not worthwhile
- if it is so large that virtually the whole population is included (for example, mass merchandising)
- if heavy users account for such a large percentage of the market that they are clearly the only worthwhile target
- if the total market is geographically local
- where the brand has an overwhelmingly large dominance in the market.

There are situations where statutory requirements decide the segmentation process. For example, local authorities have been affected over the years by statutes such as the Education Act 1944 (children aged 5 to 16), the Control of Pollution Act 1974 (segments for refuse collection), and the Chronically Sick and Disabled Persons Act 1970. In non-statutory situations (and sometimes even within them), segmentation can be classified into two broad categories:

- *general personal variables*   where people are described by broad personal characteristics such as where they live
- *situation-specific variables*   where people are described according to their consumption patterns (e.g. lager louts, aircraft model makers).

Marketers spend a lot of time analysing data, of which there is a plenitude, and are delighted if segments coincide. Happiness to a market segmenter would be to discover that 80% of lager louts are aircraft model makers and that 90% of them live in bungalows in Anglesey, especially if nobody else had discovered it. The decision to segment might be based on a number of criteria:

- there is a statutory obligation
- the segment has one or more characteristics that distinguish the segment from the total market; the characteristic(s) should preferably be stable over a reasonable time span (e.g. people living in rented council accommodation)
- the segment should be of significant size (e.g. parents with children of school age). An exception might be a segment of particular influence, power or income such as members of a pressure group
- the segment is reachable through communication channels

- the segment has a specific need or want (actual or inventable) and are likely to respond to a tailored marketing mix
- it is a plus point, but not a necessity, for the segment and its potential to be measurable in a robust manner.

Basis for segmentation

For our purposes, *organisations* can be segmented by the categories of:

- geographical (country, a part of the country, cities, distance)
- form (central Government, local authority, commercial, non-profit, charitable, religious, political, trade union, pressure group, special interest, co-operative)
- characteristics (size, structure, ownership, industry type, technology)
- usage (heavy/light, call-off, new/existing, purchase centralisation)
- policies (benefits pursued, in-house/out-sourcing preferences, product knowledge).

However, *people* are usually segmented along different lines:

- socioeconomic (social class, income, occupation, education, home ownership)
- demographic (age, sex, race, ethnic origin, marital state, family size, family life cycle, number of income earners in family)
- geographic (country, part of country, cities, distance, part of council territory)
- psychographic (hobbies, interests, activities, value systems, religion, politics, intelligence, personality, psychological needs and preferences)
- behaviour patterns (consumption patterns, buying patterns, brand/idea loyalty, media habits)
- predisposition (product knowledge, benefits sought, problems owned).

It should be pointed out that, as with so much in marketing, these main categories are not used universally but the overall pattern will be familiar to most marketers. The growth in segmentation has been massive since the 1960s. So has been the growth in data available to marketers. Few of us are unaware of the increase in direct mail that is sent to us. A high percentage of direct mail is targeted at the recipient for a reason. Often it is because of some action that we took in the past, giving money to a charity, buying from a book club, or sending off for a free sample. Any of these will have resulted in our name being put on a list somewhere and our becoming part of somebody's idea of a potentially worthwhile segment.

❏ Socioeconomic segmentation

This remains the most widely used basic method of describing people, especially their social class and their income. This may appear strange, even morally suspect. Why should one's class or income indicate one's apparent attractiveness to sellers such as social services? Since marketers would not allow mere snobbishness to stand in the way of using the most effective tools, there must be a reason. The reason is that much research over the years has shown some remarkable correlations that marketers find attractive. This research has shown that socioeconomic factors can act as a predictor of many of our actions and attitudes and it can also help to identify the most effective channel of communication to reach us. Of course, at the extremes the correlation is self-evident and hardly arguable. Few people on income support read *The Field* while few teenagers go on Saga coach holidays.

In describing class, heavy reliance is placed on occupation; those so rich that they do not work are a separate segment but in statistical terms are small. Government statistics are published and these divide workers into six classes:

I	–	professional occupations
II	–	managerial and lower professional
IIIN	–	non-manual skilled labour
IIIM	–	skilled manual occupations
IV	–	partly skilled occupations
V	–	unskilled occupations.

The system used in marketing circles is slightly different:

A	–	higher managerial, administrative or professional
B	–	intermediate managerial, administrative or professional
C1	–	supervisory or clerical
C2	–	skilled manual workers

D   –   semi or unskilled workers

E   –   casual workers, labourers, those on state benefit.

For those interested, it should be noted that long lists breaking down these broad categories into much finer detail are readily available; these, as well as the long time that these categories have been used, enable marketers to feel confident in their use and to detect trends. The percentage of the total U.K. adult population in each of these categories is as follows:

AB   –   18%

C1   –   23%

C2   –   28%

D   –   17%

E   –   14%

AB + C1 account for 41% of adults. So when tabloid newspapers proudly announce to their readers, as they do, that '40% of our readers are in the richest ABC1 group' the boast may not be outstandingly impressive.

There are occasions when the point of interest is not so much people's income as their *disposable income*. The economists have their own definition of this term but in marketing terms it is the money left over at the end of the week to spend as one wishes – discretionary spend. This aspect is of great interest to those selling non-essentials such as the teenage market for compact discs. The money spent on the CDs has competitors trying to get attention; this is not just other CD firms but includes electronic games and cinema seats. Unsurprisingly, there is plenty of research around on disposable income sources and destinations.

❑ Demographic

Segmentation by demographics is popular not just because of the great variety of data available. It has the added advantages of being easily comparable with the total population in percentage and distribution terms, and of being easily doubled up with other segments. Thus one might be interested in people who are both under 20 years old (demographic) and homeless without regular income (socioeconomic). Indeed, a large proportion of social policy initiatives depend on such double, treble, or more segmentation.

The *life cycle* is used for some demographic data collection and use. One such cycle is the family life cycle which may be split between:

- young/single
- young/married/no children
- young/married/youngest child under 6
- young/married/youngest child 6 and over
- older/married/with children
- older/married/no children
- older/single.

The idea is that people have different needs and buying patterns at different stages within the cycle, though one must not forget that 58% of the U.K. population live in one or two person households.

Sex as a segment is usually too broad at 50% of the population and so is normally used in conjunction with another segmentation. There are times when it is the main determinant such as users of Hormone Replacement Therapy and woman's magazines – nobody has yet managed to sell a male equivalent of the weekly female-dominant Woman, Woman's Own and Woman's Weekly. There are some goods which identify themselves as sex-dominant through image-building advertising; among cigarettes, Virginia Slims are smoked mainly by women and Camels by men.

Age segmentation has fallen from favour slightly over the last thirty years as people no longer stick so rigidly to their stereotyping. Nowadays, some researchers talk about psychological age instead of chronological age though this is obviously more expensive to uncover. Other marketers continue successfully to pursue the over-50s or the young ('yoof') markets. Thus one company decided to position pocket pagers as a 'trendy, must-have product that gives you the freedom to communicate on your own terms' instead of being a 'dog-collar tying you to the office' – 'Mercury Paging is reinventing the pager, targeting the youth market' and spending £3 million doing it (Marketing, 1994). On the other hand, one large company found that they were selling more pre-prepared baby food than was possible from market share statistics. Research found that elderly consumers were buying it since it was nutritious and did not require chewing (Mueller-Heumann, 1992).

❑ Geographic

The idea of segmenting people by where they live is in essence straightforward. The complexity that has arisen over the last twenty years or so lies in the subtleties of use and cross-segmentation. These complexities have taken shape in the use of the idea of *geodemographic* segmentation, which relies on the relative homogeneity of people living in *neighbourhoods*. At one time, the unit of a neighbourhood was based on individual census EDs (enumeration districts) which was an average of 150 households. The country-wide use of postal codes in Britain meant that one could use a subdivision of the old ED – an individual postal code covers an average of 15 households. Both ED and postal code neighbourhoods can be related back to the Ordnance Survey grid references, which makes for easier computer analysis.

To classify sections of the community it is first necessary to describe them in specific terms such as 'living in Lincoln', 'family size greater than seven' and so on. It is then possible to analyse the clusters of people who share a set of descriptive terms. This process is known as *cluster analysis*. In the 1970s cluster analysis was widely used in the public sector, especially at that time for defining the location of areas of maximum social deprivation. For this, R. Webber (at the Centre for Environmental Studies) developed a census classification system at ward level. This system was later renamed ACORN and is still used for housing analyses. Other classification systems followed such as Pinpoint (1983), PiN (1985), FiNPiN (for financial services selling, 1986), MOSAIC (1986) and DEFINE (1989). Some of these systems use the census data alone (ACORN, PiN) while others also use data such as the electoral roll, the postcode file, specific research data and even bad debt information from the Lord Chancellor's office.

Such systems have advantages (low cost, reasonable accuracy, ability to overlay with other segmentations) but they also have disadvantages. The main one of these is the problem of updating with a census taking place only every 10 years. They represent an area in which the public and private sectors coincide. Technical details are available in a most useful Admap article (Sleight,1992).

For a while geodemographics was particularly used for media selection. It was claimed that even ACORN was a better discriminator between say *Telegraph* and *Guardian* readers than the standard demographic segments. However, this enthusiasm appears to be waning in recent times.

❏ Psychographic

Psychographic segmentation, of which lifestyle analysis is part, caught the imagination of many marketers during the 1980s. This was a reflection of other concepts such as New Women (and New Men), green concerns, the baby boomers and various social trends. It was accompanied by a rash of acronyms and idioms for various segments – Yuppie (young upwardly mobile professional people),

Dinkie (double income no kids), Woopie (well-off older people) and so on. There was an inevitable reaction against these ideas during the economic downturn. Between the hype and the horror it should be said that some useful correlations were found. For example, six groupings of 15 – 44 year-old women with attitude descriptors were found to be correlated with both purchasing and media behaviour (Bowles,1988). The groupings that were used give an interesting insight into the way researchers work. They were:

- *self-aware* (concerned about appearance, fashion and exercise)
- *fashion-directed* (concerned about appearance and fashion but not about exercise)
- *green goddesses* (concerned about fitness but less about appearance)
- *unconcerned* (neutral attitudes)
- *conscience stricken* (too busy to act but would like to)
- *dowdies* (indifferent about fashion and exercise, dress for comfort).

At the same time, ecological matters were selling well and looked like the next USP (Unique Selling Proposition) in much product positioning and selling. A USP is an attempt to make your service or product stand out from the crowd by endowing it with some unique selling point. Lifestyle niche marketers prospered, such as the Body Shop retail chain who added ethics in their 1991 slogan, 'the most honest cosmetic company in the world' (Dibb and Simkin, 1991).

❏ Behaviour

Most behavioural segments are straightforward since these are consumption patterns, idea/brand loyalty and media habits. They can be important to those in the public sector, however, for two special reasons. First is the fact that idea loyalty can be very strong – how do you persuade the lager lout to change behaviour patterns when the nightly drinking with friends is such an ingrained habit reinforced by strong peer pressure? Second is the problem of reaching the target population. Which channels of communication would reach the homeless, those on income support or those who are blind? It may be possible one day not to have to rely on media habits if we were to attain a social service all-embracing database. This is currently unlikely and anyway would not catch everybody. From personal experience the writer knows that many blind people are hidden, not being on any register, and they have widely different media habits.

Other behaviour segments include *product-specific occasions* (when do people drink orange juice, receive their state pensions, obtain a white stick) and *critical-event occasions* (reach pension age, retire, become unemployed, marry). On such occasions, service providers may need to move into action (e.g. bereavement counsellors).

Normally, some other perhaps more mundane segmentation is included under the 'behaviour' heading. These include:

- *user status* (non-user, first-timer, regular user, potential user, ex-user). Often the need is to turn a potential user into a regular user (diabetics and insulin) or a regular user into a non-user (addicts). Social service agencies make widespread use of this type of segmentation for drug rehabilitation

- *volume segmentation* (light, medium, heavy users). Heavy users often provide the bulk of consumption such as insulin or beer (some 88% of total beer consumption is by the top fraction of drinkers). Social marketing may find this a problem. Family-planners may target large families but these are the most resistant to birth control propaganda. Additionally, concentrating too much on the heavy users may actually result in a loss of the low and medium users who may conclude that a message is not for them, or even decide that they do not want to be like the heavy users

- *loyalty status*. If we call alternative ideas or products A, B, C, etc. then we can differentiate patterns as being hard-core (A, A, A, A, A, A pattern), soft-core (A, A, B, B, A), shifting (A, A, A, B, B, B) or switching (A, B, C, D, E, B). One has to be careful not to confuse loyalty status decisions with other factors such as low price, non-availability or not caring.

❏ Predisposition

Some commentators do not show this as a separate segment, preferring to put it into behaviour or psychographic. Those commentators who do use it include:

- *product knowledge* when a consumer needs further information about a service or product being offered (knowing what housing benefit is applicable, how to use contraceptives, how to plan a healthy diet)

- *problems owned* when a consumer has a problem and is looking for a solution (how to get to the Post Office to draw a pension)

- *benefits sought* by buying a service or product (why buy expensive electronic games – to keep children quiet, to teach children about computers, to relieve peer pressure or to impress the neighbours through conspicuous consumption).

A famous study on 'benefits sought' some years ago concerned toothpaste. This threw up some odd correlations including the preferred brand of toothpaste (Haley, 1963):

Benefits sought	Demographics	Behaviour	Psychographics	Favourite brand
Economy *low price*	Men	Heavy users	High autonomy, value orientated	'Own-brand'
Medicinal *stop decay*	Large families	Heavy users	Hypochondriac, conservative	Crest
Cosmetic *white teeth*	Teenagers, young adults	Smokers	High sociability, active	Maclean's, Ultra Bright
Taste	Children	Spearmint lovers	Hedonistic, high self-involvement	Colgate, Aim

Figure 8.1. Segmentation and toothpaste.

Segmentation in practice

Within the public sector, segmentation has to be applied with care. For many services the public expectation of fairness may imply that people should receive the same quality of service whoever and wherever they are. In other cases, it may be accepted that needs vary and that service should vary according to that need. Expectations may be strongly influenced by past experience. Where segmentation is appropriate, the secret of good segmentation usage is to look at one subdivision below that initially considered. Thus if the segment is 'blind people', one would think of registered/unregistered, living alone/living with other(s), wheelchair-bound/ambulatory and so on. This enables one to home in on benefits and other cross-segments with much greater clarity resulting in far better and more discriminatory service. This can be particularly advantageous where cash is short in social services funding, as it usually is.

Not every segment is relevant in every situation. Thus it would not be useful to divide coffee drinkers by height or eye colour when looking at the split between decaffeinated, non-decaffeinated and ground, though there are statistical differences between age, income, marital state, and ethnicity. For segmentation to be relevant, it needs to be:

- *measurable* If it cannot be measured and quantified, then it is not data. There is no value in knowing that 'some' users want a public library to be open every day. There would be more value in knowing that 84% of users wanted it

- *substantial*   The largest *homogeneous* group that it is worthwhile going after
- *actionable*   If truly nothing can be done for or about a segment, leave it alone

    accessible   It has to be possible to reach a segment once it has been identified.

It is also advisable to look at three other factors – segment size (large organisations tend to go for large segments while small ones go for smaller segments because of resource allocation), growth potential (most universities favour growing faculties), and organisational attractiveness (how well it fits with our organisation's core purposes).

Staff concerns

If we assume that the average stay of an employee is fifteen years, then the salary cost over that time is likely to be in the order of not far short of £200,000. If we add the costs of National Insurance, pension (notional), accommodation and other costs, then the total cost over the fifteen years will be in the order of £300,000. The purchase of a piece of equipment costing £300,000 with an expected life-span of fifteen years would cause one to think about it very carefully indeed. Is it suitable for its purpose? Can it handle other products? Will it need adjusting or add-ons to improve flexibility? How can we avoid obsolescence? With time, machinery tends to decrease in value and eventually becomes almost worthless through obsolescence. On the other hand, correctly handled staff actually increase in value to an organisation with the passage of time. This odd dichotomy may be due to the fact that so many people regard staff as a cost rather than an investment.

This is not a human resource textbook, and there are some first-rate ones on the market. It is not proposed, therefore, to cover in depth the aspects of personnel management. However, there are certain aspects that are of particular concern to those concerned with marketing in the public sector.

It is usual to consider human resource matters under six main headings, some of which are of greater concern to us than others. These headings are as follows.

- staff planning
- recruitment and selection

- salaries and benefits
- working conditions
- development
- training.

Staff planning

To the outsider, the public sector may seem like an ideal venue for the ultimate in staff planning. After all, nothing changes in the public sector. The picture is different to the insider. The demands of Government change all the time and will continue to do so, which effectively removes the possibility of the extremes of planning. It is true that particular areas of the public sector suffer at times from a shortage of special skills, though the blame for this is not usually placed on a lack of planning. The public sector is helped by an accustomed degree of flexibility in its normal method of operating. Staff rotate after a limited time in post, service-wide trawls for positions ensure a deep reservoir of available staff, and people are accustomed to changes in their duties. For those organisations with a need for greater attention to planning than is usual in the public sector, the planning is considered in three stages:

(a) developing staff objectives

(b) administration of resources

(c) feedback and evaluation.

Developing staff objectives is based on the organisation's objectives, policies and forward plans. Based on these, one can develop forecasts of staffing requirements. These forecasts will concentrate on total staffing levels, skills required, organisational groupings and costs.

The *administration of resources* concentrates on secondary level of plans such as recruitment plans, training and development plans, appraisal systems, and so on.

Feedback and evaluation is usually based in the civil service on the well-established system of annual assessments. A recent trend that has become noticeable in some departments is the growth in the use of psychometrics as a tool. These are based on questionnaires aimed at revealing personality traits.

It may be felt that short shrift has been given to staff planning, especially by those who believe in it strongly. In reply, it has to be said that staff planning does not seem to be an outstandingly major shortcoming in the public sector.

Recruitment and selection

The main trend in recruitment in the recent past is increasing decentralisation. Executive agencies can recruit their own staff, within agreed parameters. The main decision that affects us is whether or not (and to what degree) staff with specific marketing experience should be recruited. The alternative is to train existing staff in marketing. The bulk of the public sector has mostly stayed with the latter. By and large, this seems to work satisfactorily, though one would wish that the amount and level of training were higher. Where an organisation is in a competitive situation, then it will be tempted to look outside for marketing staff. The problem with this solution is that it is difficult to offer such outsiders good career prospects. One group that has looked outside more than most is universities (and charities).

The stages of recruitment can be expressed as follows.

(a) *Preparation*   A job description and specification, with attendant grade, is written. The public sector are practised at doing this and do not usually encounter problems. The only difficulties likely to be encountered concern marketing qualifications (still rare in the UK) and how to define the practical marketing experience that is appropriate. The job is then advertised internally (through a trawl) and externally if that is needed.

(b) *Interviews*   We all think that we are good at conducting interviews, though results demonstrate that this is not universally true. A interviewer for a marketing position should obviously know about the theory and practice of marketing; practical experience would be even better. We have seen above (chapter 6) that good face-to-face sales staff have specific traits though these are not always easy to uncover in an ordinary interview. It is therefore likely that close questioning will be needed about past experience.

(c) *Follow-through*   The selected interviewee will need to be properly introduced to the new organisation. This is particularly so for somebody with no previous experience of the public sector. Later, it will be necessary to monitor progress, both in the new environment and in achieving marketing success.

Salaries and benefits

For many in the public sector, these aspects are standardised and well-known, though there are changes in many agencies. There is now a greater degree of flexibility, as well as the possibility of performance pay. To those from the private sector even this flexibility will be less than they are accustomed to, and this will have to be explained to them.

Working conditions

Office standards in the public sector are definitely improving, too much so for some of the tabloid press who will castigate any semblence of luxury. Even so, parameters are reasonably standardised. There is one aspect of working conditions that marketing staff will press for. That is the provision of good database access. This is of greater importance to those coming from the private sector since they may miss the networking that they are used to.

Development

Marketing staff (especially if from the outside) will need careful development if they are to avoid becoming fixed in a role for a long period of time. Face-to-face sellers, in particular, need development if they are to avoid becoming stale in their work.

Training

In the field of marketing, this is vital. Selling skills need constant refining, replenishment and updating. In most European countries, the majority of organisations spend less than 2% of their budgets on training (Holden and Livian, 1992). The main exception is France where a third of organisations spend 4% or more. This may be connected with the fact that legislation is in force that compels organisations to spend 1.2% of salary and wage costs on training, or be subject to extra taxation.

A formalised approach is the Training Needs Assessment (TNA). This aims to study and identify any problems or potential problems among the staff regarding their performance and skills development, and then to design ways of overcoming these through training. This is initially addressed through the use of surveys, observation, feedback from seniors and focus groups.

A recent trend is the concept of the *learning organisation*. One aspect of this is the deliberate attempt on the part of the organisation to learn lessons from its performance. This performance is then enhanced through the use of better information and staff training.

References

Bowles, T. (1988) *Does Classifying People by Lifestyle really Help the Advertiser?* European Research, February.

Dibb, S. and Simkin, L. (1991) *Targeting, Segments and Positioning* International Journal of Retail and Distribution Management, Vol. 19 No. 3.

Haley, R. (1963) *Benefit Segmentation: A Decision Oriented Research Tool* Journal of Marketing, July.

Holden, L. and Livian, Y. (1992) *Does Strategic Training Policy Exist? Some Evidence from Ten European Countries* Personnel Review, Vol. 21 No. 1.

Marketing *(1994) Mercury Ditches Dog Collar for Youth Look* 8 September.

Mueller-Heumann, G. (1992) *Market and Technology Shifts in the 1990s* Journal of Marketing Management, No. 8.

Sleight, P. (1992) *Where they Live* Admap, May.

Smith, W. (1956) *Product Differentation and Market Segmentation as Alternative Marketing Strategies* Journal of Marketing, July.

Chapter 9

Market research and market information systems

Risk varies inversely with knowledge.

I. Fisher, The Theory of Interest, 1930.

Enough research will tend to support your theory.

Arthur Bloch, Murphy's Law, 1979.

Who needs it?

In a book for marketers and the public sector, the answer expected would be 'everybody'. If you provide a service or goods, then the more you know about the environment in which you work, the better. Everybody in the public sector does provide a service or goods, so the response is what you would expect. Everybody needs market research:

- it can improve the level of service provided to the customer
- it helps to ensure that what is provided is what people need or expect
- it helps to improve the way in which the service or goods are delivered.

This is not to claim that it is infallible, or that it cannot lead you astray or that it can never be a waste of money. Even the weekly journal Marketing (1994) acknowledges some of the difficulty:

From the outside, market research can appear fiendishly complex. It's loaded with jargon and staffed, so it seems, by a mixture of psychologists and mathematicians. Technology, and in particular computers, is transforming the business. Clients need to know where to turn for help.

As already stated above, the more information that you have about the environment in which you operate, the better life is. This leads on logically to the best attitude when thinking about market research. It should be thought of as being part of the information needs within the organisation. It is often tempting to carry out research for ad hoc reasons or because it might be interesting. Instead one should consider what information is needed for success and then, if it is not already owned, go out and buy it. This may not be the most exciting approach, but it is the best.

A second less-exciting truth is that many organisations have within their boundaries vast amounts of useful information which is poorly organised and so not used. Bad information technology has in some places made things worse, hence the jibe of:

> I'm getting too much data when what I need is knowledge.

The customer care managers in the marketing department of one state-owned organisation received a 2cm. thick print-out every Monday. One day, a consultant found one of the managers hiding, crouched under his desk where he was perusing some A.5 pieces of card. Seeing the consultant, the manager smiled wanly and said that the printout was useless to him compared with his own private control figures.

This manager was regarded as being one of the best ones around and was certainly not computer illiterate (he used the databases for most of his figures). At the other extreme, some organisations use their I.T. as a major tool in their marketing and market research and we will consider them later.

Market information systems

Some organisations fail miserably to exploit the information that they already possess. The example usually quoted is the poor organisation of data within hospitals and GP practices. This may not be good enough for decent resource allocation let alone customer care (Rea, 1994). The proposals for an internal market in health care were originally published under a new style of title – *Working for Patients* (Department of Health, 1989). These proposals were based on the RMI (Resource Management Initiative) of the 1980s. Similar proposals were made for the social services provided by local authorities and volunteers (Department of Health, 1989a). These sets of proposals were brought together in the National Health Service (NHS) and Community Care Act 1990, under which health authorities and local authorities purchased services from providers who should compete, in other words market themselves. In the first years after the act, various studies suggested that the development of decent information systems remained sub-standard (Royce, 1993).

Historically, the NHS had introduced a very broad department-based information system in the 1950s. This (except for a few experimental health districts) lasted almost unchallenged until the 1990 Act. Even the use of Diagnostic Related Groups (DRGs) was strenuously resisted, DRGs being a system of 468 categories of patients used for Medicare in the U.S.A.

A very different picture exists elsewhere. Rank Xerox know how many copies their individual customers make through the charging system based on number of copies made. From this they calculate when the customer should buy the next load of paper. Each day, the tele-sellers see on their screens who should be con-tacted about ordering more paper. The next order is taken over the phone; this triggers the order assembly, delivery and account charging. Many customers like this system because they no longer have to take stock or take the time and effort to order. This is an effective marketing system. It also integrates the infor-mation system with selling, and tells Rank Xerox quickly about trends in the marketplace without paying for market research (e.g. whether people are mov-ing from 80gm to 70gm paper, which colours are increasing in appeal).

A second example is Viking Direct, a successful mail-order office supplies seller. Viking attracts customers with attractive pricing; it then tries to hold the cus-tomer through good service. Selling has to be through direct mail catalogues. The frequency of a customer getting a catalogue is related to how active the account is, with very active accounts getting a catalogue every week since (Sta-tionery Trade News, 1993):

> the object is to mail the fewest number of catalogues to achieve the most business.

Customers get a personalised message on the cover based on internal data, such as 'Dear Mr. Titman, you last ordered fax rolls from us eight weeks ago'. The same single edition of a catalogue is not the Viking way. Customers will get one of 71 different catalogues, all individually targeted. Which one of the 71 cata-logues you receive depends on which products are felt to be most appropriate. The ultimate is the customised catalogue for a specific customer, and Viking's headquarters (in Los Angeles) could do it now if they decided that it was worth-while. Viking know the profitability per square centimetre of advertising space in their catalogue, and are working on relating customers to pages. The chair-man of Viking in the U.K. says (Stationery Trade News, 1993):

> Profit is in segmentation of the database. We can evaluate the lifetime value of a customer; for example a hospital with 100 staff will provide a certain level of sales over a year, and we know what the profitability of those sales will be.

These two examples (Rank Xerox and Viking) show how it is possible to exploit internal data by being innovative. Another way of getting useful information is through the 'swapping' and 'giving' of information within the public sector by networking, though internal constraints may create countervailing pressures. There are plenty of examples of the value and problems of non-commercialised networking. Three such examples (Talbot and Harrow, 1993) are:

- a district health authority prepared a training pack in patient ethnic monitoring. It was realised that this should be sold rather than given to other DHAs. The problem was that the DHA had no practical experience of costing, hard charging or pricing and so the price seemed much too low. So low that it looked like 'a successful swapping exercise, dressed up in entrepreneurial clothes'

- the Local Government Policy and Performance Review Network (300 members, founded in 1989) flourished in spite of there being more official channels, in exchanging information. This was probably because the quality of information was felt by participants to be better. The ethos of swapping and sharing data overcame the 'commercialisation of knowledge in public services management'

- a civil service Agency had at one time made its knowledge available reasonably freely to universities and others, but had to put this on a commercial basis. The move from swapping/giving to selling should have been easy except that the Agency had poor costing systems in place. Rather than making some improvements, the practice was in effect discontinued.

The examples of both exploiting internal information and of non-commercial swapping could be multiplied many times over. The lessons seem clear and unavoidable:

- use the information you have in smart ways
- exploit Information Technology in smart ways
- if you need extra information, get it by buying, swapping, networking, or begging
- install good robust systems, especially a good costing system.

Learning these points can lead to happiness; not learning them can lead to frustration.

We are now in a position to define a marketing information system as:

> the method of gathering, sorting, analysing and distributing necessary, accurate and timely information to the marketing decision makers.

The basic source of information has to be, as we have seen, the internal records system backed up by a good costing system. The nature of this information depends on the type of organisation. At the Civil Service College, it will include reporting on orders in hand and sales to date (overall; by course; compared with target; compared with last year), prices, stock levels, finance, labour utilisation. By analysing this information, it is possible to locate areas needing special attention and to highlight opportunities and threats.

For many organisations, such as the College and health service providers, the kernel of the internal records system is the Order – Delivery – Billing system. This just has to be smooth, accurate and fast, if possible in real time. If the number of hiccups in this system becomes noticeable then the cost escalates as individuals try to cover the deficiencies by devising personal back-up systems that will operate in tandem, even if they are officially forbidden.

Depending on circumstances, there may also be a separate sales reporting system. If the output from this system is received by the staff later than that from the order/delivery/billing system then the only helpful course of action is to pray to the gods on Olympus for mercy. It should be noticed that this prayer is rarely answered, so the only alternative approach is to do without sleep. The AHS (a hospital supply organisation) equipped the purchasing departments of its customers with computer modems. Hospitals then sent their orders direct to the AHS sales section through the computer link. This gave AHS immediate access to information concerning who was buying and what they were buying. The system used by HMSO for much of their selling is similar in concept so it is certainly not a one-off approach.

❏ Setting up a system

Setting up a market information system is always a balancing act, and a balancing act in several dimensions:

- first there is a balance to be struck between what managers really need to know and what some of them think they need. This problem should not be dismissed as trivial but since it has to be faced with all I.T. based information systems is one that many people have experience in handling, but there is still no easy answer
- second, a balance often has to be struck between accuracy and timing; which of these predominates depends on the circumstances
- a third balance that often has to be faced is that between desirability and cost.

A common cause of high capital cost as well as running costs is the inability of many organisations to use standard software to its full. The wishes of individuals and internal groups to tweak the software continuously has been revealed in study after study. This can actually cost more than using inadequate software though this fact will continue to be ignored.

It is usual to hold meetings with the relevant managers or to send them a questionnaire. If meetings are the chosen vehicle, then employ a good facilitator. The facilitator will distribute a paper beforehand containing notes on the background, the objectives and any other relevant data. At the meeting the facilitator will have a higher profile than usual to try to reduce the blue skies demands and the wishful thinking, but must still listen carefully.

A questionnaire approach starts in a similar fashion. But the facilitator has to be prepared for the fact that a number of people will fail to respond. These same people will nevertheless be vocal in their opposition to any system that does not include their pet wants. Facilitators are used to this fact of life. How they handle it depends on the culture of the organisation and may be anywhere on the spectrum of ignoring all late appeals completely to incorporating everything. The sort of matters that have to be covered at both the meetings and in the questionnaire methods include:

- what sort of decisions do you have to make (a) regularly (b) occasionally
- what sorts of information do you need to make these decisions
- please say which information you need daily, weekly, monthly, yearly, as available
- is the timing of getting some of this information vital? If so, please describe
- do you periodically ask for special studies? If so, please describe
- what information would you like to get that you do not get now, and if so, when
- which magazines, intelligence/trade reports, etc, do you wish to be routed to you
- which specialised software do you need at your station or on the network
- which three or four changes would you most like to see introduced to the current market information system?

Analysing the responses enables one to build up a system that will satisfy everyone. It is quite easy to make a statement like that, to carry it out is in practice more difficult. There are always some people who are adamant that they cannot operate without some arcane (and expensive) data. There will be some who use the opportunity to get their hands on software that they have previously been refused. There will be some who 'don't know what they don't know'. One of the best defences against the last mentioned is to have somebody on the staff who delights in keeping up to date on absolutely everything. Such people will happily spend much of their spare time at home reading everything about marketing information. These people are sometimes called *cosmopolitans* or *gatekeepers*.

Some organisations find the whole process so complex that they will place the decisions in the hands of an outsider. Experience suggests that the worst candidate for this task is the head of computing. The best answer is usually to employ an effective facilitator who can find a way through the minefield of outraged egos. A chess grandmaster once said that he was always looking for that one move that would make future generations put a '!' after it to show what a fantastically good move it was (Kottnauer). In the same way, one looks for a '!' use of information technology and other market information systems. We have seen how Rank Xerox and Viking have managed this. They and others (such as the ticket telesales at American Airlines in Pittsburg) have shown that it can be done.

Market research

First, a piece of semantics. There are some people who dislike the term market research, preferring to use the term 'marketing research' or 'research for marketing'. A few people in the public sector do not like to use any of these, preferring to call all such work 'social research'. *Marketing research* is often defined to give a wider span, and to include:

- *market research* which covers studying market segmentation, market share, competitors' market share, customer location, industry logistics, and analysing economic and other environmental factors that may affect the market
- *product research* covering the comparison of one's own products with the competition's, product and product concept testing, variety reduction and expansion, packaging, and testing new applications for existing products
- *advertising research* which covers the measurement of advertising and promotion effectiveness, studying media effectiveness, copy quality and the possible use of alternatives
- *sales research* which analyses sales by many dimensions (geography, product, individual sales staff, outlets, distribution channels) to assist

in better planning of sales responsibilities, calls, selling methods, and control mechanisms

- *business economics*   which studies trends, supply/demand curves, profit/price trade-offs, econometrics, input-output analysis, scenario alternatives, assumptions, short and long-term forecasts, etc.
- *motivation research*   which looks at the social and psychological reasons for customers making a buying decision, and for accepting or rejecting social messages and campaigns.

It is sometimes felt desirable to carry out *exploratory research* before committing oneself to more specific market research. Exploratory research may try to help define a problem that is proving elusive to agree upon. Or it may help to set the parameters for later studies. For example, before researching the design of the Lexus car, Toyota sent 20 designers out of Japan to talk to dealers and potential buyers overseas. This was to try to assess just the type of thing that buyers of luxury cars look for in their cars. By its nature, exploratory research should not try to reach any definite conclusions. It is usually carried out the way Toyota did it, by talking to people and listening.

While the above description is framed very much in the traditional marketing context of products and competitors, the concepts apply equally well to services in a non-competitive situation and to policy development. What are the factors which affect people's needs, how will economic trends affect perceptions, which media are most effective in getting messages across, how far are present services satisfying people?

❏ Key stages

A lot of market research is carried out for reasons that are based on intuition or gut reaction. There is, however, a more rigorous approach that is recommended by the majority of commentators. This approach is not startling in its individual stages, so there is a temptation to feel that of course one knows it so well that it is used as part of one's sub-conscious working. Observation suggests that this is not entirely true; either that or the sub-conscious workings can be well hidden from view. This more rigorous system follows five stages:

- define the problem
- design the research
- collect the data
- analyse the data
- present the results.

Define the problem

In marketing terms, Einstein and Infield (1942) may have gone too far when they said that:

> the formulation of a problem is often more essential than its solution

but they were on the right lines. A careful definition of the problem, and from this a statement of the research objectives, results in a proper focus being given to what can otherwise become a messy process. 'Find out everything you can about our customers' has no such focus and has nothing to do with a problem. Such a kick-off will result in plenty of data, most of it useless. Knowing that one's customers cut their finger nails on average every 8.2 days or that their average length of pace is 75cms will not be too useful. Going too broad is not the only failing, going too narrow can be just as bad. The College might research the question, 'How many course members would be willing to pay £10 to have a haircut in their bedroom?'. This would beg too many other points. Would competitors copy the idea and if so how many? Would the thought of in-room haircuts tempt people who would not take up the offer? Why choose £10? A better question would be, 'could in-room haircuts give the College a competitive advantage and profit to justify the cost against other investments that the College could make?'.

The College is not alone in having to take care when defining the problem as the first stage in collecting information. The public sector is generally much more concerned nowadays in getting advice by collecting information and carrying out research to this end. Initiatives such as the Citizens' Charter have accelerated this tendency. In the formulation and ongoing monitoring of the Citizens' Charters, asking people the right questions is a key point. How satisfied are they? Are they getting what they want? Are the indices valid?

Design the research

This consists of developing the research plan and costing it. It will involve decisions concerning:

- the nature of the data to be uncovered
- the sources of that data (*primary* data is new information that has to be gathered specially, *secondary* data is stuff that already exists somewhere such as internal knowledge, Government publications, books, journals and commercial data)
- research approaches and techniques to be utilised

- the sampling plan (who is to be sampled, what size will the sample be and what procedures will be followed?)
- the contact methods (mail, telephone, personal interviews, special established groupings).

Collect the data

This step is where the costs start mounting so, unless the collection is for a fixed lump sum fee, the control mechanisms have to be in place and used. The important task for the researcher at this stage is to reduce any errors being introduced. The most famous example was in 1936 in America. The *Literary Digest* magazine carried out a poll to forecast the winner of the presidential contest between Alf Landon (Republican) and Franklin Roosevelt (Democrat). As a result they forecast a landslide win for Landon. They were wrong. The error was in using the telephone as the sole collection method. In 1936, telephone subscribers were predominantly more affluent and more Republican. Some errors can be reduced by carrying out a pre-test before the main collection to iron out any difficulties.

Analyse the data

This is likely to involve some mathematical and statistical treatment. This is not done to make the results more palatable or to blind the marketers with science, but to extract additional meanings from the data. It is also likely at this stage that some subjective analysis will be introduced. On the other hand, some existing secondary data may be used to expand the comparisons that can be seen emerging.

Present the results

Management usually want the results presented straight and will resent a paper over-larded with detailed descriptions of how the results were obtained. The usual rules for a paper apply. It should be clear, fairly short, well written, have a summary and all the clever stuff should be in the appendices if present at all. In all this, it can help considerably if the management and the researcher know and trust one another.

These stages can appear deceptively easy to perform. The need for such research is now widely accepted for policy work, the Citizens' Charter and other public sector interests. These two factors (the accepted need and the apparent simplicity) may lead public sector staff to decide to do all the research themselves. This would not always be a wise move. There is often a need to utilise specialist expertise.

147

❑ Some tools and techniques

A wide range of tools and techniques is potentially available. In this section we explain briefly the key elements and uses of:

- focus groups
- decision support systems
- experiments
- mystery shoppers
- panels
- technical market research
- databases and lists.

Those wishing to lead the use of any of these techniques will find more information in specialist texts. The *Market Research Encyclopedia* is not a book but one of the most referred to articles on market research. It was published some years ago in the Harvard Business Review (Barabba, 1990) and consists of several tables explaining many approaches that are used in market research plus a short glossary of terms. Although it was not actually used in preparing this book, it is recommended reading.

Focus groups

Focus groups were originally regarded as an approach under the exploratory research umbrella. A group of, say, 10 to 12 people sit down with a facilitator and several members of the research staff for a discussion. The discussion is only loosely structured in that a question will be put to the group who can then go in any direction. The question might be, 'What do you think of this product or idea?' To this the answers might include looks old-fashioned, over-priced, not kitschy enough, or it would break easily. The skill of the facilitator and research staff lies in being able to lock onto a comment that is important or new. Sometimes there is a general air of agreement about a response in which case this becomes the lesson. This skill is somewhat similar to that required by a good brainstorming facilitator and indeed some of the additional techniques can be common to both. The company called 'Arm & Hammer' used focus groups when looking for new uses of bicarbonate of soda and heard that people thought of it as freshening. This led ultimately to the launch in the U.K. of bicarbonate of soda for teeth cleaning.

During the Bush v. Clinton presidential election in the U.S.A. in 1992, the Clinton camp used focus groups in connection with reactions to TV election broadcasts and to policy statements. This proved so successful that its use spread to many political parties throughout Europe. Some may recoil from the thought of policy formulation or product development being decided by the off-hand remark of one person. Generally, it is preferable to think of focus groups as being the precursor of other, more robust, research that should follow it. More ideas on the conduct of focus groups are offered in Smith (1994).

Decision support systems

Decision Support Systems (DSS) are computer-based mathematical analysing systems. They tend to be held on a central computer accessed by staff through a network, and are based on a vast database of information. In use, the staff call up the DSS and move around the database. As they do this they can ask the computer to carry out a number of statistical techniques such as goodness-of-fit, regression analysis, factor analysis, cluster analysis, conjoint analysis or discriminant analysis. The users can also ask the computer to use a number of modelling techniques such as macromodels, micro-analytical models, behavioural models, optimization models, heuristic models, queueing models and so on. These techniques are all used to sort, categorise and analyse relationships in data. A good DSS can be useful in reducing uncertainty, (it can also occupy an underemployed 'techie' for hours on end as an innocent plaything).

Experiments

Experiments are carried out in a laboratory or controlled environment. Members of the public are brought together to test their reactions to advertising copy, actual products or ideas' campaigns. New television shows are regularly tested in this way. People indicate on press buttons when during a screened pilot programme they are amused, or bored.

Mystery shoppers

The *mystery shoppers* in the 1960s and 1970s went round retail outlets in the role of observant customers. They would watch the operation of the shops for such matters as customer care, speed of response and short-changing. Since those days their scope has been enlarged to act in the role of a complainant at a police station, somebody trying to get on a GP's register, a potential litigant at a solicitors, testing the telephone response at switchboards of an agency, or observing sell-by dates of food. It should be noted that in Britain mystery shoppers are resisted by many in the health and social services fields. It is said that the author Jeffrey Archer used to act as a one-person mystery shopper, going round booksellers to see if his new books were displayed prominently enough. (This rumour is not meant to be pejorative or libellous, but is repeated as a mark of admiration for his marketing skills).

Panels

Panels are the obverse of mystery shoppers. A panel is a group of people with well-tested attributes such as class, education, habits and attitudes. They are then asked for their reactions to products, ideas or advertising. This is usually done by using questionnaires or completing sheets describing their weekly actions. Panels are different from focus groups in that they are much larger, there is little if any discussion and information is collected by mail. An extension of this is (for example) Behaviour Scan where shopping lists are collected electronically and analysed against individual advertising messages that went to targeted individuals.

Another extension is *exploratory extended creative groups* which are like panels but which use a broad variety of approaches. An example was their use by Conoco in researching sales of their Jet petrol (Chambers, 1993). The group were given *bubble cartoons* and asked to fill in the bubbles. What is the customer thinking? And what is the petrol pump thinking? Members of the groups were also asked to look quickly through magazines, tearing out pictures that reflected what they thought about petrol buying (this is known as *picture search*). Then the people were given a construction toy and asked to *model build* different types of station (e.g. where you would never go, a friendly station, a typical petrol giant station). The same (well-established) approaches were repeated with Jet stations as the example.

The resulting findings were that people tended to think of petrol stations as threatening places, with antagonistic staff who might short-measure you, fiddle the change, or even make you feel a fool. Jet stations in particular were seen as cramped, dingy, cluttered, cheap-and-nasty but independent. As a result, more detailed research was carried out. This led to a new upgraded design for the sites, the cost of which was recouped within a year due to higher margins and increased throughput. Other petrol firms promptly followed suit, as usual.

Technical market research

Technical market research (TMR) is a branch of market research aimed specifically at new product development. It tries to understand what consumers need, want and expect of a new product and then to translate this into R and D and manufacturing input. Since, as we have seen, consumers frequently find it difficult to think or articulate what they do want from the future, they are given helpful prods. These include mock-ups, three-dimensional drawings and 'what-if' brainstorming sessions. Some organisations take this further by setting up *antenna shops* where consumers can try new prototypes and, importantly, data are collected on people's responses (Laulaug, 1993). Mazda call this whole approach *kansei* or sensory engineering (Japan Automotive News, 1990).

Databases and lists

Databases and *lists* are often the first building block in any market research. There are hundreds of such available on the market, so it can be important to get under the sales blurbs and analyse exactly what each one contains and the source. There are lists of millionaires, people who shop at Sainsbury's, and people who are thinking of getting a hearing aid. One of the more expensive is that of unmarried women aged 30 – 44 who are vegetarians and support charities and green issues. There are analyses of the last census on CD-ROM (such as 'Cenario'). There is one ('Portrait') with a four-digit analysis code for each of the 1.5 million residential postcodes in the U.K., e.g. '0102 – Affluent families with pre-school age children'. So there is plenty of data about data.

Market research is continually changing and trends can be seen. Local authorities appear not to use it much even for policy evaluation though this may be increasing (Severljen, 1994). Posting questionnaires through e-mail should increase in suitable segments, though one study found that response can still be inferior to postal mail, 19% against 56% (Schuldt and Totten, 1994). The availability of vast consumer databases will be further exploited for accurate targeting. Some already contain several million entries. Questionnaire design will improve as information about good design becomes better known (Vittles, 1994). None of the improvements will protect us from the occasional glitch. Good market research requires a number of specialist skills, for example, sample design, questionnaire design, facilitation skills, statistical and qualitative analytical techniques and information systems. While managers need an overview of various approaches and of the techniques available, such as that which this chapter has attempted to provide, this is an area (as we have said) where they will need to employ or buy-in specialist expertise.

References

Barabba, V. (1990) *The Market Research Encyclopedia* Harvard Business Review, Vol. 68 No. 1, January-February.

Chambers, S. (1993) *Research and Jet: In Site, in Mind, in Business* Admap, January.

Department of Health, (1989) *Working for Patients* CM555, London, HMSO.

Department of Health, (1989a) *Caring for People: Community Care in the Next Decade and Beyond* Cm 849, London, HMSO.

Einstein, A. and Infield, L. (1942) *The Evolution of Physics* New York, Simon & Schuster.

Japan Automotive News – Overseas Edition, (1990) *Mazda eyes Niche Markets* December.

Kottnauer, K. in a private conversation.

Laulaug, A. (1993) *Technical-Market Research – Get Customers to Collaborate in Developing Products* Long Range Planning, Vol. 26 No. 2.

Marketing (1994) *Choosing and Using Market Research* Supplement, 25 September.

Rea, D. (1994) *Better Informed Judgements: Resource Management in the NHS* Accounting, Auditing & Accountability Journal, Vol. 86 No.1.

Royce, R. (1993) *DRGs and the Internal Market* British Journal of Healthcare Computing, Vol. 10 No.1.

Schuldt, B. and Totten, J. (1994) *Electronic Mail v. Mail Survey Response Rates* Marketing Research, Vol. 6 No. 1.

Severljen, P. (1994) *Local Authorities and Market Research* Local Government Studies, Spring.

Smith, R. (1994) *Strategic Management and Planning in the Public Sector* Harlow, Longman.

Stationery Trade News (1993) *The Honesty of 71 Catalogues,* July.

Talbot, C. and Harrow, J. (1993) *Sharing or Withholding Organisational Knowledge?: An Exploration of Changing Values in Managerial and Organisational Learning* British Academy of Management Conference, September.

Vittles, P. (1994) *Question Time* The Health Service Journal, 12 May.

Chapter 10

Statistical and forecasting techniques

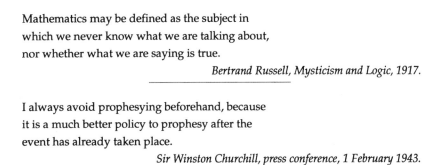

Mathematics may be defined as the subject in
which we never know what we are talking about,
nor whether what we are saying is true.

Bertrand Russell, Mysticism and Logic, 1917.

I always avoid prophesying beforehand, because
it is a much better policy to prophesy after the
event has already taken place.

Sir Winston Churchill, press conference, 1 February 1943.

Whilst having a quiet drink in a pub one evening, you hear somebody say, 'Coventry will beat Tottenham easily on Saturday'. Is this a forecast? Is it a gamble? Is it defence of a loved one? Is it an attempt at sympathetic magic by a supporter? If it is a forecast, then a professional forecaster would have some further questions. What is the probability being claimed for accuracy of the statement? What data were used? Are there trends that support the statement? What research was carried out beforehand? Does the speaker have special expertise or knowledge? Which mathematical techniques were used in arriving at the result? This just goes to show, of course, what terrible spoil-sports professional forecasters are, always dubious, always wanting facts, and insisting on a robustness of approach. One should be grateful that they are indeed like this, since the world is full of pseudo-forecasts and hopes masquerading as expectations. The truth is that we should all try to emulate our spoil-sport forecaster. These are just the sorts of questions that we should always ask when presented with a forecast that is of importance.

A food manufacturer called its sales' staff together for an inspirational meeting to announce a wonderful new opportunity. Laser lights swung and flashed, a pop group played, wine flowed, the inevitable (alas) underdressed models wafted across the stage. Then graphs were produced proving positively that sales were going to be astounding, new sales targets were shown leading to extra bonuses. The thought of imminent riches had the sales' staff on their feet, cheering and waving their arms aloft, so certain were they that the sales forecasts were correct.

This whole extravaganza was because this baked beans manufacturer was going to change the taste of its tomato sauce. Sales did not rise, in fact they fell. The graphs were purely and solely a wish, a hope, on the part of the sales director and had absolutely no factual basis at all, though they were beautifully drawn. It should not be thought that such an act is unusual. It happens every day, especially, it has to be said, in the world of marketing, though it is not unknown even in budget preparations.

Bases of forecasting

Forecasts are built upon three inputs:

- *what people tell you* in response to questionnaires, interviews and published data. 'What do you need? What would you like? What are you expecting to buy, and when?' As every researcher knows, none of this is foolproof. People may find a potential action very attractive in prospect, but then change minds when actually faced with the factual decision later. This does not mean that we do not ask people. It means that we have to be very careful with the design of surveys and questionnaires, and put our own caveats on the results
- *what people do* in response to, for example, a test market study, though again this is by no means foolproof and it does alert the competition
- *what people have done*, from which we try to extrapolate trends and study past behaviour patterns. This often involves statistical demand analysis or time-series analysis.

Some of the specific approaches that may be used include:

- *employing indicators* (This will usually involve building an econometric model). An example of this approach is the forecasting of U.K. sales of management consultancy. It has been found that this follows closely the response of organisations to question 2b of the CBI survey with a time lag of nine months (this relates to the anticipated change in capital expenditure)
- *trend extrapolation* In this approach a graph is prepared of past behaviour and this is compared with known types of curves to find the 'best-fit' between the shape of the past and a standard curve. If a straight line looks close this fact is best ignored except over the short term. Instead, use may be made of quadratic or S-curves, reflecting the idea of the product life cycle discussed in chapter 4. Hysteresis curves

and even the discharge from a triode have been used but these are usually (justifiably) rejected by sales management. The assumption is made that the best-fit curve will be followed in the future enabling one to forecast that future

- *asking expert opinion*   The basis for this method is that experts in any field keep up to date with developments and may thus be better placed then a layperson in making prognostications about the future. One method using this approach is the Delphi method where experts go through several rounds of expressing their opinions, at the same time being given fresh data and feedback about the opinions of the rest of the panel of experts

- *dynamic modelling*   Sets of equations are prepared that model the basis of the system under consideration. The coefficients, the impact of each explanatory factor on the final result, are calculated statistically. HM Treasury's model for forecasting the U.K. economy uses this approach

- *building scenarios*   A scenario is a picture of the future with its implications, based on agreed data. Scenario building has passed through several stages in the past twenty years. At one time, many people would rely on two scenarios which were 'most optimistic' and 'most pessimistic' pictures. Then a third one was added, a sort of middle picture where life continued much as at present. Dissatisfaction with this approach led to people trying to build up a 'most likely' picture. Some organisations, notably the oil giants, now build up an overall most-likely scenario based on an atomised technique; this builds up the whole picture by combining a lot of lower level forecasts. These lower level forecasts are a combination of products and countries. Other scenarios are then built based on assumptions of major upheavals such as a collapse in the price of oil.

Forecasting methods are discussed in more detail in Smith (1994). The art of forecasting can drive staff into two opposite camps. There are those who avoid any arithmetic, preferring the 'wet finger' approach (based on long experience, of course). Some others place implicit faith in statistical methodology believing that figures cannot lie. The most successful, such as the oil giants, take great care but keep their ear to the ground the whole time for those events that can upset all the calculations.

Probability

You have three dice which you throw one at a time. The first time you try this, the first die shows 5, the second 1 and the third 3. You try the whole thing again when the first die shows 6, the second 6 and the third also shows a 6. Which of these two events is the more usual? This question has been posed by researchers on a number of occasions. The answer is that the two events are equally likely. When one throws dice, the chance that a particular face will be on top is the same for each face, a fact that should be obvious if instead of numbers the faces were adorned with, say, different fruits. The odds that a particular fruit (or number) ends up being on top has to be 1 in 6 since there are six faces on a cube. We can express '1 in 6' as either saying a particular face will be the top one $1/6 \times 100 = 16.7\%$ of the time, or as being 167 in a thousand. When you throw the second die, it does not know what the first die showed nor can the first throw affect the second throw. So the odds against two particular fruits (or numbers) coming up are $1/6 \times 1/6$ or nearly 28 in 1,000. Similarly, if you throw a third die the odds against three fruits (or numbers) has to be $1/6 \times 1/6 \times 1/6$ or just over $4\frac{1}{2}$ in 1,000.

This concept is blindingly obvious to many people. However, research shows also that many people refuse to accept this reasoning. To them the 6-6-6 result is much less likely than the 5-1-3 result. What has provoked interest among researchers is that this second group of people are different in another way. They are more likely to be superstitious, to be susceptible to fringe religions, and more prone to accept advertisements at face value. In other words, such people do not have a general feel for whether something is likely to be true. In the jargon, they have a poor *life probability faculty*. Such people may be optimists in life or pessimists. They may even be able to handle mathematics; it is the implications that they cannot handle.

❑ Decision trees

One way to handle this situation is to use an approach that is a good presentational tool, the *decision tree*. A decision tree is a graphical way of showing the effect of probabilities. For example, suppose the Civil Service College is thinking of launching a distance learning pack about 'The Use of Spreadsheets in Marketing'. This product would have certain costs up front (writing, making a video, advertising, management and staff time, etc) as well as revenue costs (production, etc.). We can also identify the costs and income at various sales' levels. This could then lead us to calculating that if the product floats like a lead balloon and sells only 10 copies then the loss would be £100,000. If the product does very well, then the profit could be £300,000 for 2,000 copies. If sales are middling at 250 then there would be a loss of £50,000. We can now draw a decision tree as in Figure 10.1.

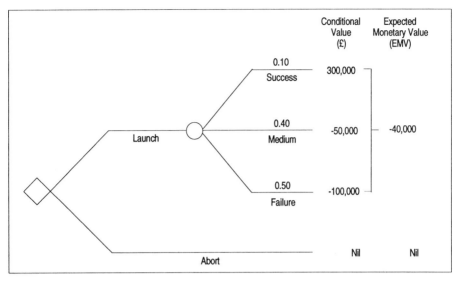

Figure 10.1 Decision Tree.

In this diagram, some probabilities have been allocated to the three different results. The likelihood of a resounding success is given as 0.10 (10%), that of a flop as 0.50 (50%) and that of a middling result as 0.40 (40%). These figures must add up to 1 (or 100%). We can multiply each of the financial results by its probability and then add up the outcomes to arrive at a final figure. This figure is known as the EMV (*Expected Monetary Value*) thus:

$$\text{Success} \quad + \quad \text{Medium} \quad + \quad \text{Failure}$$

$$\text{EMV} = [(0.10) \times (300{,}000)] + [(0.40) \times (-50{,}000)] + [(0.50) \times (-100{,}000)]$$

$$= 30{,}000 - 20{,}000 - 50{,}000$$

$$= -£40{,}000$$

This then is the probabilistic outcome of going ahead and launching the idea, a loss of £40,000 which is distinctly unattractive if the mesmerising potential of a £300,000 profit has been dangled in front of people. The problem can now arise of somebody suggesting that the probability of success is really 20% rather than 10%, and the probability of failure is really only 40%. If these figures are substituted in the decision tree then the launch EMV is exactly break-even. There is then the distinct possibility of somebody saying, 'Let's go ahead, then, and try to reduce the costs'. Making re-calculations using different figures is known as *sensitivity analysis*. Given the uncertainties, sensitivity analysis is an essential step, it should add to the understanding of the potential implications of the decision. The danger is that it can lead people to choose the probabilities which give the answer they intuitively want rather than realistic probabilities

The decision tree approach can be much further refined in every aspect. One can even incorporate that pang of regret felt when one makes the wrong decision, by using a technique known as the 'Savage criterion of minimax regret' (Peppers and Bails, 1987). At one time, decision trees were widely discussed in management training schools, such as on the managerial economics course at Harvard Business School. This is less true now since it has been found that most Chief Executives prefer a more discursive approach. However they are very useful for getting one's thoughts down on paper.

❏ Venn diagrams

Another device for getting thoughts down on paper is the Venn diagram, named after John Venn (1834 – 1923) who developed this graphical method. This arose out of *set theory*, which is now taught to children at primary school, much to the surprise of many parents and grandparents. A set is a group of objects, such as all the books in the North Totteridge public library. A sub-set is a group within a group, such as all the Mills and Boon published books within the total stock of books in the North Totteridge public library. The sets and sub-sets are not the same as the actual books themselves but the concept of the books.

So we could draw a circle and say to ourselves that the circle represents the set of books in the aforementioned library (Figure 10.2, drawing No.1) . The Mills and Boon books in the library could also be represented by a circle. However, since all the M & B books are part of the total stock of books, we would have to put the second circle inside the first circle since this is the only way of representing the situation (Figure 10.2, drawing No.2).

We can use two overlapping circles where only some items are in both of two sets. Thus we could use one circle to represent the books that Jean Bloggs has read while still keeping the other circle for the library books. This means that Jean Bloggs has read some books that are in the library (but not all of them), and some books that are not in the library at all (Figure 10.2, drawing No.3). We can use three circles to show that there are overlaps between three groups (Figure 10.2, drawing No.4). If we say that circle A represents all the Albanians living in Albania, circle B people who speak Belgian and circle C people who play cricket, then there are some people who are in all three circles, those right in the middle of all three circles. This select group are Belgian-speaking, cricket-playing, Albanians. The use of three overlapping circles as in drawing No.4 is very common in the representation of probabilities. Four overlapping circles is the effective maximum.

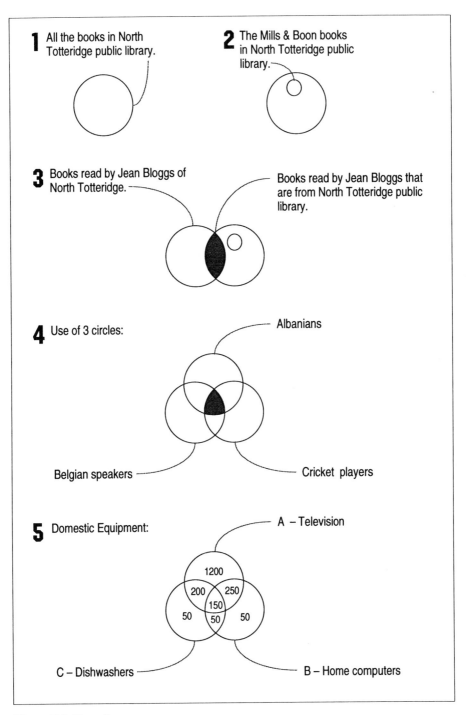

1 All the books in North Totteridge public library.

2 The Mills & Boon books in North Totteridge public library.

3 Books read by Jean Bloggs of North Totteridge.

Books read by Jean Bloggs that are from North Totteridge public library.

4 Use of 3 circles:

Albanians

Belgian speakers

Cricket players

5 Domestic Equipment:

A – Television

1200
200 250
150
50 50 50

C – Dishwashers

B – Home computers

Figure 10.2. Venn diagrams.

In expressing probabilities, there are some graphical conventions that are always used:

P(A)   is the probability of A,

A∪B   is the set of all the elements in A, in B or both,

A∩B   is the set of all the elements in both A and B and

A/B   is the set of elements in A which are not in B.

Let us consider some market research that was carried out on a sample of 2,000 homes. The following ownership of domestic equipment was observed:

Televisions	1800	Television and computer	400
Computers	500	Dishwasher and computer	200
Dishwashers	450	Television and dishwasher	350
		All three	150

If we wanted to calculate the probability of homes having only a television then we would have to say that it is:

$$P(A\backslash B\backslash C) = P(A) - P(A\cap B) - P(A\cap C) + P(A\cap B\cap C)$$

$$= \frac{1800 - 400 - 350 + 150}{2000}$$

$$= 0.6$$

Instead of doing this calculation, it will be found that a three circle diagram can be drawn from the data provided. This is shown in Figure 10.2, drawing No.5, from which we see that the probability of homes having just a television is 1200/2000 = 0.6. (The diagram shows why the final term in the above equation has a plus rather than a minus sign; that segment has been deducted twice in the previous two terms).

If it is true that mathematicians use probability and marketers abuse it, then philosophers worry about it. Mackie (1973) called it 'slippery and puzzling' because it hovered uncertainly between objectivity and subjectivity:

> Talk about something being probable or likely seems to reflect some mixture of knowledge and ignorance.

In the face of this, all that we should remember is the golden rule of probabilities in marketing:

Don't guess, calculate.

In other words, always try to base your conclusions on hard data, especially robust market research. This does not remove the need for subjective judgement, but it provides a better basis for that judgement.

While the above illustrations have concentrated on products and hard facts, the approaches are equally valuable in assessing the likelihood that a new policy or service will be successful in achieving its objectives.

Statistics

The Crowther Report (1959) was quite definite:

Statistical ignorance and statistical fallacies are quite as widespread and quite as dangerous as the logical fallacies which come under the heading of illiteracy ... The educated man, therefore, needs to be numerate as well as literate.

Since few of us manage to keep abreast of all of the developments in statistical thinking, this sort of comment causes most of us a feeling of unease. This is compounded by the fact that unless one is continuously using it, statistics must rank as one of the most easily forgotten areas of knowledge. There are plenty of sound books on statistics so in this section we will merely touch the surface.

❏ Central tendency

This is not, as might be thought, a clique within a political party but the name given to types of 'average'. Here, the word average is put into quotation marks since statisticians try to avoid using the word. Instead they talk of the mean, the median and the mode.

The mean

The arithmetic *mean* is what is called the average in normal conversation. Five people in an office are aged 20, 30, 45, 40 and 35. If we add all five figures together and divide the result by 5, we get the average, or *mean* as we should call it, of the five figures. The mean of the ages is $(20+30+45+40+35) \div 5$ or 34. If just one extra person, aged 65, joined the group then the mean would become $235 \div 6$ or 39.

The advantages of the arithmetic mean are:

- it is understood by most people
- the calculation is easy
- it can be calculated precisely
- it includes the whole group by using all the data
- to calculate it one only needs to know the number of items and the total value.

The mean does have some disadvantages. A few items that are exceptionally high or low can change the descriptive nature of the mean. In our example, the addition of a 100-year old would distort things giving a mean of 45, where most people in the group are younger. The mean may not be like one of the items and this can confuse some people.

The median

The *median* is the value of the middle item in a group of items that have been put into ascending (or descending) order. Our five office staff are, in age order, 20,30,35,40,45 so the median is the one in the middle which is 35. The advantages of the median are:

- any very high or low values do not distort it. It is therefore useful when describing groups (such as home distance from an office) where a few extreme values *would* distort our mean value
- since it is usually an actual value it appears realistic and even representative.

The disadvantages of the median are that it cannot be used for further calculations based on all the data, it may not be representative if the spread of values is erratic and if values are grouped into sub-groups then the median may become just an estimate.

We have seen how a median divides a distribution into two halves. In the same way we could divide values into four quarters if we used three *quartiles*. We could, of course divide the values into any division we liked such as 10 (deciles) or 100 (percentiles). Thus Mensa accepts as members people in the 98th and 99th percentiles of I.Q. (the top two percent).

The mode

A *mode* is that value that occurs most frequently in the group being considered.

In general conversation people sometimes say 'most' when they wish to imply the mode, for example, 'most families have two children' although the mean is about 2.3. A list of values in a group with their frequency of happening is called a *frequency distribution*. A frequency distribution of how long our staff take to travel to work might look like this:

Time taken in minutes	Number of staff taking that long
20	10
30	30
40	60
50	30
60	20
70	10

In this example, the mode is 40 minutes, even though this is less than half the group. Advantages of the mode are:

- it can often be a representative value, because it occurs most frequently
- in some situations, it can represent a 'fair' figure, such as in staff negotiations
- the mode is usually an actual value and so appears realistic.

Disadvantages include a lack of usefulness if the values are widely dispersed, it is difficult to use for further calculations, and it can involve a degree of judgement in some situations.

❏ Dispersion

After cutting the lawn, it would be possible to measure the length of each piece of grass cut. We could then draw a graph of the result. To do this, we could decide on certain *intervals* such as 5 millimetres, and then count how many pieces of grass were 25 – 30 millimetres, 40 – 45 millimetres and so on. The length of each blade of grass is known as the *value*. The number of pieces of grass within each interval is known as the *frequency*, the number of times a certain value was observed. The result might look like the graph in Figure 10.3. It will be seen that this is a nicely regular graph, with the same shape to the right of the middle as to the left. In this case, it will be realised that the position marked '✳' is the mean.

In this case it is also the median and the mode. This tells us that the lengths of grass pieces were *dispersed* regularly on either side of our measures of central tendency.

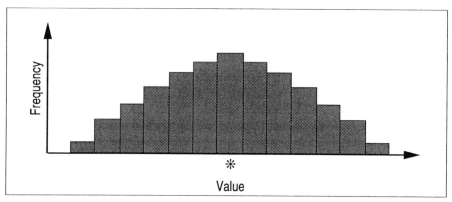

Figure 10.3 Frequency histogram.

The type of graph that we have drawn is known in general terms as a *frequency distribution* because it shows us the frequency of the distribution of lengths, how often we observed certain values. Specifically, this type of graph is known as a *histogram*, a series of vertical bars. If we counted every piece of grass and plotted the result individually then we would not be using any intervals, and should end up with a smooth curve instead of one with straight lines. We would, in fact, get a graph like the one in Figure 10.4.

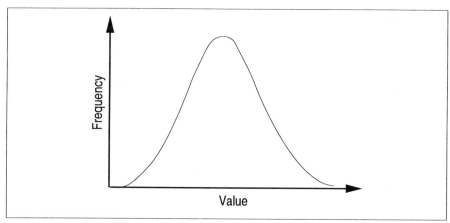

Figure 10.4 A normal distribution.

Again, this is a smooth and symmetrical graph. It is just the sort of graph that one gets when measuring pieces of cut grass as well as other items in life such as the heights of people. This symmetrical smooth graph is named after Herr Gauss and so is known as a *Gaussian distribution*. It is also called a 'normal' distribution.

Range

In looking at any distribution of values, the first measure that we can see is the *range*. We can calculate the range by taking the lowest value away from the highest. The range of lengths of cut grass would merely be the shortest to the longest. Range is an everyday way of describing the dispersion or scatter or spread of values that have been observed. We might say that the range of fees charged by consultants is from £300 to £5000 per day. If the range is very large then it may not tell us very much. In such cases we would probably like to know the average, or mean, as well to give us a better feel for the spread of values.

We would also get a better feel for the values if we could be more precise, which means being more arithmetic. One such measure is the *interquartile range*. We have already seen that we can divide a distribution into four equal parts by using three dividers called quartiles. It is usual to refer to the lower quartile position as 'Q1' and the upper quartile as 'Q3'. We get the interquartile range quite simply by subtracting the lower quartile value from the upper quartile value. This is usually expressed as Q3 – Q1. This measure can be useful since it means that we are not influenced by any extreme items such as the £5000 per day for consultancy, which few public sector organisations would expect to pay for general consultancy. Both the range and the interquartile range have their uses and tell us something about the dispersion of the values. However, in many cases they do not tell us enough. We may need something that is more precise.

Standard deviation

The way we measure the variability of the values is the *standard deviation*, two words that seem to strike fear into many marketers. The problem is largely one of feeling or intuition. We can instinctively feel that measures such as the range or the average say something to us. This instinct may fail us if we are told how useful it is if we get the square root of the mean of the squared deviations of a set of values about its mean. Unfortunately, this is useful in marketing. It has become one of the most influential concepts in modern statistics. It is the basis (practically, the justification) for opinion polls, taking samples, comparing market segments and much of the market research that is done.

In the last paragraph, the standard deviation was described in words. A more certain definition is to go through how it is calculated. For this, we only have to remember four things:

- a square root is a figure which when multiplied by itself gives us the figure we first thought of
- a mean is an average

- a deviation of one figure from another is the difference between them, and
- a distribution is how values (such as our pieces of grass) vary from one another.

Step 1: Calculate the average (mean) of all the items of whatever we are looking at.

Step 2: List the difference (deviation) of every item from this mean.

Step 3: Calculate the square of each of this list of deviations, giving a second list.

Step 4: Add up (sum) all these squares to give one figure.

Step 5: Divide this sum by the number of items.

Step 6: Find the square root of this amount. This is the standard deviation.

If we call: this standard deviation 's',

the number of items 'n' (if we are dealing with a frequency distribution, this would be called 'f'),

the squared deviations from the mean 'x', and

the sum of anything 'Σ',

then we can express the basic formula for calculating the standard deviation as:

$$s = \sqrt{\frac{\Sigma x^2}{n}}$$

As stated, this is the basic formula. There are complications in certain situations such as when one is dealing with items that are in groups, as in the histogram that we looked at above. The above explanation helps to show why the standard deviation does measure dispersion. The wider the variation of individual figures from the mean, the greater the standard deviation will be. Moving away from the complexity of the calculations, however, it is possible to interpret the results in useful and simpler ways.

If we have a Gaussian curve then the standard deviations have a useful property. Approximately 68% of the items lie within ± one standard deviation of the mean. Similarly, approximately 95% of the items lie within ± 2 standard deviations of the mean, and approximately 99% of the items are within ± 3 standard deviations of the mean. Actually, this figure of 'approximately 99%' is really 99.74% but not many marketers seem to know this. One of the many uses of this fact is in the introduction of management controls. Suppose that we have analysed the number of patients picked up and later returned home by community service transport each month. We find that the mean is 320 patients per month and that the standard deviation is 40. We would expect that 99% of the staff would serve 320 ± 3x40 patients per month, which is 200 to 440. If an individual attendant falls outside these limits then it is possible that too long or too short a time is being spent on each call. This may indicate a need for re-training. It is possible that you may think of other reasons for somebody being outside the limits, such as a difference in geographical density of customers being covered by individuals, or a difference in the percentage of people in wheelchairs.

This shows how careful one should be before installing controls. In this case (as in so many) the data must be homogeneous. A similar rigour must be applied in using the standard deviation for sampling, for comparison of groups, for budgeting, etc. This all involves a degree of detail beyond that considered here. To move beyond this basic consideration of statistics, it is necessary to consult some of the many specialist books on the subject, for example Greensted, Jardine and Macfarlane (1974), Hannagan (1982), and Bondi (1991).

Finally, for those who find the art of forecasting a fascinating business, especially when backed by research and statistical analysis, here are four such forecasts (Fleet Street Letter, 1994):

By 2010 the EU will have fallen apart under internal pressures from its quarrelling member states.

The value of the pound will continue to decline, until by 2010, it reaches parity with the Swiss franc.

Ordinary shares will more than double by the year 2000 (which would seem to imply an FT-SE 100 index of 6,000).

Gold will go above $1,000 an ounce by 2000.

Those who doubt the forecast concerning the future of the pound should be reminded that as recently as 1938, the pound stood at 21 Swiss francs.

References

Bondi, C. (Ed.) (1991) *New Applications of Mathematics* Harmondsworth, Penguin Books.

Crowther Report (1959) *15 to 18: A Report of the Central Advisory Council for Education* London, HMSO.

Fleet Street Letter (1994) *'1994 – 2010'* direct mail shot London, Fleet Street Publications, September.

Greensted, C., Jardine, A. and Macfarlane, J. (1974) *Essentials of Statistics in Marketing* London, Heinemann.

Hannagan, T. (1982) *Mastering Statistics* London, Macmillan Press.

Mackie, J. (1973) *Probability, Truth and Paradox* Oxford, Clarendon Press.

Peppers L. and Bails, D. (1987) *Managerial Economics* Englewood Cliffs, Prentice-Hall.

Smith, R. (1994) *Strategic Management and Planning in the Public Sector* Harlow, Longman.

Chapter 11

Using consultants and agencies

In the multitude of counsellors there is safety.

Bible, Proverbs 11:14.

Look busy, here come the suits.

M. Johnson, Business Buzzwords, 1990.

While most senior managers involved in the provision of services, the promotion of ideas and the development of policies need an overall appreciation of marketing, it is clear that this general understanding will have to be backed up by others with more detailed and specialist knowledge of particular approaches and techniques. In many cases this may require the use of consultants from time to time to back up the capability of a specialist marketing department.

In the field of marketing, there are two distinctly different types of consultancies. First, there are the general consultancies; by and large, these include the best-known names, large companies operating internationally. Second, there are the specialist firms many of whom tend to concentrate their expertise on one of the six Ps. The first decision, therefore, is to decide exactly why one is considering the use of consultants. Is it to look at a specific area of marketing such as direct mail, or is it to look at marketing strategy and to integrate marketing with overall organisational strategy. It should be borne in mind that any consultancy salesperson worth their salt will be tempted to try to convince you that their expertise covers absolutely everything. This claimed expertise is true for a very few firms but is the exception.

General marketing consultants

General marketing consultants can be engaged for such purposes as:

- studying overall corporate strategy, overall marketing strategy and the correct amalgam of the two so that an organisation has clear marketing objectives

- carrying out broad brush research. This may concern the general state of an industry and its future, the actual and potential activities of competitors, the parameters and nature of customers current and potential, looking at trends, studying other countries and the global situation, and carrying out economic analyses
- carrying out specific research. This research can be into any area of the market and will often involve a measure of subcontracting and hence co-ordination of the specialists involved. For example, a study for the Government into the future of Information Technology involved the services of seventeen organisations and consultants
- general investigations into the internal efficiency of the marketing function
- carrying out a *marketing audit.*

The public sector has a special responsibility for using consultancy advice effectively. There have been occasions when, according to a newspaper report (Independent, 1994) departments and agencies appoint:

> as project managers civil servants who are too inexperienced, too busy or who change their jobs too often. Only limited attempts are made to assess the benefits consultants bring or their value for money.

These comments were based on a study carried out by the Cabinet Office Efficiency Unit (1994). This study gives nine golden rules for the cost-effective use of consultants:

- see consultants as a potentially valuable if costly resource
- use them only on matters of real importance to the organisation
- use them only where management is committed to bringing about change
- be clear about why they are being used, and identify the work that needs to be done
- make sure that the problem cannot be solved in-house or in some other less expensive way
- select the right individuals at the right price
- manage the consultants effectively, and work closely with them
- implement the results of their work.

The point about working with the consultant is one that the public sector too often ignores. Some project managers regard buying consultancy as being akin to buying photocopier toner. Get a low price and then make sure that there is no cheating. In fact, the best return on fees is attained when the client and the consultant think of themselves as a team (a view expressed to the Efficiency Unit by the Civil Service College in their discussions). Admittedly, this approach can lead to the buyer having a sense of unease if there is any disagreement; one has to steel oneself to this fact while at the same time co-operating. This is not as difficult as people seem to imagine in prospect.

❏ The marketing audit

A marketing audit is a comprehensive review of the effectiveness of an organisation's marketing. It is as long as a piece of string, so the point made by the Efficiency Unit about being clear as to the work that needs to be done is very valid. Consultants adore the marketing audit, because:

- it is almost unthinkable that there is absolutely nothing that could be improved
- most such assignments lead naturally on to extensions (follow-on work).

On the other hand it can be very advantageous for an outsider, unblinkered by internal past thinking, to look closely at all aspects of one's marketing. The items that constitute a Marketing Audit can vary widely but are likely to include some or all of the following (McDonald and Leppard, 1993):

- strategy (corporate, marketing, SWOT, objectives, options, selection, assumptions, anticipated results, controls, progress tracking, forecasts and budgets)
- the Marketing Plan and the Marketing Mix
- Critical Success Factors
- market (definition, market share, trends, competition, innovation, technology)
- customers (segmentation, behaviour, trends, retention)
- products (product lines, portfolios, life cycle, gap analysis, after-sales service)
- advertising and sales promotion effectiveness
- price (strategy, levels, discounts, trends)
- channels of distribution, delivery efficiencies
- branding
- market data, market research, trend analysis

- sales force management and effectiveness
- costs and profitability, budgets and controls in practice.

A list of such length emphasises again how important it is for a consultancy purchaser to be clear as to the aims of a marketing audit assignment.

❑ Choice

Legally, anybody can call themselves a management consultant. All it takes is some headed notepaper saying 'Jean Bloggs, Management Consultant' and an address. Inevitably this means that there are some charlatans out there waiting for the unwary. This thought worries some purchasers, not unnaturally. The other worry can be summed up in the aphorism:

> Plumbers, dentists, lawyers, consultants, you know how good they are; after you have used them.

So the first problem is choosing your consultant, the first stage of which is selecting a short list. The best source for a short list is to use the various networks that abound in every part of the public sector. The second source is the index. An index of management consultants is maintained by the *Accountancy Advice Division* of HM Treasury. This is a listing of hundreds of consultancy firms and individuals. It is definitely *not* a recommended list in any sense although the blatantly sub-standard are removed.

Many public bodies have a member of their staff who has been nominated to act as a link with the Accountancy Advice Division, a fact that is not always known to all of their colleagues. Such staff are known as 'members of the consultancy community'. They all have an up-to-date copy of the index for consultation. Entries in the index state the claimed expertise of the consultants and some examples of their recent work for the public sector. Some public bodies maintain a register of past work that they have paid for and this is also normally held by the nominated member of staff. A few such registers contain a form of de-briefing for each assignment. Another source of potential consultants is to ask the Institute of Management Consultants and the Management Consultants Association (see below).

A mnemonic that assists the purchasing process is the acronym PURCHASE:

P – Price.	The level of charges, whether per diem or a lump sum, the presence of any escalators, the level and method of calculation of expenses, how fees are to be invoiced and paid.

U – Understanding.

How the consultants understand the problem, its implications, the environment and stakeholders, the client culture and management, the overall strategy, the politics involved, the industry and the techniques to be used.

R – Reputation.

Overall experience, knowledge, integrity, orientation, internal administration.

C – Contract.

Nature, restrictions, confidentiality, terms of business, the resolution of any conflicts, impact of the Official Secrets Act.

H – Human Relations.

With client's staff and Unions, future needs, consultants themselves.

A – Availability.

Of consultants and own staff, whether client will have to provide a team, assignment control, project control.

S – Service.

Pre-, post- and during assignment.

E – Excellence of service.

Breadth and depth, back-up facilities, databank availability, will the consultant go the extra mile?

Care must be taken to follow set procedures in those bodies that have a carefully prescribed methodology and format for buying consultancy. These normally follow the pattern of:

- specification preparation
- specification despatch
- bid receipt
- compliance check
- bid comparison.

Some public bodies have been observed that use universal specification documentation when buying, say, print, as well as consultancy. Care must also be taken over those cases that will be affected by EC or GATT regulations. Technical aspects are covered by various publications from HM Treasury Central Unit on Purchasing (C.U.P.), two of which are particularly appropriate (1989, 1990).

There are some other publications to help one find one's way around the consultancy world. One that is strongly recommended is a booklet that was written by HM Treasury (1990a) and which in a few pages explains how to get help from consultants. There is also a history of consultancy in the U.K. which contains some interesting tit-bits of near-gossip (Tisdall, 1982), a book written for practising consultants which explains much of the way they do things (Markham, 1987), and a book on purchasing different types of consultancy as well as marketing (Bennett, 1990).

The consultants' proposals will usually follow the pattern of:

- a description of the current situation
- an appreciation of the problem
- the scope and objectives of the assignment
- the proposed methodology of their approach
- the programme of work
- a summary of benefits to be gained
- the resources required, including the fees and costs
- appendices covering a capability statement (how they have done similar work in the past), C.V.s of those consultants who would be doing the assignment, an outline plan usually in the shape of a Gantt chart, and, where applicable, the terms of business.

To choose one from a group of competing offers, it is desirable (and sometimes obligatory) to use a weighting-and-ranking system. In this, a selection board will consider each proposal and rate them by allocating points to each under a set of heads. These criteria will include such factors as:

- understanding of our problem
- approach/proposal/presentation
- availability
- general reputation
- price and other costs
- assessment of individual consultant(s)
- firm's knowledge and database
- knowledge of our industry.

These factors are listed on a form that is used by each member of the board. Points (out of an agreed maximum) are allocated by each member to each factor for each firm. These are weighted according to a pre-agreed scheme, and to-talled for each firm in the usual manner. A contract is then drawn up for the winning firm, a project manager appointed, and a project control system initiated for running the assignment.

Specialist consultants

The specialist consultancies are treated in the same general manner although briefing will be more specific and constraining. A good brief is essential. This means that a purchaser must think through the implications beforehand (changing one's mind is expensive) and must make sure that the briefs are consistent, co-ordinated and clear.

Sales promotion consultants usually implement their suggestions and have in-house facilities or preferred subcontractors. This means that it is possible to inspect previous work that they have done. A brief to a sales promotion consultant should include a statement of objectives, details of assumed targets, aims of a specific campaign, any no-go areas of taste or culture, and an agreed maximum spend. In return, the consultant should be expected to suggest a set of approaches, the channels of distribution, a promotion mix, an indication of measurable results and a timetable. Names of consultants can be obtained from the *Institute of Sales Promotion*, who have a Code of Practice. Within the public sector, sales promotion campaigns have not been very common in the past. They are more likely where organisations are in a trading situation, something which is becoming more frequent nowadays with arms' length relationships and internal trading.

The same factors are leading to an increase in the use of direct mailing within the public sector. Direct mail consultants can advise on mail shots, telemarketing and flyers. Results of direct mail are quickly and accurately measurable. This leads to a quite fast turnover of such firms; profits are high if the firm gets it right, losses are high if not. Many firms draw a distinction between consultancy and supply with the supply firms trying to achieve a slick operation side and competitive cost. Suppliers consist of *fulfilment houses* who handle responses to advertisements and direct mail, *telemarketers* who will phone offices and people at home to sell or interview, *mailing agencies* who send out promotional and similar material and *computer bureaux* who maintain databases of names and addresses. *Mailing lists* can be the life blood of a campaign. Many organisations, such as just about every charity, will keep their own lists which can be quite valuable. Others will buy or rent standard lists which are categorised by market segment. These standard databases are often built up from people's responses to surveys and special offers and can run into millions of names. Lists are available as esoteric as potential buyers of a particular make of car, or millionaires.

Public relations consultants can help to create awareness of a campaign, place releases in the media, lobby on your behalf, prepare sales and in-house literature, help establish brand image, train staff, write speeches, assist with stakeholder relations, help deal with adverse publicity, and generally obtain favourable publicity. Some of these are long term in nature so there may be a suggestion that a retainer be paid; this is fine unless one finds that one has ended up by paying for not much more than a cuttings' service. Those in the public sector have to make it clear to the consultants what is acceptable and what is not, otherwise some stunts may rebound. It must also be remembered that consultants should not be used in a representational role by a Government department or agency. That task should be undertaken by civil servants who are directly answerable to a Minister. The lead in this would normally be taken by a department's information office, which is experienced in dealing with the media.

Market research consultants undertake a wide range of research connected with market segmentation, new product introductions, the likely effect of price changes, consumer motivation, an organisation's image, and so on. They will undertake interviewing and often know about published research data that will be of use. In spite of initiatives such as social trends research, some people in the public sector still hold a poor opinion of market research firms. This is unfortunate since there are many other people with a much more positive story to tell. With a good brief they can be very useful indeed. The professional body is the Market Research Society and they publish an annual listing of members with outline details. Also in this annual are the names of some of the *public opinion poll* firms. Many of these firms also provide research facilities that are very useful and far removed from those polls so popular with the tabloids at general election time.

Advertising agencies

To many people advertising agencies are the glamorous face of marketing. It seems as though they are the places where creativity is high, salaries are high and recognition is high. Certainly, advertising agencies can be exciting and enjoyable places to work; on the other hand they are also the places where one has to deliver, or else. Moreover, no bushels are available under which to hide one's light.

A brief outline of how advertising agencies achieve their income has already been given. A comprehension of the way the agencies operate is important so that one can understand their point of view, and improve one's negotiating abilities. As already stated, agencies were originally agents who sold space in the media to advertisers and were rewarded with the payment of commissions by the media owners. Nowadays, agencies continue to earn income from the media or else to get fees from the advertiser, or a mixture of the two. Suppose an advertiser spends £1 million on television time. Buying this time from the television company costs the straight £1 million and buying it through an agency still costs £1 million. The agency lives off the 15% (say) rebate paid to the agency in return for their success in selling the TV time:

Cost of advertising time	1,000,000
Less 15%	150,000
Charge paid by the agency	£850,000

It is out of this £150,000 that all the costs have to come as well as the agency's profit. These costs include the cost of producing the actual advertisement such as a film. This means that cost control is vital to an agency. It also explains why so many agencies regard size as important. A large agency can afford ever more attractive services to clients, can spread costs over more campaigns, and can attain better scheduling of its staff. Since the different operations within an agency need differing types of staff, they are usually organised into four divisions:

- *creative* who actually produce the advertisements
- *research* who do what their title suggests
- *media* who select and place the advertisements
- *admin* (or 'management' or 'business') who hold everything together.

The level of charges can also be affected, at the margins, by whether the industry is in a boom or slump condition. During a boom there is a tendency for extra fees to appear while in a slump they vanish.

When an advertiser talks with an agency, it will give the agency a *brief*, the parameters of the campaign. The brief should contain details of the advertiser's thinking, clearly stated objectives, the target segment(s), the product specification, the preferred style and image, price (if applicable), and details of all research carried out previously. It should also contain the criteria for evaluating the advertisements' effectiveness in reaching the objectives, which should themselves have an element of measurement. The question of effectiveness measurement will often be resisted by the agency. Alternatively they may wish to substitute a softer measurement such as *penetration* (percentage of target segment exposed to advertisement) or *awareness* (percentage of people who can recall having seen the advertisement). It is a standard defence by agencies that public sector advertisements are inherently less easy to measure for effectiveness than those for the private sector.

Selecting an agency to handle one's message is done in the same way as any other public sector option appraisal. One selects factors and uses a weighting and ranking system. The factors used are likely to include:

- does the agency understand our problem
- have they done good work in a similar area previously
- do they have a good reputation with others in the public sector
- is the range of services compatible with our needs
- do they understand the public sector, especially our part of it
- do we seem to get along well (ignoring professional charm)
- was their presentation impressive and show that they have thought about us?

For the rest, the comments on choice of consultants (above) apply.

Fees and charges

Fees for professional advice are too high in the eyes of many clients, though the providers see things differently. If one understands the cost structure and constraints that underpin consultants, then one can negotiate more meaningfully as well as getting value for money. Providers (for which we will use the generic term 'consultants') have in their minds two all-important break-even points. These are:

- fee rate
- utilisation rate (known colloquially as being 'on the clock').

If the consultancy can keep above both of these break-even points then profitability beckons. Stay below both and bankruptcy beckons. It is the basic marketing problem writ large and simple, price and volume. The basic calculation (and this is inescapable) is the number of days that a professional can earn fees in a year:

Aspect	Days p.a.
Total days = 52 weeks x 5 days per week	260
Statutory holidays	8
Annual holidays (maximum 5 weeks)	25
Sick leave (covered by insurance for long-term illness)	5
Training (in-house and external, plus staying up-to-date)	10
Total time not available to earn fees	48
Net days available	212

This represents a days-on-fees of just over 80% (212/260 x 100); in practice such a figure is just not possible. There is selling time, preparatory non-fee time, scheduling slack, periods for which no work is sold, and admin time. Most firms work on a figure of 65% (169 days) or 70% (182 days) and even this latter figure is not easy, needing constant pressure to achieve. If the professional earns £50,000 p.a. as salary and bonus, then the cost of that person is likely to be £170,000-200,000 because of the cost of selling, other employees, buildings, production facilities, pension, National Insurance, interest on capital employed, and so on.

The first break-even is fee rate. If we assume a 65% utilisation rate, then income per professional at various fee rates would be:

Fee rate £ per diem	Revenue £ p.a.
1100	186,000
1200	203,000
1300	220,000

The second break-even is utilisation rate. If we assume a fee rate of £1,000 per day, then the income per professional at various utilisations would be:

Utilisation %	Revenue £ p.a.
70	182,000
75	195,000

This shows why professionals have to keep costs down (without sacrificing extra services), keep utilisation high, and try to keep the fee rate as high as possible.

Qualifications and memberships

As already stated, anybody can call themselves a consultant. Unlike the Chartered Accountants, passing examinations is not mandatory. There are, however, a number of organisations around, some of which have been mentioned. Some of these are professional bodies, some are rather akin to trade associations and some are groupings of like-minded people.

In talking to people in the public sector, it is clear that there is considerable confusion about the two main consultancy organisations. The *Institute of Management Consultants* is for consultants as individuals. It is a professional institute with a code of standards and retains the right to eject from membership anybody who fails the ethical standards. Perhaps the worst sin would be to accept money in return for recommending particular equipment to a client. There are two grades of corporate membership, member and fellow. The main difference is the length of experience. So if one employs a person with 'FIMC' after their name, this is a person who has some years experience as a consultant and who has satisfied various criteria. The IMC publish an annual Yearbook which includes the names of its members as well as the IMC Code of Conduct.

The *Management Consultants Association* is for corporate bodies and so is a sort of trade association. Membership of the MCA tends to be concentrated in the larger consultancy practices. Both bodies try to keep out the charlatans. Conversely, there are certainly many excellent consultants who are in neither body.

There are few British marketing consultants who have academic marketing qualifications. This is because few British public sector higher education institutions find it possible to conceive of marketing as being an academic subject. Aspects of marketing are included in MBA degrees, general business degrees and various schemes for certificates and diplomas. The *Chartered Institute of Marketing* (C.I.M.) and the *Communication, Advertising and Marketing Foundation* (C.A.M.) have examination courses leading to the award of a diploma. Anybody who passes the CIM examinations, for example, will have a good grasp of marketing which is likely to be superior in many respects to somebody who has an MBA with marketing as one of the subjects.

References

Bennett, R. (1990) *Choosing and Using Management Consultants* London, Kogan Page.

Efficiency Unit (1994) *The Government's Use of External Consultants* London, HMSO.

Independent (1994) *Government Wastes £40m on Consultants* 5 August.

Markham, C. (1987) *Practical Consulting* London, Institute of Chartered Accountants in England and Wales.

McDonald, M. and Leppard, J. (1993) *The Marketing Audit* Oxford, Butterworth-Heinemann.

Tisdall, P. (1982) *Agents of Change: The Development and Practice of Management Consultancy* London, Heinemann.

HM Treasury (1989) Central Unit on Purchasing Guidance Notes, *No. 13 The Selection and Appointment of Works Consultants* London, HMSO.

HM Treasury (1990) Central Unit on Purchasing Guidance Notes *No. 23 Model Forms of Contract*, London, HMSO.

HM Treasury (1990a) *Seeking Help from Management Consultants* London, HMSO.

Chapter 12

Lessons from success and failure

Go to now, ye that say, To day or to morrow we
will go into such a city, and continue there a
year, and buy and sell, and get gain.

Bible, James 4:13.

Make your decisions with your heart, and what
you'll end up with is heart disease.

H.B.Mackay, Swim with the Sharks, 1988.

The two chapters concerned with 'Illustration' give examples of marketing in action. Chapter 13 concentrates on three major case studies from the public sector. This shorter chapter goes through the alphabet (nearly) with a miscellany of examples from a wide range of organisations and a longer time span. Each example of success or failure highlights a lesson that has been discussed earlier.

❏ A & P prices

The Great Atlantic and Pacific Tea Company was founded in the mid-nineteenth century. By 1971, when William Kane was appointed chief executive, it was better known as A & P. It had also become known for receding profitability. In 1972, Kane decided to convert the supermarket chain into superdiscount stores. He was quoted (Business Week, 1972) as saying:

This is a business based strictly on volume, with sales measured in tonnage.

The stores were called WEO, standing for either 'Where Economy Originates' or else 'Warehouse Economy Outlet'. Prices were reduced on 90% of lines, from an industry mark-up norm of 20 – 22% down to a mark-up of 9 – 13%. As usual, this meant that a truly massive increase in turnover would be needed to maintain profits. Also as usual, the competition fought back. Some (like Pantry Pride and Kroger) tried to match the prices. Others went different routes. Pathmark and others went to 24-hour opening, some started to stock non-grocery lines, some added service items like buses for the elderly, some (like Jewel) actually put a few prices up. The bad news for A & P was that inflation started up again, making price comparisons fairly meaningless. The even worse news was that, although sales volume increased by $800 million, A & P went into the red by over $50 million.

Lesson:

It is not volume or turnover that matters, it is the balance of revenues (or benefits) and costs.

❑ Beecham's Pills

Thomas Beecham started making and selling four products at his initial base in Wigan. Three of these were Royal Toothpowder, Gold Tooth Tincture and a 'tonic for women' called Female's Friend. But it was the fourth product, a laxative sold as Beecham's Pills, that made him rich. By 1859 he had moved to St. Helens which became the headquarters of the Beecham organisation. The famous slogan, 'Worth a Guinea a Box' originated in an advertisement in a local newspaper in August 1859. Since a box cost only $2\frac{1}{2}$ p they must have seemed a bargain; anyway, the pills were a runaway success. Beecham believed in the power of advertising, more advertising, and still more advertising. Thirty years after the launch, by 1890, Beecham's had the biggest advertising spend of any British organisation. They advertised in an unbelievable 15,000 newspapers world-wide. Acceptance was so good that there was even a dance called *The Guinea a Box Polka*. By 1890 it was Beecham's proud boast that the St. Helens' factory was making 15,000 pills a minute. What makes the Beecham story fascinating is that the pills still sell, at the rate of 50 million a year.

Lesson:

If you have something that the public accept and trust, then the product life cycle can be extended for longer than the theoreticians would believe possible. Indeed, in the public sector, it is sometimes the public themselves who seek to prolong the availability of a service that they accept and trust.

❑ Coca-Cola

On 23 April 1985, Coca-Cola announced that after 99 years it was going to change the taste of its drink to New Coke. On 11 July 1985, it announced that it was bringing back the old coke as Coca-Cola Classic. After £3 million and two years of research, a mistake had been made. Pepsi had been taking market share from Coke and this was reinforced by a 'Pepsi Challenge' in which comparative taste tests showed that people preferred the taste of Pepsi to Coke. The same results were obtained by Coca-Cola when they tried them. So research was undertaken to find a new, better taste. This was tried out on 191,000 people who backed the new taste. So New Coke was introduced, and soon brought an avalanche of protests. 40,000 protest letters were received as well as 5,000 phone calls a day. The media had a field day. New taste tests went the wrong way. Eventually, Coca-Cola gave in and brought back the old Coke.

Lesson:

However careful you are, you cannot be sure. Monitor carefully, have a back-up plan, and be prepared to admit it quickly when you have got it wrong, especially on matters of policy.

❏ De Lorean

John Z. De Lorean was brilliant at publicity and promotion. He was also an enthusiastic supporter of what he called 'The Dream', an expensive gull-wing car. He was not alone in his enthusiasm. The Northern Ireland Government, the trade unions, the management and the backers all desperately wanted the project to succeed. The flamboyance and drive and glitz all militated against anybody daring to say that the Emperor was short of a suit or so. One of the advertisements ran:

> Your eyes skim the sleek, sensuous steel body, and all your senses tell you 'I've got to have it' . . . Of course, everyone stares as you drive by . . . After all, you're the one Living the Dream.

There were stories soon after the launch that the cars were selling so fantastically well that they were attracting a premium. The De Lorean car achieved amazing levels of recognition. It did not reach the same levels of distribution, engineering, quality, cost structure and control, and so on. In the event, over half the cars ever made in Belfast stayed in stock.

Lesson:

As has been said many times, the service or product must match the promise. This is particularly true in the public sector.

❏ Electric razor

As he repeatedly said in a long-running series of television commercials, Victor Kiam liked his Remington razor so much that he bought the company.

He bought it from the Sperry multinational that had lost $30 million in Remington in the previous four years. Kiam soon doubled the total sales and was making $12 million a year profit. This is often used as an example of the benefits of being a dedicated independent compared with being part of a large conglomerate. The marketing (which was part of this) changed completely. Kiam went round the retailers to find out why stocks were not being held. Then he introduced a new, simple model at a charm price that was around half the competition's. He maintained a heavy advertising spend even at the expense of short-term profits. He got the public to accept the razor as a suitable product for a gift. Any of this could have been done by Sperry. But there is a world of difference between a multinational regarding a subsidiary as a loss-making investment and a marketing man who has put $1 million of his own money into a product.

Lesson:

Big Goliath may have clout but may not be able to match an independent David with determination and marketing skills.

❏ Fund-raising

The Yorkshire Building Society was looking for a new product, something that was both new and that would appeal to young savers. Four teams of advertising agency account executives presented their ideas. The team whose ideas were accepted was led by somebody who had worked at Saatchi and Saatchi as account director. This team was from the NSPCC (National Society for the Prevention of Cruelty to Children). Their idea was for a new account under the NSPCC 'Happy Kids' brand name. For this the NSPCC would receive £1 for every new account opened plus 10% of the gross interest paid. This bid by the NSPCC is far from being unique. Charities now employ agency-trained staff who know that if they are to succeed in getting a share of marketing budgets, then they must offer a service which helps their 'client'. This means that the competition between charities for private sector/charity relationships can be intense. As the head of NSPCC corporate fund-raising put it (Marketing, 1994):

> When it comes to the actual pitch it is probably as competitive between charities as it is between advertising agencies.

Lesson:

Even for those not in the private sector, professionalism in marketing is necessary.

❏ Ginger wine

Stone's Original Green Ginger Wine was first produced in London in 1740. So it may not be entirely unexpected that 240 years later it was losing a little of its early popularity. The owners refused to accept that the life product cycle might be taking its toll, even though posters and press advertising had failed to stem the fall in sales. A small agency did its homework and decided that certain aims were in order. These were to appeal more to the 24 – 44 age group across the socio-economic groupings, to sell outside the Christmas/New Year season, to use the product as a mixer (Whisky Mac). It was decided that television would have to be used, and an inexpensive animated film was made using the slogan 'It's what winter was invented for'. Sales went up instead of down, while maintaining the premium price level.

Lesson:

Do your homework, know your market thoroughly, play to your strengths.

❏ Harley Davidson

During the 1940s and 1950s, the public perception of motor cyclists was of dirty drunks as seen in *The Wild One* with Marlon Brando. The manufacturer's perception of motor cyclists was of fanatics who liked getting oil on their clothes and who tended their machines with tender loving care. In 1960 there were less than 400,000 motorcycles registered in America, mainly from Harley Davidson, Norton and Triumph (U.K.), and BMW (Germany). Four years later the figure was nearly a million and a decade later it was 4 million. The difference was Honda who sold lightweight machines to the young as fun objects to be enjoyed not fussed over. Harley Davidson's reaction was minimal. Bikers would not buy light machines, especially in bright colours and, anyway, Honda were an unknown foreign make. The old bike makers were guilty of the 3 C's, complacency, conservatism and conceit, which in marketing is a heinous sin. By 1977, Honda had 45% of the U.S. market while Harley Davidson had 6%.

Lesson:

Never underestimate a competitor. Success awaits those who spot that the traditional service is not meeting a widespread need.

❏ Iacocca and the Mustang

The Ford Edsel is often quoted as being a marketing fiasco, one that scarred both Ford and the car industry. People still shudder at the mention of the name. So it is interesting how only four years afterwards the Ford Mustang was launched. This is in large measure due to the drive of one awkward product visionary, Lee Iacocca. In its first four months of sales, the Mustang sold more than the Edsel did in its more than two years life span. The Edsel followed prodigious research efforts and was new from the ground up. More circumspect research showed that the Mustang should be a sports car in appearance, low priced for the young, a back seat for a family car appeal, in other words, all things to all people. A daunting prospect. Iacocca took parts from existing cars; these were the Falcon (a compact) and the Fairlane (a mid-size), and added a sporty shell. The basic Mustang had a low price but came with the offer of a wide range of options. The advertising campaign was massive and omni-present. It had been hoped to sell 75,000 Mustangs in the first year; it took 92 days to sell the first 100,000. In its first two years it generated profits of $1 billion. Many factors helped. Market Research was kept current, the styling had wide appeal, quality was kept high, promotion was effective, production costs were kept low.

Lesson:

Costly research, detailed planning and long lead-times do not guarantee success. Good marketing and a quality service or product that people desire are the priority.

❏ Johnston's Fluid Beef

Johnston's Fluid Beef was a drink invented by John Johnston of Edinburgh. He changed the name in 1884 to 'Bovril'. The quotation marks were kept for the next half a century to show that the word was synthesised and to emphasise its importance. Johnston made the word from Bo (from the Latin *bos*, an ox) and Vril (the 'life force' in a novel written a decade earlier). The USP (*unique selling proposition*) was that the product was a product made from strong bulls and was therefore obviously good for you, especially if you were too poor to afford expensive cuts of meat. An early advertisement showed one bull saying to another apprehensively:

I hear they want more BOVRIL.

Many Victorian advertisers liked to link their products with the Pope; one Bovril poster showed the Pope holding a mug of the liquid with the line:

The Two Infallible Powers – The Pope and BOVRIL.

The most famous poster showed a man in the middle of the ocean, floating on a giant jar of Bovril with the line:

Prevents that sinking feeling.

This slogan was first used in 1920 and continued until 1958. Bovril had a USP that they used for almost a century until public beliefs changed whereupon the product projection changed as well.

Lesson:

If as an agency you have a strong USP, stay with it as long as it works, but be ready to change it when it stops working.

❏ Kiwi fruit

Actinida chinensis was better known as the Chinese gooseberry but not much better known, since it stayed stubbornly low in sales to the public. Somebody in New Zealand had the brilliant idea of re-naming it Kiwi fruit, whereupon the sales obligingly took off (62,000 tons in 1984). It sold particularly well in Germany and Japan. So well, that growers in other countries decided to get in on the act in spite of the fact that the plant takes six to eight years to reach maturity, and that the early 1980s heralded the spread of a kiwi disease. Demand went up, supply went up (much of it local by now) to reach a world-wide usage of 370,000 tons by 1992.

Lessons:

Two lessons. First, if the public does not like your offering, it could well be worth looking at the packaging (verbal and visual). Second, success will usually bring in competition.

❏ Lead lining

At the start of the 19th century, most grocers kept commodities such as sugar in large bags from which they weighed out the needs of individual customers. Tea was sold similarly but had the reputation of being grossly adulterated. (One report suggested that only 6 million pounds out of ten million was actually tea, with the rest being dust, hawthorn, etc). A Quaker, John Horniman felt that there was a market for pure quality tea. He sold tea in sealed packets under his brand of Horniman's Pure Tea. His USP was that the containers holding his tea were 'lined with lead'. This revolutionary concept was backed up with massive advertising. In 1902, coronation year, an advertisement showed King Edward VII in full regalia with a cup of tea in his hand with the slogan:

A Right Royal Drink.

This habit of using royalty, the Pope, and others in pseudo-endorsement poses was not made illegal until 1930. The Horniman USP worked. By the 1890s his company was the biggest tea trader in the country.

Lesson:

If the public are convinced that your's is a quality service or product, then they will willingly pay a premium price, either directly or through their taxes.

❏ Mercedes cars

One company that has consistently maintained the necessary relationship between promise, product, image and sales is Mercedes-Benz. It has stayed constantly in the segment of up-market cars that are solid, reliable, comfortable, well-engineered and with a definite design style. New models are at rare intervals which reinforces the image of consistency. British firms have sometimes lost high volume by moving up-market for higher added-value, while Mercedes have succeeded in achieving volume as well as quality. During 1982 – 83, Mercedes sold 450,000 cars; this was almost two thirds of all British cars sold in Britain. Mercedes have a clear image – a high-quality one-brand product line. Having all one's eggs in one basket is not universally popular but Mercedes have made it work better than many of its competitors and for longer. Only time will tell if the 1996 introduction of the A-Class small cars will damage their image.

Lesson:

A one-brand product line can be made to work, especially in up-market areas, but it takes consistency, quality, and effort.

❏ Now!

There is something about magazine publishing that can cause great enthusiasm in spite of the long history of loss makers. Sir James Goldsmith launched *Now!* magazine in what one unkind commentator (Heller, 1987) called:

> a foolhardy attempt to mimic the success of *Time*.

The advertising rates for the new magazine were set high by the standards of the competition (e.g. the colour supplements of the quality Sunday newspapers). This meant that the socio-economic profile of readers had to be kept high although it was felt that the break-even circulation might be as low as 250,000. A television campaign might deliver too diluted an audience at too high a cost. A press campaign or direct mail could be better targeted but might well not deliver the response needed. A test of the direct mail approach suggested a 1.6% response rate but the actual mailing that followed is said to have achieved only half that. The pre-tax loss on the magazine has been estimated as being over £10 million.

Lesson:

One may have what seems like a wonderful idea for a new service or product, but if the facts are against one, it will be to no avail.

❏ Osborne computers

Osborne Computer Corporation was founded in 1981. It rose meteorically so that within a year and a half it was turning over £60 million. In September 1983 the firm moved into a form of bankruptcy. Adam Osborne spotted a niche market, the first portable *business* computer. He priced it at £1795 (way below the competition) and this included a claimed £1500 worth of software. Osborne had a flair for marketing that had a splash of showmanship. The writer and a friend nearly put their future at risk for British rights but fortunately could not agree terms. There is no doubt that the machine sold, and sold well, but a number of things went wrong. Osborne was an entrepreneur and as we see time after time such people do not always make good administrators. Costs went too high, competitors came in almost overnight, stock control was well-nigh nil as was spending control. So the euphoric profit forecasts failed just as a public placing of shares was coming up. This effectively stopped cash injections from other sources.

Lesson:

A good product and good marketing still need good management behind them to last the course. And never let expenses get out of hand.

❏ Pears' soap

In the thirty years between 1861 and 1891, the sales of soap in Britain doubled. This brought into the market a large number of competitors, all fighting for market share. The old family firm of Pears was changed out of all recognition when the super-salesman Tom Barratt married into it. Barratt has been called the father of modern advertising; his startling innovations certainly made him a king of stunts. One of these was to import a quarter of a million ten centime pieces from France (these were widely accepted at the time as being equivalent to one British penny). All these he stamped with the word Pears and put them into general circulation. It took an Act of Parliament to stop this stunt, the publicity from which helped him even further. He used a massive poster campaign with the words:

> Good morning! Have you used Pears Soap?

This caught the public's fancy to such a degree that for a time it was impossible to greet someone with 'Good morning!' without running the risk of the slogan's riposte. But the action that caused most furore is one that seems fairly innocuous from our current vantage point. In 1887 he purchased the famous painting 'Bubbles' by Sir John Millais (a baronet and a Royal Academician). 'Bubbles' was a picture of a small child sitting on a log blowing bubbles. Barratt dared to use this painting as a poster, just by adding the words 'Pears' soap'. This association is still used in amended formats by Pears' soap today.

Lesson:

No matter what the situation is, it is always possible to be innovative in one's marketing.

❏ Quencha thirst

Advertising has always had its share of copywriters who became famous novelists. It has also had its share of apocryphal stories as to the true identity of the originators of famous slogans and copy. In 1806 Charles Lamb may have promoted a lottery ticket with the less-than-pithy, 'the smallest share may gain near two thousand pounds'. Fay Weldon may have coined 'Go to Work on an Egg' for the Egg Marketing Board; Salman Rushdie may have coined 'delectabubble' for Aero chocolate and 'Naughty but Nice' for cream cakes though there have been objections to this attribution (Times, 1994). One of the most odd of such phrases was 'Drinka Pinta Milka Day', followed by 'Drinka Pinta Quencha Thirst'. This was used by the Milk Publicity Council. It has been claimed (Coren, 1994) that the advertising agency originally came up in 1958 with 'Drink at least one pint of milk each day' but that a member of the client's staff (Bernard Whitehead) changed it. The purists hated it but during the early 1960s the impact was considerable. Milk consumption throughout Europe was declining but in Britain there was a sales increase of 1.5% per annum.

Lesson:

A good easily-repeatable slogan can catch the public's imagination.

❏ Rowntree's Elect Cocoa

Two artists, James Pryde and William Nicholson, got together and formed an advertising partnership to produce posters. They called the partnership 'Beggarstaffs'. The posters they produced were minimalist and, at the time, revolutionary, semi-silhouettes, usually monochrome and without the exaggerated hype that was the norm. In 1896 they produced a poster for Rowntree's Elect Cocoa which showed three black and white figures without any obvious connection with the product. The poster has since become internationally praised. But the client did not like it and it failed to sell the product. Rowntree withdrew it whereupon other clients followed suit. The partnership ended.

Lesson:

You can produce brilliant stuff but to no avail if the public do not like it or it does not work (even if history vindicates you, it is no help at the time).

❏ Skegness

Skegness, on the Lincolnshire coast, had a problem in promoting itself as a holiday resort. This was a stiff east wind that holiday makers swore never stopped blowing. At the same time, the Great Northern Railway wished to promote excursions and holiday travel to as many resorts as possible, including Skegness. In February 1908, the GNR bought a painting by John Hassall. This was of an overweight, smiling, pipe-smoking fisherman bounding joyfully along a beach. The painting was used to promote day excursions from King's Cross to Skegness for three shillings (15p). The original 1908 poster had no slogan but somebody (possibly from the Skegness Advancement Association) thought up the slogan:

Skegness is SO bracing.

Bracing is a far better word than windy, from a promotional viewpoint, and the slogan plus visual caught on with the public. Cartoonists liked it as well and continued to use it over the years, such as one in 1994 (Times, 1994a) of the Chancellor of the Exchequer.

Lesson:

Sometimes a negative feature can be not merely neutralised but actually turned into a positive selling point.

❏ Tinned cat food

The name of Forrest Mars is printed two million times a day on chocolate Mars bars. A thrusting if somewhat autocratic entrepreneur, he built up a fortune from sweets and pet food. One of these pet foods, Kit-E-Kat, achieved a position of outstanding dominance. It outsold every other canned pet food in the country. It even sold more cans than baked beans. At this time, the advertising spend was £2 million a year and Kit-E-Kat seemed unassailable. So it seemed to Mr. Mars who decided to stop all the advertising, a decision that could not be overcome by anybody, including the advertiser Jack Wynne-Williams. Not surprisingly the sales plummeted until within less than a year Kit-E-Kat was down among the also-rans instead of being at the top. Mars admitted his mistake. He even returned the advertising to rescue the product to Wynne-Williams, whose admonition to Mr. Mars provides the lesson:

Lesson:

'Sometimes you've got to spend money to defend money'.

❏ Underground

The London Underground started in 1863 and for some decades produced rather insipid advertising. This consisted in the main of 'gravestone' style newspaper announcements of new lines opening and the train timetables. Then in 1907 Frank Pick was made General Manager. He realised that since it was possible to charge money for selling poster space, it was also possible for the Underground to use posters on its own account. The first poster, in 1908, had the slogan 'Underground to Anywhere'. From this it was a short step to having posters featuring some of the attractions in London that could be reached by Underground, such as museums. This was followed by featuring the countryside which, in a less built-up era, could be reached for a day out away from a foggy capital. By the 1930s, the posters had become art unashamedly. Painters such as Graham Sutherland and Paul Nash did work on the Underground posters which were changed monthly to retain the public's interest. This all helped to build up a powerful and positive image for the Underground as being effective, a source of wonder, almost a treat.

Lesson:

There is more than one way to create a positive image for a public service, and an enthusiastic innovator is worth having.

❏ Velocipede

Raleigh bicycles were at one time as apparently unassailable as Kit-E-Kat. Their position was continually eroded during the 1960s and 1970s until it seemed that their only safe haven was their exports to Nigeria. A strike in 1979 led to a flood of imports into Britain and a loss of over £10 million. The parent company, Tube Investments, put in new management who cut costs, rationalised, shut five factories, and reduced the range by 80%. This did not work so a new new management were installed. They let the Huffy Corporation have the American market. They also undertook a major automation project which became a famous fiasco when production stopped completely. The lack of any marketing strategy seemed obvious to commentators but not to Raleigh. The head of the firm (Heller, 1987) said:

> We are now trying to pursue a well-thought-out strategy, one that will stand the test of time. Previous ones didn't.

Lesson:

Success will not beckon unless there is a good marketing strategy backed up by a good overall corporate strategy.

❏ Whisky

The Distillers Company Limited (DCL) was an independent organisation whose constituent parts were also independent, of each other as well as of the parent. DCL brands had at one time been unbeatable – Johnnie Walker, Black & White, VAT 69, Haig, Dewar's – but the marketing had hardly been updated in fifty years. The advertising had stayed static, the product line the same, the distribution poor (which latter was to cost them dear in America). One by one, the market leadership fell. First, it was America which fell to J&B and Cutty Sark, both owned by St. James's Street wine merchants and both light Scotches. In England the lead was lost to Teacher's, a heavy Scotch. In Scotland the market leadership went to the once far smaller Bell's. At no stage were competing light or heavy Scotches brought to the market. Eventually, in 1985, the sleeping giant awoke and tried to gain control and improve the subsidiaries. But it was too late. In 1986, Guinness (then half the size of DCL) won control.

Lesson:

Give the public what they say they want, and still you have to market it.

❏ Express

The founder of People's Express, Donald Burr, did not sell the airline as just being price-cutters. They were ethical, crusaders and 'smart'. Smart was a favourite word at People's Express, even to their sales' slogan 'Fly smart'. Initially, it is not difficult to cut prices and get away with it for a while. The higher-price competition, in this case largely British Airways and American Airlines, do their sums, (a small loss of market share still represents more profit than cutting prices). There comes a time when the loss of market share starts to hurt. This hurt is either to profits or to an over-weaning sense of self-esteem of a chief executive, or both. It is then that the competition retaliates by cutting its prices in line with the price-cutter. In the case of People's Express this led to a lower seat fill which led to higher costs. Since they offered minimal service, were infamous for overbooking, and tried to operate out of Newark, the only thing they were forced back on was price. When that advantage went, they were sunk.

Lesson:

Be very careful before making price your main weapon. Some people in the public sector seem obsessed with low price.

❏ You too can have a body like mine

Angelo Siciliano was born in 1894 but is better known as Charles Atlas. He won a competition in 1922 run by a magazine called Physical Culture. On this basis, advertisements for his body-building course bore the imprint:

Awarded the title of *The World's Most Perfectly Developed Man*.

Siciliano devised a method of body-building known as Dynamic Tension which was sold by mail order. The first journal advertisement, as well as later innovations, were composed by Charles Roman. Many of these advertisements were based on the strip cartoon format, including the well-known one of a bully kicking sand in the face of a scrawny youth while in the company of his girl friend. After taking the home course, the youth punches the bully thus becoming the Hero of the Beach. Over the years the cartoon strips were changed marginally (the girl's swimsuit was altered in 1946 and a picture of Charles Atlas acquired leopard spots on his shorts). However the basic idea continued until 1972 when Atlas died. The Charles Atlas advertisements were well-known for more than their lack of change. They almost always made use of two words which marketers believe are particularly powerful – FREE and YOU.

Lesson:

Tying in to a single personality can be a powerful aid, until the personality is no longer available for some reason.

Lessons from the front line

Some people view marketing from a Clausewitz-like point of view. Competition is war, the market-place is the battle field, and all lessons must be stated in military terms. Such thinkers are likely to find attractive the Barrie 'ten traps to avoid' (1986):

* preparing to fight the last war rather than the next
* concentrating on fighting for the objective rather than on fighting the enemy
* underestimating the magnitude of the task and overestimating your capabilities
* relying on size and resources rather than speed and mobility to win battles
* being unprepared for combat
* following traditional, rather than new and creative, strategies

- choosing the wrong enemy at the wrong time in the wrong place
- staying in static positions that invariably lead to neglect of combat efficiency
- being discontinuous in the conduct of combat
- being unable to concede an engagement.

It is not surprising that so many marketing books quote Sun Tzu's *The Art of War*.

References

The material for this chapter came from a large number of journals including the Harvard Business Review, the Financial Times, the Journal of Marketing, Fortune, Forbes, Advertising Age and Business Week. It also used material from four main books (those by Hartley, by Heller and by Healey) of which the two by Professor Hartley are highly recommended.

Barrie, G. (1986) *Business Wargames* London, Penguin Books

Business Week (1972) *A & P's Ploy: Cutting Prices to Turn a Profit* 20 May.

Coren, G. (1994) *Going to Work on a Slogan* Times, 24 August.

Hartley, R. (1985) *Marketing Successes* New York, John Wiley.

Hartley, R. (1989) *Marketing Mistakes* New York, John Wiley.

Healey, T. (1992) *Unforgettable Ads* London, Reader's Association.

Heller, R. (1987) *The Supermarketers* London, Sidgwick and Jackson.

Times (1994) *Working on Slogans* Letters to the Editor, 27 August.

Times (1994a) Peter Brookes cartoon magazine, 27 August.

Chapter 13

Case studies

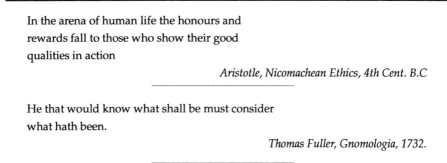

In the arena of human life the honours and
rewards fall to those who show their good
qualities in action

Aristotle, Nicomachean Ethics, 4th Cent. B.C

He that would know what shall be must consider
what hath been.

Thomas Fuller, Gnomologia, 1732.

The three case studies which make up this chapter tackle a number of common themes from different points of view and as such highlight many of the issues which are at the heart of marketing activity within Government.

One important theme is the rate of institutional change. A change of status often provides the initial stimulus for parts of Government to set up a marketing function. In two of the case studies which follow, the Civil Service College and Chessington, it was the transition to agency status within the Next Steps programme which gave a massive impetus to the marketing effort within those organisations.

In these circumstances organisations have to reappraise their histories, especially how those histories have shaped the perceptions of customer or client groups. While history may bring problems for the present which need to be specifically addressed, it is also part of the organisation's core identity. This identity cannot be revised beyond a certain point without damaging relations with existing clients. On the other hand, for some products and markets a complete break with the past is exactly what is required, as the Training Credits case study illustrates. Getting the balance right between continuity and change is a key strategic decision for the marketing and communications strategy of an organisation in this situation.

The high rate of change and succession of reform initiatives within Government also means that the market place itself is changing dramatically. New

197

organisational customers and customer groups are being created with new needs as they acquire new roles and responsibilities. Commercial success often relies on being able to anticipate these changes and deploy new products and services accordingly.

Getting to grips, often on very short timescales, with new techniques and new ways of working is another key theme. The selection of partners and contractors is vital here. How much outside expertise should be brought in? Can outside experts be relied upon to provide value for money, especially on unfamiliar topics and issues? Will their recommendations reflect sufficient understanding of the particular culture of Government? Given that funds are inevitably limited, which tasks are best tackled internally albeit on a trial and error basis and where is outside assistance going to be most valuable?

It is not always easy to assess whether the right judgements have been made on these and related points, even after the event. However the case studies which follow provide an opportunity to review how three organisations have gone about tackling these challenges.

The Civil Service College

The Civil Service College was opened in 1970 as part of the Government's response to the Report of the Fulton Committee on the Civil Service. Fulton had identified the need within the Civil Service for a more professional approach to management and better use of staff with appropriate skills and training. He saw the establishment of a Civil Service College as an important means of achieving these ends.

Some of the approaches adopted during the early years of the College were not popular with those who attended courses, especially young fast-track recruits. Many of this cadre in the intervening years reached influential top management positions within the civil service carrying with them negative perceptions of the College based on past experience.

During the 1980s the agenda of the College and its customers was increasingly shaped by a number of major Government initiatives to improve the efficiency and effectiveness of the Civil Service, in particular the Financial Management Initiative and subsequently the Next Steps programme. The Financial Management Initiative launched in 1982 emphasised the need for clear organisational objectives, measurable outputs and well defined responsibility for resource utilisation. It ushered in a wave of financial devolution with line managers being given budgets for many elements of running costs. During this period the College began to charge customers for its services, although not initially at least to recover the full costs of provision.

The Next Steps programme flowed from a report published in 1988 by the Prime Minister's Efficiency Unit entitled *Improving Management in Government: The Next Steps*. It recommended, inter alia, that agencies should be established to carry out executive functions of Government within a well-defined policy and resources framework. By mid-1994 some 64% of the Home Civil Service were working on Next Steps lines i.e. in units with a clear mission and objectives, and performance targets and standards to ensure effective and efficient delivery.

The Civil Service College was one of the first wave of agencies to be established in 1989 and it is this development that provides the over-arching context for the College's marketing activity of recent years.

❏ The agency framework

As an executive agency within the Next Steps programme, the College was given a clear mission:

> to provide a centre of excellence for developing the managerial and professional skills amongst civil servants, and promoting best practice throughout Government.

Its core activities were broadly defined as:

- management training for civil servants, particularly those at or aspiring to relatively senior positions
- specialist training in key areas or at advanced levels
- related consultancy and research.

A number of more detailed objectives were set, including:

- supporting the initiatives and policies of Government, in particular those affecting the management of the Civil Service in departments and in executive agencies
- improving the quality of its training and its service to customers, and
- improving the efficiency and effectiveness of all its operations and covering its full costs with income.

All of this was underpinned by a set of quantitative targets covering relevant outputs such as the number of students in senior grades and the number of students attending courses which lead to an externally validated qualification.

A way of measuring the value for money of the College was introduced taking into account both the efficiency of the operation and quality of the output. The overall objective of achieving a 10% improvement over a period of five years was set.

❏ Redefining the College's organisational identity

In the run-up to the launch of the College as an agency, priority was given to analysing and improving the way that the College expressed its identity as an organisation. It was felt that the College would be unable to make any progress towards its new aims, objectives and targets without first understanding how it was perceived by different stakeholder groups and then actively managing those perceptions in a way more appropriate to its redefined role and objectives.

External consultants were appointed who started by carrying out a SWOT exercise on the College as a whole. The results raised a number of strategic issues for the College:

- STRENGTHS
    - knowledge of Government and how the Civil Service works
    - privileged access to Civil Service departments
    - the site of the residential centre at Sunningdale Park in Berkshire

- WEAKNESSES
    - a poor built environment, particularly the residential facilities
    - product-oriented organisation with a lack of balance between the College as a whole and its component parts
    - non-competitive attitude and a tendency to undersell itself
    - an image reflecting the position and objectives of a number of years ago

- OPPORTUNITIES
    - the chance to move up-market
    - the chance to be a visible champion of change in the Civil Service
    - premium pricing based on a premium position

- THREATS
    - private sector providers developing public sector specialism
    - the proliferation of course titles.

The consultants were particularly critical of the way that the College expressed its product-based and bureaucratic organisational structure visually. Each of the four teaching directorates had its own primary colour used within the corporate prospectus, for the directorate-specific literature and even on each directorate's business stationery. This approach restricted cross-selling between directorates, potentially threatening repeat business, weakened what little external image the College possessed and more generally was symptomatic of a disadvantageous organisational mind-set.

Transition to agency status offered the College the opportunity to lose some of the negative baggage from the past and to re-position itself at the leading edge of civil service reform.

To express this in visual terms the consultants recommended a design solution which aimed to be elegant, classic, have a lightness and finesse and was explicitly non-bureaucratic in tone. They recommended against a change of name as it would threaten one of the College's key strengths, its link with its core market.

They provided the College with corporate colours, corporate typefaces, business stationery, a set of design conventions and a typographic logo with the strapline:

Management in Government

a phrase taken from the title of the original Next Steps report. A number of non-typographic logos were considered but none emerged which commanded sufficient support from all the key stake-holders for it to be selected.

❏ Market developments

The management reforms within the civil service certainly offered the College the chance to reposition itself but they have also had a radical impact on the College's customer base and its relationship with that base:

(a) the reforms undoubtedly have provided a stimulus to demand for the College's services. Civil servants have had to master a number of new techniques and approaches to their work and a common response in this situation is to see training as part of the solution;

(b) the broad theme of devolution has greatly increased the number of customers and changed the nature of the College's relationship with them. Prior to devolution training funds tended to be managed centrally by a Departmental Training Officer, a training and development specialist who as often as not also ran an in-house training unit. With these arrangements, the College was in a similar position to the manufacturer who sells through retail outlets which have competing own-label brands. Increasingly, training budgets have been devolved away from the central specialist units within departments and been given to line managers i.e. non-specialists. The line managers, generally have the freedom to switch funds between budget categories according to local need so the level of training spending has become much more sensitive to the needs and perceptions of operational managers;

(c) over a period of years, the number of organisational customers has increased as Departments have formed agencies (around 100 new organisations so far) and new tasks (such as regulating privatised utilities) have been tackled by the establishment of new organisations. The growth in the number of organisational customers has taken place despite the reduction in the total number of civil servants overall;

(d) the pressure on organisations in Government to do more with less has resulted in a substantial growth in the demand for tailored training to meet specific organisational objectives. This training is generally cheaper than that offered via open programmes and should be more relevant to the organisation. (The disadvantage of this approach is the loss of opportunity to exchange ideas and experience between organisations);

(e) competitive forces have greatly increased, partly as a matter of deliberate Government policy but partly because of the general pressure on resources. Customers are thinking much more carefully about their precise requirements before they commit to a training purchase. As far as individuals are concerned increased pressure of work has intensified the competition between time spent on training and time spent in the office, leading to increased demand for shorter more specific courses.

Much of this was foreseen in the strategic analysis which was carried out in the run up to agency status and the immediate aftermath. But it is one thing to anticipate an environmental trend and another accurately to assess the scale of its effect.

❏ Research and market models

The College gained substantial benefit from the research element in the organisational identity exercise, but as it moved into a much more commercial environment it needed to deepen its understanding of its market place and the critical factors in customers' purchase decisions. As a medium-sized organisation there are strict limits to the size of its marketing budget and to the proportion of that budget which can be devoted to customised research. It has coped with this by:

- buying into published or collective market research wherever possible
- making the most of internal systems to get feedback from customers
- focusing commissioned market research on non-users and non-core markets.

Drawing on this material the College has acquired a much clearer understanding of the dynamics of the market in which it is operating. Training is a complex and intangible professional service. The purchaser may not experience the product directly if he or she is buying on behalf of others. If the purchaser is buying on his or her own it can be difficult to visualise clearly the actual benefits of the training in advance of experiencing them.

Purchase decisions are likely to be quite lengthy and involve a number of stages of search and assessment, especially when the complete purchase cycle is taken into consideration including further purchase of tailored courses. During the purchase cycle, purchasers will be influenced by everything they know about potential providers, even those aspects of the service package which might be thought of as incidental or non-core. High standards are vital at every stage in the transaction because purchasers will tend to see poor standards in one phase or service element as representative of a poor product overall. All human contact between purchaser and provider organisation will be particularly critical.

The initial results of the customer feedback survey put in place to support the College's value for money measure showed that users in fact rated the non-training elements in the service package, accommodation, catering and support services, much lower than they rated our training. If the total-service concept was correct, this meant that the weaknesses on the non-teaching side were artificially lowering the level of repeat-business and might well be lowering the overall effectiveness of the training itself.

❏ Strategic change

This overall marketing analysis provided the basis for a number of strategic changes at the College, changes which went a good deal wider than the marketing function itself. They included:

- re-organisation of the teaching effort into seven market-oriented business groups
- a major programme of capital investment on both the residential and the teaching facilities

- reformulating and re-tendering service contracts including hotel and catering
- use of the customer feedback data to identify priority areas for action often undertaken by cross-functional project teams
- a deliberate policy of increasing average course prices above the rate of inflation.

❏ Reaching out into the core market

These changes would gradually build the College's reputation as a provider of high quality training within a contemporary service framework and this should substantially increase the level of repeat business. However, the situation was more serious than this. Research of civil servants who had not used the College recently revealed:

- they had very little impression at all of the College, its products or facilities
- where there was an impression it tended to be based on experience of how the College was five or more years ago
- training courses tended to be selected and judged to be of interest through personal recommendation.

The researchers concluded that the College needed to devote much more effort to distributing literature about its product range to non-users and that the literature needed to communicate the whole service package available from the College, not just the content of the courses.

These recommendations were confirmed by published and collective research which the College accessed which showed that generally, in the training market, product literature was as important as personal recommendation as a source of information in training purchase decisions. With so many more budget holders and purchase decision makers in the College's core market it became clear that literature production and distribution would be a strategic marketing issue for the College if it was to grow the business in the way required by the agency targets.

Making progress in this area involved a number of steps:

- finding a local design firm to help take forward the College's visual identity and to project a high quality and innovative image for the College

- recruiting specialists to use cheap desktop publishing technology to provide an in-house typographic capability
- using magazine and journal inserts to raise awareness of the College and via a response mechanism to build up a substantial mailing list for the Prospectus
- contracting out literature distribution to a specialist firm used to handling complex bulk tasks
- increasing the range of product literature, complementing the general Prospectus with a number of brochures targeted at particular market segments.

Between 1990 and 1994 the number of College prospectuses produced and distributed to the market has doubled. The number of delivery points has grown by over three quarters and the proportion of the delivery going in small numbers to individual purchasers has sharply increased. The time taken to complete the initial distribution of the prospectus following publication has dropped by two thirds. In short, delivery of College literature has become much more direct, much more effective and much less reliant on intermediaries.

❏ Marketing instruments for non-core markets

Improving the overall service package and supporting this by strengthening the production and distribution of literature has had a positive business outcome for the College's open programmes. Income has grown at a compound rate of about 12% per annum over a four year period in the core market.

However, the College has been presented with opportunities and challenges in non-core markets:

- there has been a substantial growth in the organisational buying of tailored training packages
- as part of the agency target framework, the College has been encouraged to seek business from private sector firms.

Approaching these non-core markets has involved the College in experimenting with new marketing instruments. While the two non-core markets are not identical, an important common theme has been the need to work with marketing instruments which facilitate the development of inter-organisational relationships. This involves creating opportunities for face-to-face contact between the College and prospective clients so that the client can explore in some detail what the College has to offer to meet his or her organisational need. This has involved:

(a) developing an *exhibition programme*. Organisational buyers often use exhibitions as an opportunity to survey the market and see what is on offer from different providers. The College has invested in its own portable stands which can be refurbished each year to reflect the current Prospectus design. It has built up a knowledge of the exhibition events which offer the best contact with the markets that it is interested in and developed staff skills in manning the stand and dealing with enquiries;

(b) developing a *seminar programme*. As an intangible professional service, training is quite difficult to display to prospective purchasers. Seminars offer a way round this. They provide a rationale for prospective clients to visit College premises which stand as an effective proxy for the quality of services available. Perhaps more important, different seminar formats offer an opportunity to display different aspects of the College's training capability, e.g. using role-play in skills training or its ability to access authoritative presenters from within Government;

(c) experimenting with a *client manager*, a paid external consultant with knowledge of training managers and management development specialists within blue-chip organisations. The aim is to use the consultant to establish awareness of the College as a provider of certain kinds of specialist training services, to identify organisations with specific needs for those services and to develop the relationship to a point where there is a brief which can form the basis of a proposal from one of the College's experts.

The College has also concluded that its progress in both core and non-core markets would be helped by adopting a more pro-active approach to its dealings with the press. The College cannot afford very much in the way of an advertising budget, especially for titles which are read outside the core market. Editorial coverage in the right titles can be very effective at improving awareness of the College and enhancing our credibility amongst organisational buyers of training. It can also enhance and reinforce the spread of the College's reputation by 'word-of-mouth'. After an extensive search of the market the College has appointed a *press relations agency* to advise it on which aspects of its activities and operations are most likely to interest the media and to help secure the appropriate coverage.

❏ Evaluation

Since the College became an Agency it has enjoyed considerable business success. The number of students (including the number of students in senior grades) and total income from services have increased by around 75%. The College will soon be in a position where it completely covers its costs from income from services.

Measurable service standards have increased by about 25% and the disparity between the customer evaluation of teaching and the other elements of the total service package have been greatly reduced and in some instances eliminated. The level of repeat business has increased so that on open programmes just over half the students say that they have attended a College course some time in the previous three years.

There has been three- to four-fold growth in the non-core markets for tailored training and private sector business.

It is hard to quantify the extent to which particular elements of the marketing programme have contributed to the progress of the business. The College has sought to follow a programme of marketing activities based on a coherent analysis of the nature of its product and the way that it is viewed and assessed by potential purchasers, its place in the market and the changes taking place within it. There has been a conscious attempt to link the marketing portfolio to broader strategic developments within the business.

However, the College cannot afford to stand still in terms of its strategic thinking. Its market-place is becoming ever more competitive as the rate of change within its core market increases, its customers become more sophisticated and under ever greater pressures to control costs and secure greater value for money, product life-cycles shorten, the boundary between the civil service and other sectors becomes less clear-cut and the civil service itself goes into a period of contraction.

Against that background the College is currently re-considering many of the components of its marketing and business strategy. For example, is a more distinctive identity and corporate personality appropriate to these more competitive conditions. Are 'elegance, lightness and finesse' sufficient to project the College in more turbulent and competitive market conditions?

Chessington computer centre

Chessington Computer Centre was formed in 1957 as one of a number of Government pay centres. Over the years Chessington became the largest supplier of administrative computing in Government, not only processing payroll but providing personnel information, pension calculations and financial management and accounting systems.

Chessington became an executive agency and a Trading Fund in April 1993, the first organisation to achieve both at the same time. As part of the preparations for this management recognised that the new business needs, and the changes to Chessington's traditional market resulting from the civil service reform, continued to build upon Chessington's successful market penetration. The new freedoms afforded by the changed status led directly to the formation of a marketing team.

❏ Setting up a marketing team

Formed in July 1992 within the Customer Services directorate, the marketing team's staff were taken from various disciplines in order to have a wide spread of knowledge and expertise within the team.

The culture necessary actively to market Chessington's services was an unfamiliar one and the lack of knowledge about a market-focused culture caused some initial concern. However, the marketing team quickly discovered that their common experience of civil service reform meant that Chessington was able to appreciate the needs of other departments.

Chessington had expanded its customer base year on year without active marketing and there was a view that this would continue. However such a view failed to take into account the changing central Government market and the new market opportunities available to public sector organisations. It also became apparent that many existing customers were not aware of the variety of services offered by Chessington. The marketing team therefore had to raise the profile of the agency, its products and services.

As part of this process a Chessington newsletter was started. Titled Chessington Today it features news of the latest product and service developments, details of new customers and articles on various areas of general interest to customers. It is written with the intention not only to inform people about but also to 'personalise' Chessington. Issued on a quarterly basis the newsletter quickly evolved from a desk top published A4 sheet to a full colour eight page paper. Chessington Today has proved to be very popular.

❏ Launching the agency

The change to agency status was seen as the most significant event in Chessington's long history. Senior management were agreed that a special event would be held in order to announce the new chapter in Chessington's history. This would be used to promote the prime message, 'Evolution not Revolution'. This approach enabled Chessington to reinforce the friendly yet professional attitude towards its customers. The overall aim was to emphasise the fact that Chessington was not rejecting all that had gone before but would be continuing to build upon its success. Agency status was to begin on 1 April 1993, as was that of a number of other organisations. To avoid any conflict with other launch arrangements the event was scheduled for the 31 March.

The marketing team were set the task of organising the launch in just four months. This was to include not only the event itself but a new corporate look, the first ever promotional literature and a new marketing approach to business.

A number of organisations were briefed on the launch requirements and were requested to submit proposals. The Central Office of Information (COI) were successful with their bid and worked in close collaboration with the marketing team.

One aspect that needed careful consideration was the name of the agency. Staff at Chessington usually referred to themselves as CCC. When the customers were approached it was found that the opposite applied, with CCC being used in correspondence but Chessington in conversation. COI were commissioned to design a new logo which placed the emphasis on Chessington, thereby reflect-ing the customers' view. The design team submitted a number of suggestions which evolved over the weeks into the current logo, selected because it was a clear, clean design with the 'device' indicating forward and upward movement. The logo is a stylised form of CCC looking somewhat like a sail.

COI also produced a 'style guide' to help staff identify and use the logo correctly on literature, promotional items and stationery etc. The use of the logo was monitored by the marketing team during the initial stages of its introduction to ensure correct usage.

For the launch itself Chessington held two events, the first for its customers and key stakeholders and the second for its staff. It was decided that event should take place at Chessington by utilising the 'sports hall' adjoining the staff restau-rant. The effect created by COI by their use of drapes utilising the corporate colours was a spectacular success.

❏ A new range of literature

COI designed an entire range of literature for the Centre. A hierarchical approach was adopted with a corporate brochure at the top working down to in-depth fact sheets for those who wanted specific product, or service related, informa-tion. In order to produce these COI looked at the material already available, interviewed the various Directors and key staff and, in conjunction with the marketing team, produced draft documents for consideration. The design was finalised following a presentation by COI staff.

The corporate brochure was designed to 'personalise' the organisation. It focused on the people at Chessington rather than the products. Entitled 'Putting a Face to the Name', it contained sections on those involved in strategic new products, customer services, marketing and the pay sections.

The product information pack covered each aspect of Chessington's products. Each 'fact sheet' had to be informative but easily accessible. If the customer needed further information this could be obtained from the marketing team. From this initial approach the 'fact sheet' has evolved into a new general product booklet covering all Chessington's products and services.

❑ New product developments

New products, introduced after an intense period of research and planning, were a tangible sign that the organisation was continuing to move forward. An online superannuation estimate service designed to meet personnel managers' needs was launched to great acclaim at a series of seminars. Within one month of these taking place over 50 departments had signed up for the service and the customer base has continued to grow.

After careful consultation with actual and potential customers, Chessington also made the decision to implement an integrated pay/personnel system using Open Systems technology. The initial phase was the development of the personnel system based upon an established product developed for use within the public sector. Scheduled for introduction in April 1994 the first customer received their system on time, and successive customers have had their systems 'rolled out' on time. This collaboration between the public and private sectors is an important strand in the continuing evolution of Chessington and its services.

The new product needed a name and this presented another task not encountered before. Initial searches made using the Patent Office's online enquiry system confirmed that a number of suggested names had already been registered. The marketing team therefore employed a Patent Agent to check out a number of alternative names. From these the name 'Argosy' was chosen, not only for the pay/personnel system but for the entire range of Chessington's products and services.

❑ New promotional techniques

The marketing manager also became responsible for dealing with press enquiries, an activity not previously undertaken by Chessington staff. The various launches and seminars staged by Chessington proved ideal events for promoting the agency and its new products. Chessington introduced press releases for important issues to ensure that the targeted publications were presented with the relevant information and contact details.

The skills learnt by the marketing team in organising the launch proved useful at exhibitions. It was decided that the effectiveness of exhibiting needed to be tested carefully. Two exhibitions were selected, one for central Government and the other for local authorities. The team also attended a number of shows to see the different types of stands available in a working environment. It was also useful to see how different organisations presented themselves. The events attended by Chessington proved useful in terms of business leads and as part of the learning curve for the marketing team.

During the eighteen months of marketing effort a substantial number of leads were generated from different kinds of promotional activity. As the marketing function continues to evolve it may prove necessary to introduce a commercial marketing database system to support the various activities.

❏ Evaluation

The success which the agency has achieved in the first eighteen months is closely intertwined with the marketing activity in its various guises. As the team members found their feet and developed different areas of expertise, the opportunities to build on Chessington's successes increased. As this learning process continues, marketing activities will become increasingly proactive. The key point is that during this initial phase the new marketing function has been able to establish itself within the agency as being essential to the future business development of the organisation.

Training credits in South East London

South Thames Training and Enterprise Council serves the four London boroughs of Lambeth, Southwark, Lewisham and Greenwich. All four boroughs are classed as urban priority areas and suffer from many social problems including poor housing and homelessness. Negative perceptions of South London need to be countered, particularly in relation to levels of crime and the quality of life for residents and employees.

The South Thames area has many strengths which include:

* its universities and colleges of further education

- attractive tourist and leisure amenities
- the benefits which should flow from Waterloo International Terminal.

The mission statement of South Thames Training and Enterprise Council is:

In partnership with the community, public and private business and other organisations to create the climate, culture and infrastructure which will:

- sustain and regenerate the area's economy and promote profitable, new and revitalised businesses; and
- maintain and improve standards in education and training to give local people better opportunities for self-development, jobs, and an enhanced quality of life.

The Council has four main objectives. Objective Two is:

To enable local people to achieve more and maximise their choices for self-development through education, training, access to jobs and to help inform their personal choices.

❑ Training Credits

Training Credits are part of the Council's work under Objective Two. Training Credits are an Employment Department national initiative and South Thames was chosen as a second round pilot. The first round was the previous year and about ten Training and Enterprise Councils (TECs) participated with a similar number involved in the second round. In 1993–94 the Council introduced Training Credits for young people as entitlement to vocational education and training for all young people who have not completed two years of post-compulsory full-time education. The Council's aim was to play its part in the delivery of the Secretary of State's guarantee to young people, in collaboration with the Careers Service, and the achievement locally of the National Education and Training Targets. During that first year the Council provided approximately 5000 Training Credits opportunities.

❑ Market research

Before South Thames began marketing Training Credits, it needed to find out more about young people's perceptions of training, and what they thought of the Government's training schemes available to them. South Thames began by inviting tenders for the Training Credits project, and contracted with a research company with a track record in working with young people.

The company carried out a series of interviews with groups of 15 to 17 year olds, parents, careers teachers, training providers and employers. The research concluded:

- training in the South Thames area had a very negative image
- Youth Training/YT/YTS was 'only for people who can't get a job' and not an attractive option. It was seen as a last resort rather than something people asked about
- benefits of training and the link between training and employment were not fully recognised
- Youth Training was seen as 'just another government scheme' and 'cheap labour'.

Training Credits are for all young people, whether in a job or not, and therefore it was important to raise the profile of training, to make training seem more attractive and give it a 'street-cred' image. It was also important to raise awareness amongst young people and others, for example parents, employers and teachers, that Training Credit leads to nationally recognised vocational qualifications (NVQs) and therefore would enable a young person to obtain employment, or to progress further if they were already with an employer. Training Credits 'empowered' young people to seek their own training from providers of their own choice.

❏ Visual identity

The research had highlighted the fact that young people in the South Thames area stayed away from anything to do with the Government. A specialist design firm was contracted to produce an image and identity which young people could relate to. A steering group was set up by South Thames to look at the designs (and other issues related to introducing Credits). This group was made up of representatives from training providers, Careers Service, employers, teachers and the Council's own project group.

Based on the research of what would appeal to young people, the brief to the design agency was they should produce something in 'rave' colours (based on rave flyers), in user-friendly language, which could be used by careers teachers in schools to introduce Training Credits, but would also appeal to the young person so that if they came across the literature they would want to pick it up, and even put it on their bedroom wall! The literature for young people would be supported by a video and an exhibition stand for use in schools, careers offices and careers exhibitions and would carry the same visual theme. The words 'scheme' or 'programme' would not feature anywhere in the literature, because this would turn people off and it would give the impression that Training Credits were just a replacement for Youth Training.

The young person would be issued with a 'credit card' when taking up Training Credits, and this would also carry the created visual image, a personalised number and an entitlement to about £2000 worth of training. This was based on the research findings that young people liked to have something to keep.

After several attempts to 'get it right' and many long discussions on the issue of male/female and ethnic minority representation, a logo image was agreed. The literature (in bright vivid colours) showed young people squashed up and restricted until they found a new lease of life with their Training Credits.

❑ Getting the message across

A video was produced using a combination of a young presenter acting out different roles to highlight the benefits of training, and graphics similar to a computer game. 'Get a Life' was the main theme, to encourage young people to think that training was the 'in' thing to do and would lead them to better things.

The main 'Get a Life' brochure was translated into the principal languages spoken in the four boroughs, so young people could inform their parents. About ten languages were used. There are over two hundred languages spoken in the South Thames area.

For employers, a separate identity was developed, to project a more professional image that would appeal to an employer. The literature 'My First Big Break' contained case studies of local employers (for example the Senior Personnel Manager of Sainsbury's) talking about who gave them their first break, and encouraged employers to consider employing a young person. The literature would be mailed to the area's 18,000 employers, but not immediately. The campaign needed to be planned carefully to ensure effective follow-up. A radio campaign aimed at employers was carried out on a local music station with response to a freephone Training Credits Helpline. This freephone line was set up to deal with any Training Credits enquiry.

After the launch of Training Credits in April 1993, another group which had been identified was targeted. Up to April, the literature had been aimed at 14 to 16 year olds in school. South Thames also needed to communicate to young people who had left school, did not have a job or further education to go to, and so could benefit from training. A cinema and poster campaign was launched aimed at this group, using graffiti style images. (This attracted some national press interest, especially as graffiti writing on trains is known as 'training'!)

An advertising company produced a 30-second cinema advert for South Thames TEC, which was shown with selected films in the four South Thames boroughs. It showed fast images of young people trying to achieve different tasks, namely sports, driving and 'scratching'. The theme of 'The Harder You Train The Better You Get' was developed, and carried through the cinema advert and the 48 sheet posters and ad shells. A 'street artist' was used for the graffiti writing, to authenticate it. This campaign contributed to the achievement of raising the profile of training and giving it an image which would appeal to young people.

❏ Evaluation

Training Credits have now been operating in the South Thames area since April 1993. The next step is to carry out detailed evaluation to gauge response to the marketing campaign and to see if the campaign helped to increase the take-up of Training Credits places. Other activities have taken place to raise awareness of Training Credits and South Thames Training and Enterprise Council has been working in partnership with its local community to raise standards, develop quality training and work towards achieving National Education and Training Targets. With the introduction of Pan London Training Credits (now called Youth Credits), South Thames Training Credits' marketing activity may need to be reassessed to take into account the ever-changing youth market and the effect of Training Credits being available in London and nationally.

Selected bibliography

> The printing-press is either the greatest blessing or
> the greatest curse of modern times, one sometimes
> forgets which.
>
> *J. M. Barrie, Sentimental Tommy, 1896.*

The following list is but the merest abbreviated selection of the thousands of books available on marketing. The objective is to help on the next stage of acquiring knowledge.

P. Kotler *Marketing Management: Analysis, Planning, Implementation, and Control* Englewood Cliffs, Prentice Hall, 1991.

There cannot be a writer (or lecturer) who does not owe a debt to Kotler, and most are willing to admit it, too. Most of the examples are American and from the private sector, but it would have to be a rather narrow-minded person who would reject the book on these grounds. Try to get the latest edition. Strongly recommended.

W. G. Zigmund and M. d'Amico *Marketing* St. Paul, MN, West Publishing, 1993.

Another general marketing book, again with plenty of examples and charts. Together with Kotler, the two books provide an excellent introduction. Of particular interest to those in the public sector is the discussion of ethical considerations at the end of many of the chapters.

M. H. B. McDonald *Marketing Plans: How to Prepare Them: How to Use Them* Oxford, Butterworth-Heinemann, 1993.

One of a series with the imprimatur of the Chartered Institute of Marketing, this is aimed at examination students. It is therefore rigorous and informative.

M. H. B. McDonald and J. W. Leppard *The Marketing Audit: Translating Marketing Theory into Practice* Oxford, Butterworth-Heinemann, 1993.

Another book in the Chartered Institute of Marketing series. Consists largely of what is really a set of check-lists, so it should help prevent one from omitting some vital aspect. If you like check-lists, you should like this.

N. King *The Last Five Minutes* **London: Simon & Schuster, 1991.**

For those who have difficulty with the close in 'sales, business and interviews'. This is a book on personal selling. Like so many it has a touch of go-go and the 1930s about it but should provide plenty of ideas. The same author wrote *The First Five Minutes* for those who find the introduction to the presentation stage a problem.

J. Winkler *Pricing for Results* **Bicester, Facts on File, 1984.**

If one ignores the first two chapters, this book has plenty of thoughts that might otherwise escape one. Not new but the main reason for recommendation is that it is often seen on marketer's bookshelves.

J-P Jeannet and H. D. Hennessey *Global Marketing Strategies* **Boston, Houghton Mifflin, 1992.**

One of the comparatively few robust books on global marketing. Not many laughs in it but if one needs it, one needs it. Anybody coming new to this area will learn something. The book is heavily slanted towards the private sector but, since one of the authors was at Ashridge, there is a British dimension to much of the material.

M. J. Baker *Research for Marketing* **Basingstoke, Macmillan Education, 1991.**

Gives an overview of market research. Good for those not working directly in this field but who need to know most of the techniques and jargon. As a Professor at Strathclyde, the author includes the University's 'marketing information leaflet'. This is a first rate listing of sources of information for research.

R. F. Hartley *Marketing Successes* **New York, John Wiley, 1985.**

R. F. Hartley *Marketing Mistakes* **New York, John Wiley, 1989.**

Two books which give the backgrounds and details of past marketing case studies together with some notes on marketing theory. Lively reading for people who like to learn from other's experiences.

MRS *Orgs Book 19--: Organisations and Individuals Providing Market Research Services* **London, The Market Research Society, Annual.**

An annual reference book giving details about market research organisations.

CIM *The Marketing Manager's Yearbook 19--* **London, Chartered Institute of Marketing/AP Information Services, Annual.**

Over 1,000 pages of data, which means that it contains plenty of information that may not be of immediate direct help; but it also means that there is plenty that *will* be of help. For example, an index of 5,000 advisors plus suppliers of services should enable one to build up a short list for tenders.

G. Bolt *Market and Sales Forecasting* London, Kogan Page, 1994.

Another book that has gone through several editions, which is often a good sign. Covers the basic methods, with some elementary arithmetic, as well as how to prepare a total forecasting plan. More readable than many in this field.

P. Doyle *Marketing Management and Strategy* London, Prentice-Hall, 1993.

This book looks at strategy as such and will be very useful to anybody taking examinations in marketing. The author is a professor at Warwick and his clients include the Cabinet Office.

Index

D

K

L

M

Marketing audit, 170, 171-172.

Marketing Mix, 27, 40, 41, 42, 46, 105, 171.

Marketing plan, 36-40, 171.

Marketing research, 144.

Marketing strategies, 3-6.

Market information systems, 138-144.

Market price, 82-84.

Market related prices, 82-86.

Market research, 138-151, 171, 203, 212-213.

Market Research Encyclopedia, 148.

Market Research Society, 176.

Market share, 80.

Markham, C, 174.

Marks and Spencer, 50, 81, 90.

Marn, M, 88.

Maturity, 47, 50-51.

Mazda, 151.

McCarthy, E, 105.

McDonald, M, 38, 49, 171.

McKinsey, 84.

McLuhan, M, 105.

Media, 97.

Median, 162.

Medicare, 140.

Memorandum Trading Accounts, 72.

Mensa, 162.

Mercedes Benz, 189.

Mercer, D, 52.

Mercury Paging, 128.

Mesmerists, 43.

Meterological Office, 70.

Metropolitan Police, 109.

Michelangelo, 8.

Ministry of Defence, 52.

Ministry of Housing and Local Government, 109.

Ministry of Pensions and National Insurance, 56.

Missionaries, 99.

MMM, 98.

Mode, 162-163.

Model building, 150.

Monopolies and Mergers Commission, 85.

Moral price, 84.

Morris, M, 4, 6.

MOSAIC, 129.

Mueller-Heumann, G, 128.

Multi-channel conflict, 121.

Museums, 79.

Mystery shoppers, 149.

N

National Health Service (NHS), 6, 7, 16, 66, 68, 79, 92, 111, 139.

National lottery, 121.

National Savings, 58.

National Savings Bonds, 38.

National Savings Certificates, 49, 54.

National Savings Stock Register, 54.

National Society for the Prevention of Cruelty to Children, 185.

National Vocational Qualifications (NVQs), 213.

NewProd, 62.

News conferences, 93.

Portfolios, 39, 52-54.

Portrait, 151.

Post Office Counters, 41.

Post Office, 117, 131.

Pre-approach, 101.

Presentation, 101.

Prestige price, 84.

Price-sensitive users, 119.

Price, 171.

Price, types of, 80-86.

Pricing, 65-89.

Price wars, 19, 49, 86-88.

Pricing points, 85.

Primary suppliers, 61.

Privatisation, 6, 7.

Probability, 155-161.

Problem children, 53.

Proctor & Gamble, 59.

Product, 45-63.

Product champion, 62.

Product development, 56-63.

Product gap, 54-55.

Productivity, 22-23.

Product life cycle, 47-52, 54, 56, 154, 207.

Product-market approaches, 4.

Product range, 39-40.

Product portfolio, 52.

Product-specific occasions, 130.

Project Industriele Innovatie, 63.

Promotion, 90-112.

Promotion boards, 8.

Promotion price, 85.

Prospecting, 101.

Public goods, 9.

Public Expenditure Survey (PES), 42.

Public Health Laboratory Service, 45.

Publicity, 91, 92, 113.

Public relations, 49, 91, 93, 94.

PURCHASE, 172.

Q

Quartiles, 162, 165.

Quinn, J, 9.

R

Radford Community Hospital, 18.

Raleigh bicycles, 193.

Range, 165.

Rank Xerox, 21, 140.

Ratners, 90.

Rat principle, 24.

Rea, D, 139.

Reemtsma, 88.

Relationship seekers, 119.

Rembrandt, 8.

Remington razor, 184.

Research and Development, 58.

Resistance, 102.

Resource Management Initiative, 139.

Resources, 43, 52.

Response hierarchy models, 107.

Retail Price Index, 47.

Reukert, R, 3.

Ries, A, 5.

RJR, 88.

Rogers, E, 106.

Role uncertainty, 121.

Rothwell, R, 63.

Rowntree's Elect Cocoa, 191.

Royal Botanic Gardens, 45.

Royal Crown, 50.

Royal Mail, 7.

Royal Mint, 5, 21, 26, 45, 65, 80, 94.

Royal Opera House, 84.

Royal Society for the Prevention of Cruelty to Animals, 94.

Royce, R, 139.

Rushton, A, 13.

S

Saga, 126.

Sainsbury, 50, 98, 117, 151, 214.

Sales people, 100.

Sales promotion, 92, 104-107.

SAPPHO, 63.

Savage criterion, 158.

Scenarios, 38, 155.

Schramm, W, 105.

Schuldt, B, 151.

Screening, 59.

Segmentation:

    basis, 125-132.

    behaviour, 125, 130-131.

    demographic, 125, 127-128.

    geodemographic, 129.

    geographic, 125, 128-129.

    in practice, 132-133.

    loyalty status, 131.

    predisposition, 125, 131-132.

    psychographic, 125, 129-130.

    socioeconomic, 125, 126-127.

    user status, 131.

    volume, 131.

Segments, 3, 20, 26, 38-39, 54, 57, 59, 63, 175, 177, 189.

Segments:

    down-stream, 26.

    up-stream, 26.

'Sell or tell', 43.

Selling-in, 17.

Selling-out, 17.

Semantic differential, 111.

Sensitivity analysis, 157.

Service level agreements, 67.

Service criteria, 22.

Service gap, 55.

Service providers, 17, 19, 56.

Services, 11-27.

Services:

    characteristics of, 12-16.

    delivery, 20-21.

    differentiation, 19-21.

    fluctuating demand, 16.

    inseparable from consumption, 14-15.

    intangibility, 13-14.

    offer, 20.

    people dependency, 14.

    perishable, 16.

    statutory, 68.

    unstandardised, 15-16.

Serwer, A, 87.

Training and Enterprise Councils, 118, 212.

Training Credits, 212.

Training needs assessment, 136.

Transport and Road Research Laboratory, 41.

Treaty of Rome, 70.

Trend extrapolation, 154.

Trial close, 103.

Two ears, one mouth, 23.

U

Ultra vires, 35.

Unique Selling Proposition, 130, 187.

Utilisation rate, 178, 179.

V

Value for money, 19.

Variable price, 86.

Variety seekers, 119.

Venn diagrams, 158-160.

Venn, J, 158.

Ventriloquistic salesmanship, 114.

Vertical channel, 121.

Vidal Sassoon, 84.

Viking Direct, 140.

Virginia Slims, 128.

Vittles, P, 151.

Vodaphone, 61.

W

Wack, P, 38.

Walker, O, 3.

Wal-Mart, 50.

Webber, R, 129.

Weighting and ranking, 174-175, 178.

Westminster City Council, 116.

Winkler, J, 82.

Woolworth, 116.

Woopie, 130.

Wright, P, 3.

Y

Yes-but, 102.

Yeskey, D, 3.

Youth Training, 213.

Yuppie, 129.

Z

Zeithaml, V, 12.

Zikmund, W, 77.